Designing and Dev
Robust Instruction

Designing and Developing Robust Instructional Apps advances the state of instructional app development using three learning paradigms for building knowledge foundations, problem-solving, and experimentation. Drawing on research and development lessons gleaned from noted educational technologists, time-tested systematic instructional design processes, and results from user experience design, the book considers the planning and specification of instructional apps that blend media (text, images, sound, and moving pictures) and instructional method. Further, for readers with little to no programming experience, introductory treatments of JavaScript and Python, along with data fundamentals and machine learning techniques, offer a guided journey that produces robust instructional apps and concludes with next steps for advancing the state of instructional app development.

Kenneth J. Luterbach is Associate Professor of Instructional Technology in the College of Education at East Carolina University, USA.

Designing and Developing Robust Instructional Apps

Kenneth J. Luterbach

Routledge
Taylor & Francis Group

NEW YORK AND LONDON

First published 2018
by Routledge
711 Third Avenue, New York, NY 10017

and by Routledge
2 Park Square, Milton Park, Abingdon, Oxon, OX14 4RN

*Routledge is an imprint of the Taylor & Francis Group, an informa
business*

Library of Congress Cataloging-in-Publication Data
A catalog record for this book has been requested

ISBN: 978-1-138-30317-1 (hbk)
ISBN: 978-1-138-30318-8 (pbk)
ISBN: 978-0-203-73150-5 (ebk)

Typeset in Bembo
by Apex CoVantage, LLC

Visit the eResources: www.routledge.com/9781138303188

To my son

To my son

Contents

Acknowledgements

First, thanks to everyone who has helped me learn: Family, friends, colleagues, and students come readily to mind. With respect to this book, the proposal reviewers provided excellent recommendations. I thank them and the people at Routledge who contributed to this book, especially Daniel Schwartz, Jamie Magyar, and Seth Townley.

Part I

Foundations of Instructional App Development

Chapter 1

Conceptions of Learning and Instruction

Enjoy creating interactive instructional apps. To begin, we may perceive of two phases to instructional app creation, design, and development. During the *Design Phase*, we make a plan to help a target group of learners acquire and retain particular knowledge, skills, or attitudes. Though rarely stated explicitly, each instructional plan asserts that engagement in the instruction by target learners will result in acquisition of particular knowledge, skills, or attitudes. In this work, we will proceed from design to development. Consequently, we will be able to test the instructional apps we create and substantiate the implicit claims of instructional effectiveness. During the *development phase* we will engage repeatedly in a build-test-refine cycle. In some cases, testing may reveal flaws in the design, which would result in redesign, as depicted in Figure 1.1.

Enjoy the instructional app creation process. If you find it challenging at times, know that you are in good company as numerous instructional designers and developers before you have encountered similar feelings. Persist and reap the benefits! There is much joy in overcoming challenges and you will forever be able to draw on your app design and development skills.

We begin this instructional design and development journey by clarifying some terms. Then we gain shared conceptions of learning and instruction,

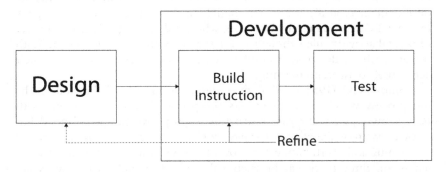

Figure 1.1 Two-Phase Design and Development of Instruction.

and draw on lessons learned by others who have previously engaged in instructional design and development. In many cases, we will consider the work of individuals who have spent their professional lives studying the design and development of instruction.

Key Terms

The meaning of the term *design* varies according to its use. One of the revelations of the study of language is that the meaning of a word can depend on the words around it. Sometimes we speak of design as a verb in order to portray design as a process. "Let's design some instruction!" Other times, we use design as a noun. "I like this design" or "It is helpful to know key principles of visual design." On other occasions, we use design as an adjective, as in *design thinking, design school, design documents*, and *design process*. With respect to *instructional design*, the process, design is often meant to include *development*. Conversely, one speaking of *instructional development* might mean to include the design stage (and perhaps even more stages of the instructional creation process). This confounding of the terms, *instructional design* and *instructional development* needs to be recognized; we should realize that mere mention of either term does not suffice to convey meaning precisely. Knowing that we need to be careful when using those terms enables us to move forward. We will discuss conceptions of instructional design and development in depth in Chapter 2. For now, in light of the work of architects, let's recognize that *design* is a planning process and that we can share plans for producing something through *design documents*, such as drawings.

Like the word design, the term *development* can also be a noun or adjective and it has the verb form, *develop*. When using development as a noun, we might say, "What an interesting development." Using development as an adjective, we might say, "My development plan includes learning to create instructional apps." Even though development is used in multiple forms and instructional development can be confounded with instructional design, as noted above, *development* seems easier to conceptualize than *design*. After all, development typically leads to a tangible artifact (though we could speak of mental development, for instance), whereas designing is largely a matter of mental activity unless thoughts of design are reified in a document. With respect to both design and development, we must rely on context (their actual use) to ascertain meaning.

Romiszowski (1981, p. 4) defines *instruction* as a "goal-directed teaching process which is more or less pre-planned." Okay, consistent with Romiszowski, we will regard instruction as purposive and pre-planned, but what are we to make of a *teaching process*? One's conception or mental model of teaching and instruction emerge over time. Section 1.1 elaborates at some length on three particular instructional methods, which in this work are called *behavioral instruction, cognitivist instruction*, and *constructivist instruction*.

You may have alternative or additional conceptions of instruction, but we use those three to establish common ground. Ultimately, you are free to implement any form or forms of instruction you wish.

For clarity regarding conceptions of instructional apps, note that any use of a computer technology to implement an instructional method results in the development of an *instructional app*. For example, a PowerPoint presentation, which poses a question on a slide and provides feedback by branching to a different slide based on the link the user clicked, is an instructional app. However, in this work, we will not develop such an inefficient app, which severely limits input and requires *a priori* branching to account for all possible paths through the instruction. Our instructional apps will implement instructional methods efficiently without strict limits on learner input.

As noted previously, development of instructional apps may be challenging at times. Indeed, any attempt to build something new is a challenge until sufficient practice has enabled mastery of fundamental skills. This is to be expected: Developing, creating, and synthesizing are at the top of Bloom's (revised) *Taxonomy of the Cognitive Domain* (Anderson & Krathwohl, 2001). Creating an instructional app involves synthesis of one's technological, pedagogical, psychological, and content knowledge. Often, instructional designers collaborate with others, in which case instructional app design and development proceed according to the team's collective knowledge.

To begin, we will create a simple, yet powerful, instructional app, which requires a little coding or programming. If coding is new to you, that's great. We begin in a simple environment, a window embedded within a web browser, to learn a couple of fundamental JavaScript commands and statements. Then, following an example in this book, you will write your first instructional app. You will discover that with about ten lines of code, your instructional app will provide accurate feedback for infinitely many practice items, though, practically, each time actual learners use the app, they might stop after encountering perhaps 50 or 100 items. Your simple and powerful app will surpass the utility of commercial development software, which requires that all practice items and feedback to possible responses be determined and linked before the instruction begins. Seymour Papert (1980, p. 5), regarded computer programming as the "art of intellectual model building." Nobel laureate, Herbert A. Simon, who with Alan Newell wrote and demonstrated the first computer program to exhibit artificial intelligence (AI), encouraged a particular form of software testing. According to Simon, "If you test your programs not merely by what they can accomplish, but how they accomplish it, then you're really doing cognitive science; you're using AI to understand the human mind" (see Herbert A. Simon interview transcript in Stewart, 1994). In my view, computer programming is both a form of problem solving and creative expression. However you ultimately resolve to test computer programs, enjoy instructional app development and learn a lot.

Instructional apps, like all application software (apps), run on some type of digital computer, whether desktop, laptop, tablet, smartphone, digital wristwatch, or virtual reality headset, for instance. Unique to instructional apps is that they implement an instructional method. Instructional apps seek to help learners acquire particular knowledge or skill by engaging learners in an instructional experience. Conceivably, one could create an app that displays facts and/or plays audio recordings of the facts. Such demonstration or "display and play" apps are not instructional apps. However, we could make a demonstration app an instructional app by adding a feature that directs the learner to repeat the facts. Providing feedback about the accuracy of the learner's recollection of the facts might enhance the instructional experience but, in many cases, learners decide for themselves when they have practiced sufficiently to recall facts or to perform a skill adequately. Hence, for recall of facts, it would be sufficient for the app to direct the learner to repeat the facts until memorized, even without feedback from the app.

Providing instruction that meets conditions minimally sufficient for learning facts would not be helpful for pursuit of other learning goals. For example, accurate feedback from an instructional app or a person, though not essential for rehearsing and learning some facts, is often very helpful in pursuit of many learning goals. Indeed, for all goals in which the learner does not know the correct answer, feedback is either critical or exceedingly important, such as when learning to calculate the area of a triangle. Further, for all goals without a correct answer or a single acceptable performance, feedback from someone who has mastered the task is often very helpful.

Since learners can adequately regulate their own learning while seeking to attain some learning goals, feedback from an external source is not always necessary, but learner practice is essential. The necessity of practice was established long ago and remains evident in the work of educational technologists (e.g., Gagné, 1965, 1985; Merrill, 1983, 1994, 2002; Reigeluth, 1983, 1999a; Reigeluth & Carr-Chellman, 2009). Learning has been a subject of formal study for centuries and pondered by philosophers for millennia. Individual differences among learners, as well as variability in learning goals and instructional methods, invite reflection on learning, which we seek to foster in the development of instructional apps. Accordingly, we will consider alternative perspectives on learning as we progress through this work. The one constant will be the necessity of practice for learning. Consistent with the French philosopher, Merleau-Ponty (1963), this work regards practice as the essence of learning. Demonstration alone is insufficient for learning, but practice is sufficient. Some might argue that there is more to learning than practice; perhaps for them, demonstration and practice are sufficient for learning. Even so, practice is necessary. Hence, our instructional apps will provide practice. In addition, for effectiveness and efficiency of instruction, our apps will also provide feedback or guidance to the learners.

Robust instructional apps implement multiple instructional methods to help diverse learners attain a multitude of instructional goals using a wide range of technologies. Though it is possible for a single app to implement multiple instructional methods and run on multiple devices, this book will guide you through the development of a set of instructional apps that collectively implement multiple instructional methods and run on multiple devices.

By progressing through this book, you will learn to create robust instructional apps, which implement multiple instructional methods to help diverse learners attain a multitude of instructional goals using a wide range of technologies. In so doing, you will become increasingly aware of the diversity of instructional apps and the tools for creating them. Further, you will become increasingly aware of the benefits and requirements of instructional app development.

Gaining the ability to create robust instructional apps will enable you to advance the state of instructional development. For instance, you may wish to pursue any of the following three goals, leading educational technologists in new directions:

- Make Instructional Apps Ubiquitous across Diverse Digital Devices
- Improve Instructional Development Tools
- Implement Machine Learning Techniques

New Directions

Make Instructional Apps Ubiquitous across Diverse Digital Devices

As learners, we should be able to engage in instruction at any time and place of our choosing. A mobile device, such as a smartphone, is helpful in this regard. However, just as all paper-based instruction should not be relegated to 3-inch by 5-inch or 4-inch by 6-inch index cards, all instruction on a digital device should not be limited to 3-inch by 5-inch or 4-inch by 6-inch smartphone displays. We should enable learners to engage in instruction using a wide variety of devices and, when possible, provide the instruction without requiring installation. For example, HP (Hewlett Packard) delivers instructional videos through a built-in 2-inch by 2-inch display on the OfficeJet Pro 6978 (and other printers). Beyond developing instructional apps for tablets, phones, desktops, and laptops, we should seek to create instructional apps for wearable devices (e.g., watches, headsets, eye glasses), TVs, cars, boats, drones, planes, 3D printers, defibrillators, telescopes, and assembly kits (e.g., to help people learn to knit sweaters, embroider blouses, build furniture, and construct model aircraft), for instance.

Devices with voice interfaces offer another platform for deployment of instructional apps. Indeed, over time, we may turn social robots into instructional robots. An instructional robot may possess characteristics of human tutors, eventually including voice and vision capabilities, along with content and pedagogical knowledge. When commanded, such an instructional robot might provide lessons in materials science, aeronautics, photography, knitting, construction management, kinesiology, and nutrition, for instance.

This book will enable you to acquire fundamental app development knowledge and skill, which you are encouraged to transfer to the development of instructional apps for diverse devices and platforms. Also in the future, as electrical engineers create new *form factors* (devices of different shapes and sizes), transfer your app development knowledge and skills to implement instruction for deployment on those devices. For example, in the summer of 2017, a company named *Neurable* made available a Brain-Computer Interface (BCI) for Virtual Reality (VR) and Augmented Reality (AR) applications (Thompson, 2017). A BCI detects patterns in brain activity to control, for instance, a prosthetic limb or a virtual keyboard. The *Neurable* software development kit translates electroencephalograph (EEG) data into user commands. Though not for VR/AR, IBM also makes available technology for developers seeking to create telekinetic applications (Domingues, Lima, & Chong, 2014).

Improve Instructional Development Tools

In some cases, an instructional developer might use a program like Microsoft PowerPoint to create an instructional app. Though generally regarded as a presentation tool, an instructional developer could use PowerPoint to include text, images, and sound, and present a question to which the learner may respond by clicking text or an image. Through hyperlinking, the selected response would display feedback to the learner. As an alternative to PowerPoint, educators may use a special purpose instructional development tool, such as *Adobe Captivate, Articulate Studio*, or *Trivantis Lectora*. Even though those tools have useful features, they have some serious limitations. First, the development paradigm for those tools proceeds from the view that instruction should present content (2D images and text) on slides. In addition, those tools require developers to predetermine all instructional stimuli and responses. Alternatively, the 2D slide paradigm for instructional development could conceivably be replaced with a Python add-on to the open source 3D graphics tool, *Blender*, which also enables use of audio, video, and animation.

By advancing through this book and learning to create instructional apps, you will become aware of the potential to automate instructional development. The extent to which the development of instruction can be automated is an open question ripe for research. Improvements to instructional development tools might also encourage deployment of instructional apps on devices other than smartphones and tablets, such as watches, eyeglasses, VR headsets, TVs, and social robots, for instance.

Implement Machine Learning Techniques

Recently, educators have been able to access large stores of educational data and have been using machine learning algorithms to find patterns in the data. The availability of large databases containing educational data and the utility of machine learning techniques have sparked interest in *educational data mining*. As a result, a small number of graduate degree programs in educational data mining have been launched in universities within the past 5 years. Applications of machine learning in speech recognition, game playing, and spam email detection are well documented, but why are educators using machine learning techniques?

Educators are turning to machine learning techniques in attempts to improve instructional apps, as well as to identify effective teachers and teaching practices, for instance. Conceivably, educators may also use machine learning algorithms to determine what courses should be taught in Massive Open Online Courses (MOOCs) or other learning environments. In the future, we may use machine learning techniques to predict which instructional methods may be especially helpful to particular learners seeking to attain particular knowledge and skills. Such predictions may be helpful to pedagogical agents and instructional robots that converse and otherwise interact with learners. As a starting place, Chapter 6 in this book introduces machine learning in the context of educational research scenarios. One scenario demonstrates how a machine learning technique could be used in an attempt to improve learner satisfaction with instruction. In the second scenario, machine learning is applied to the problem of identifying effective teachers.

In this work, we will take the following steps in our journey to design and develop instructional apps.

1. Gain shared conceptions of learning and instruction
2. Become aware of lessons learned by educational technologists
3. Follow an instructional design model
4. Heed guidelines from User Experience Design
5. Recognize real world challenges and opportunities
6. Learn the fundamentals of procedural programming
7. Practice instructional app development.

We take those steps in two parts. The first part of this book enables acquisition of fundamental knowledge and skills in pedagogy, psychology, instructional design, user-experience design, visual design, sound design, diffusion of innovations, and procedural programming. Then, in the second part of this book, we apply knowledge and skills gained in Part 1 to the development of instructional apps.

1.1 Learning Paradigms and Instructional Methods

Conceptions or definitions of learning are certainly debatable. To begin, consider the following three conceptions of learning:

- "Learning is a change in human disposition or capability that persists over a period of time and is not simply ascribable to processes of growth" (Gagné, 1985, p. 2).
- "Learning is the relatively permanent change in a person's knowledge or behavior due to experience" (Mayer, 1982, p. 1040).
- "Learning is a conscious activity guided by intentions and reflections" (Jonassen & Land, 2000, p. v).

The first two conceptions regard learning as a product; the third speaks of learning as a process. The second conception of learning requires a shared understanding of knowledge. Discussions of epistemology (conceptions of knowledge) may proceed along multiple paths. For instance, we could speak of *declarative knowledge, procedural knowledge, conditional knowledge, inert knowledge*, or consider other descriptors of knowledge. Since we must necessarily limit this discussion, we will consider perspectives that have stood the test of time; we will consider classical forms of knowledge.

Greek philosophers conceived of four distinct types of knowledge, *episteme, techne, phronesis*, and *mètis* (Baumard, 1999). We may regard *episteme* as knowledge about things, explicit facts, principles, and representations, universal truths, which are circulated and taught. *Techne*, the root word of technology, is regarded as skill or craft, which is the capability to perform or to do things. Such performances are observable. *Episteme* and *techne* are forms of explicit knowledge whereas *phronesis* and *mètis* are types of tacit knowledge. Tacit knowledge is not easily shared. *Phronesis* is quite the opposite of *episteme*. *Phronesis* is meaningful to the individual who lived the experience; it increases through trial and error and through social interactions. *Phronesis* may be regarded as wisdom gained through experience. Consider, for instance, the knowledge gained through experiencing a minor automobile accident. While everyone who analyzes car accident data knows that riding in a car is somewhat dangerous, one who lives through a car accident has personal knowledge of the risks. *Mètis* is regarded as conjectural knowledge, which is situational, unpredictable, complex, and dynamic. For example, a coach who knows the capabilities of each player on the team and has some knowledge of the strengths and weaknesses of the opposing team devises a plausible winning strategy and directs players to employ tactics consistent with the strategy. The coach may alter the tactics during play in order to maximize the likelihood of winning the game. In such light, *mètis* is foresight of continually changing circumstances. *Mètis* is also evident, for instance, in choices to present particular personal characteristics to different people in order to enhance mutual enjoyment or benefit. This is consistent with Oppien (in Baumard, 1999, p. 69): "Deliver to each of your friends a different aspect of yourself." In light of this discussion, we will proceed with the view that learning is a gain in knowledge, in any combination of its four classical forms, *episteme, techne, phronesis*, and *metis*, attained through conscious experience.

At present, three main paradigms of learning have emerged: behaviorism, cognitivism, and constructivism. We derive an instructional method from each one, which we will implement in our instructional apps.

Behaviorism

In his most influential work, John B. Watson (1913), the founder or father of behaviorism, sought to distinguish behaviorism from the view of psychology as the study of human consciousness or mental states. Behaviorists, beginning with Watson, study observable effects of the environment on animals and people in attempts to predict and control behavior. "The behaviorist, in his efforts to get a unitary scheme of animal response, recognizes no dividing line between man and brute" (Watson, 1913, p. 158). Two paragraphs later, Watson (1913) confesses that the large number of experiments he and other behaviorists had performed on animals had contributed little to human psychology. Yet Watson did not want psychology to be based entirely on perceptions of human mental states based on self-reported introspection. Watson sought for psychology to accept "facts of behavior" (Watson, 1913, p. 159) as complementary to consideration of human consciousness. Given the acceptance of both behavioral psychology and cognitive psychology for more than half a century, Watson's proposed merger seems to have been accepted. An instructional method is evident in the work of behaviorists, including the "Father of Educational Psychology," Edward L. Thorndike (1912), John B. Watson (1913), B. F. Skinner (1974), and in related work (Watson, Tolman, Titchener, Lashley, & Thorndike, 2009).

One implements behavioral instruction by presenting a stimulus, eliciting a response, and providing feedback to the learner. Owing to the association of a particular response with a specific stimulus, association learning is an alternative expression for behavioral learning. Positive feedback encourages a specific response to a particular stimulus, whereas negative feedback reduces the likelihood of a specific response to a particular stimulus.

Association learning is effective for children and adults. Teachers "shape" student behavior by rewarding children (e.g., praise, smile, congratulate, give a gold star, eliminate homework for a day) when they act appropriately and punish children (e.g., chastise, detain, exclude, suspend) for inappropriate behavior. Rewards and punishments ("carrots and sticks") also shape adult behavior even though adults are more likely to be aware of the motives. Adults are more likely to buy an electric vehicle or install solar panels in their home for a tax credit than if no financial incentive is available. The possibility to gain large sums of money by obtaining federal "Reach for the Top" funding caused some state legislators to change state education laws. Association learning is an effective instructional method to implement when seeking to help learners acquire particular skills or when helping learners acquire facts that are easily shared (*episteme*). For shaping behavior regarded as trivial by human beings, association learning is also effective for birds, dogs, giraffes, elephants, and other brutes.

Cognition

Throughout the first half of the twentieth century, behaviorism impeded the study of consciousness in learning. However, by the 1940s, Karl Lashley (who was solidly in the behaviorist camp, originally) and other psychologists would no longer accept the behaviorist belief in the "supremacy and determining power of the environment" (Gardner, 1985, p. 11) or that chains of stimulus–response associations could account for complex behavior, such as formation of language, playing a musical instrument, or problem solving. Lashley and others insisted on the acceptance of studies of consciousness. Even though introspection might always be questioned, maybe neuroscience and computing could lend objective support to studies of internal mental states. Indeed, McCulloch and Pitts (1943) had shown that a neural network, a nerve cell's operations and its connections to other neurons, could be expressed in logic. Further, logic could be realized by binary signals through a circuit. This establishes a relationship between a biological nervous system and a neural network implemented by a digital computer. Gardner (1985, p. 18) captured this relationship with the words of von Neumann: "Anything that can be exhaustively and unambiguously described ... is ... realizable by a suitable finite neural network." Further, Norbert Weiner offered that feedback loops are central to control mechanisms, whether natural (biological) or artificial (implemented by machine). Weiner originally conceived of this coherence of biological and technological ideas in 1948 and launched a new field of study in control and communication, called *Cybernetics*. In summarizing the technological and biological influences at the foundation of cognitive science, Gardner (1985) identifies Herbert A. Simon as a founder of cognitive science. Simon was a graduate student at the University of Chicago in the 1940s, working with Rudolph Carnap (a specialist in symbolic logic) and aware of the work of Weiner and von Neumann. Further, work on the nervous system was being conducted in nearby laboratories by biologists Ralph Gerard, Heinrich Klüver, Roger Sperry, and Paul Weiss. Moreover, Gardner (1985) describes the relationships, meetings, communications, journal articles, and conferences among those researchers and founders of cognitive science, such as Jerome Bruner, Noam Chomsky, John McCarthy, George Miller, and Alan Newell. Miller (2003) actually identifies September 11, 1956 as the start date of cognitive science, even though he acknowledges that the early 1950s were progressive. Miller and the others had important roles in the genesis of cognitive science, but they were part of a much larger movement of psychologists, computer scientists, linguists, and biologists within and beyond the United States.

Ulric Neisser, who wrote the book *Cognitive Psychology* (Neisser, 1967), was influential in the earliest years of cognitive psychology or, as Newell and Simon (1972) called it, "information processing psychology." Indeed, the Association for Psychological Science identifies Neisser as the "Father of Cognitive Psychology." Atkinson and Shiffrin (1968) presented a three-stage model of information processing, which posits sensory memory, short-term memory, and long-term memory. Stimuli are perceived by senses; certain of those stimuli (attenuation theory of Treisman, 1964) or perhaps a single stimulus (attention filtering theory advanced by Broadbent, 1958) is selected and advances to short-term memory. Rehearsal (practice) in short-term memory may be sufficient for storage in long-term memory. Such a view of learning is regarded as an *information processing model* and is analogous to computer functionality (input, processing, output). One criticism of the three-stage model is that it is over simplified because some recollections may occur without rehearsal. Baddeley and Hitch (1974) replaced short-term memory with working memory, which consisted of multiple components, including an executive function, as well as a phonological loop (for auditory processing) and a visual–spatial pad (for processing visual information). Research by Paivio (1971, 1986) on dual coding, as well as experiments by Craik and Lockhart (1972) pertaining to levels of processing (e.g., rehearsal strategy, such as use of mnemonics, matters), enlighten cognitive processing. Further, work by Bransford, Franks, Morris, and Stein (1979) on salience of stimuli provides additional insight into cognitive processing. According to Bransford et al. (1979), we are more likely to remember unusual stimuli than something we regard as common. Overall, the research (and perhaps your personal experience as well) persuades one to the view that salience of stimuli matters to cognitive processing, which is tantamount to saying that salience of stimuli is important for learning.

Jean Piaget (1936) was not deterred by psychologists who favored behaviorism. Using observation and interviewing, Piaget developed a stage theory of development in children, which included the *sensorimotor, preoperational, concrete operational*, and *formal operational* stages. Further, Piaget proposed that intellectual development was an adaptive process involving *assimilation, accommodation,* and *equilibration.* According to Piaget, knowledge is assimilated into existing schemata (mental models) until the learner encounters atypical cases. Such a state of disequilibrium prompts accommodation, which is the restructuring of the mental models. For example, one might conceive of chairs as having four legs, a seat, and a back support. When one encounters an object with a seat supported by three legs, it might seem like a chair. A person can sit on the object, though it has only three legs and no back support. This leads one to accommodate (refine) the conception of "objects for sitting" by forming a new concept for *chair,* which includes stools. Subsequent assimilating to the refined *chair* concept is necessary when encountering an object for sitting that has four supporting legs and no back support.

Since cognitive science has achieved much in the past half century, it may seem odd that it was ever impeded by behaviorism and that considerable and sustained support for studies of consciousness and mental states by (radical) cognitivists was necessary for the emergence of cognitive science. Such persistence paid off. A new science evolved, which we draw on now to inform development of effective instruction.

Unlike behavioral instruction, which is observable and well defined, cognitive instruction seeks to help learners develop mental models. There is no single instructional method for helping people develop mental models, but researchers have identified some effective methods for helping learners perceive, encode (store), and process stimuli, which facilitates learning. Paivio (1971, 1986) and Mayer (2009) concluded that many people benefit from presentations containing both verbal and visual stimuli. Ausubel (1960, 1963) demonstrated the effectiveness of *advance organizers,* which make use of analogies and metaphors. [Some people mistakenly conceive of advance organizers as meaning to state the learning objective in advance of the instruction. Some *accommodation* is necessary on their part in order to include the concepts of comparative and expository organizers.] One method for visually depicting relationships among concepts is a concept map (Novak & Gowin, 1984), which includes a visual representation of connected concepts; verbal expressions make the connections explicit.

Consider how a mathematics teacher might use an advance organizer to help learners extend their conception of numeric representations. When learning to count and to represent numbers in base 10 (using behavioral instruction), human beings form a concept of place value. Accordingly, elementary school children can represent a Base 10 number, such as 739, as 700 + 30 + 9, which conveys knowledge that 7 is in the hundreds place, 3 is in the tens place, and 9 is in the ones place. To help a person learn numeric representation in a base other than 10, say Base 8, an advance organizer may be utilized, beginning with explicit reminders about the place values of Base 10 numbers. The place values of Base 10 numbers from right to left, are the ones place (10^0), tens place (10^1), hundreds place (10^2), and so forth. Increasing the exponent by one determines the next place value (10^3 is the thousands place, 10^4 the ten-thousands place, etc.). To understand Base 8 numbers replace the base, 10, with 8. In Base 8, from right to left, the place values are the ones place (8^0), eights place (8^1), sixty-fours place (8^2), five hundred twelve's place (8^3), four thousand ninety-six's place (8^4), and so on. The explanation would also note that Base 10 has 10 digits, 0 through 9. Similarly, Base 8 has 8 digits, 0 through 7 (the number of digits and the largest digit in place-value number systems is the base minus one). Thus 216 Base 8 (216_8) has 2 in the sixty-fours place (8^2), 1 in the eights place (8^1), and 6 in the ones place (8^0), so 216_8 is $2 \ast 64 + 1 \ast 8 + 6$, which is $128 + 8 + 6$ or 142 (Base 10).

This type of cognitivist instruction includes an advance organizer known as a *comparative organizer*. Such an organizer is an explanation with an analogy. Other possibilities for cognitive instruction would include use of mnemonics, metaphors, or concept mapping. Unlike behaviorism, since cognition accepts that internal processing matters, cognitivist instruction can employ a guided discovery approach. That is, the instruction can present a problem without advancing an explanation or possible solution. Learners must draw on their own prior knowledge and deduce how to solve the problem. Instruction using guided discovery presents a problem and responds to the learner's problem solving attempts. We will implement this instructional strategy in Chapter 5 to help learners solve a coin puzzle and the Farmer, Wolf, Goat, and Cabbage problem.

As noted in the previous section, behavioral instruction can help learners remember facts, which is the lowest level of Bloom's Taxonomy (Anderson & Krathwohl, 2001). Behavioral instruction is also useful for learning simple skills. You may recall helping a child learn to spread butter or margarine or hummus or something on bread or a cracker. The child may hold the knife vertically initially, but such an orientation applies the substance inefficiently. Telling the child, or demonstrating, that a horizontal orientation of the knife will spread the substance quickly is often all the child needs to learn to use a knife for spreading a substance efficiently. Negative feedback about the vertical orientation along with positive feedback about the horizontal orientation is sufficient for the child to learn how to use a knife for spreading a substance.

This section discussed the suitability of cognitivist instruction for attaining knowledge by refining mental models. Place values in a number system depend on the base and the base need not always be 10. An alternative example could discuss how people who have learned some words (using behavioral instruction) would benefit from cognitivist instruction to learn the concept of sentence and the procedure to write a sentence. A parent or teacher might begin simply by describing a sentence as a group of words that makes a statement. Such an explanation accompanied by examples helps learners to gain an initial conception of a sentence and then enables them to produce *simple sentences*. Later, the concepts of subject and predicate (a group of words containing a verb and stating something about the subject) would be introduced, as would additional types of sentences. Specifically, sentences may present a question, a command, or an exclamation. Then learners could gain even more refined conceptions of sentences by learning the characteristics of *compound and complex sentences*. By helping learners gain increasingly sophisticated conceptions of sentences, the learners become able to apply their knowledge of words and sets of words to write increasingly complex sentences. In learning to write sentences, learners apply their knowledge of words and sentence formation. Application is in the middle of Bloom's Taxonomy.

In the instructional scenarios above, the learners have yet to solve algebraic expressions and to write essays, for instance. In general terms, the learners have yet to: transfer their knowledge to different contexts; justify a proposed solution to a real world problem; make decisions in uncertain circumstances; or synthesize their knowledge and skill in order to build something new. Constructivist instruction, as discussed in the next section, will help one learn how to accomplish those tasks, which are at the top of Bloom's Taxonomy.

Constructivism

People hold diverse conceptions of constructivism (Phillips, 1995), which seems rather fitting because constructivists regard knowledge as uniquely constructed by each individual (Duffy & Jonassen, 1992; Tobias & Duffy, 2009; von Glasersfeld, 1989, 1995). Constructivists assert that each person constructs her or his own reality. To discuss variability in conceptions of constructivism, Phillips (1995) created a classification system focused on three particular ideological themes, which concern: acquisition of public versus personal knowledge; knowledge construction explained by individual mental activity (cognition) versus sociopolitical processes; and ontological position, the extent to which one accepts interpretivism (reality is internal, a state of one's mind) or positivism (there exists an external objective reality). Phillips (1995) holds that, while each theme identifies two completely divergent perspectives, there is a continuum of more moderate positions between the extremes. For the purposes of this discussion, the ontological question is pertinent because it is regarded as distinguishing constructivism from both behaviorism and cognitivism. Further, according to Jonassen (1991) and Bednar, Cunningham, Duffy, and Perry (1991), such a distinction has revolutionary implications for the design of instruction.

One key implication of this learning paradigm is that constructivist instruction ought to engage learners in authentic tasks, which often involve complex fields of study or endeavors. Functioning in such ill-structured domains is challenging. After all, there is no single best way to write a novel, design a building, create effective drug treatments, compose music, play a musical instrument, invent devices, devise mathematical proofs, conduct research, collaborate, sell products, or respond to global climate change, for instance. To avoid acquisition of *inert* knowledge (Whitehead, 1929), such as trivial information one cannot apply, constructivist instruction seeks to engage learners in real-world practice, which bodes well for continually gaining knowledge, particularly *phronesis* and *mètis*.

The issue of personal versus public knowledge raised by Phillips (1995) is also pertinent. Teachers want each learner to gain personal knowledge. Researchers want to discover new knowledge for public dissemination. Professors want to achieve both of those outcomes: They want their students to learn to conduct disciplined inquiries (to gain personal knowledge) while engaged in collaborative research to discover new knowledge (public knowledge). Constructivist instruction supports ill-structured problem solving "wherein learners generate new knowledge and subproblems as they determine how and when knowledge is used" (Hannafin, Hannafin, Land, & Oliver, 1997, p. 109). Potentially, learners can generate new personal and public knowledge.

In the Phillips (1995) framework, the knowledge construction issue is also relevant because acceptance of the individual mental state perspective would make cognition the foundation of constructivism. It would be difficult to argue persuasively that constructivism is fundamentally different from cognition if constructivism is founded on cognition. Yet, that is what constructivists maintain. They do so by emphasizing the interpretivist distinction. According to Bednar et al. (1991), the objectivist epistemology is the most crucial fundamental assumption of both behaviorism and what they call *traditional* cognitive science (p. 20). Seeking to be "very clear" about the distinction between the fundamental assumptions of constructivism and both behaviorism and cognitivism, Bednar et al. (1991, p. 21) declare: "Constructivism is completely incompatible with objectivism." Yet one sentence after that declaration, Bednar et al. (1991) find constructivism and cognition entirely compatible, joining the two words in order to create the label "Constructivist Cognitive Science" and proceed to discuss the constructivist view of cognition as nothing new. That contradiction, and papers on cognition identifying the same instructional methods as constructivist (Wilson & Cole, 1991) notwithstanding, constructivists have elevated the importance of instruction situated in real-world contexts, which enables learners to grapple with complex issues from multiple perspectives (to increase *cognitive flexibility*) in order to learn.

Like cognitivist instruction, there is no single form of constructivist instruction. However, there are consistent themes across forms of constructivist instruction, such as problem-based learning (Barrows & Tamblyn, 1980), anchored instruction (Bransford, Sherwood, Hasselbring, Kinzer, & Williams, 1990; Cognition and Technology Group at Vanderbilt,

1990), and cognitive apprenticeship (Collins, Brown, & Newman, 1989). We have already encountered the situated learning (Lave & Wenger, 1990; McLellan, 1996) and cognitive flexibility (Spiro, Feltovich, Jacobson, & Coulson, 1991) themes. In addition, the learner is conceived as active and the teacher as a mentor or coach who models real-world performance and then encourages and monitors the learner, adjusting task difficulty as necessary.

Research comparing performance of experts and novices has revealed that experts have developed qualitatively distinct mental models (Bereiter & Scardamelia, 1987; Chi, Feltovich, & Glaser, 1981; Larkin, McDermott, Simon, & Simon, 1980). To help novices refine their mental models, cognitive apprenticeship is helpful, whether learning to read (Palincsar & Brown, 1984), write (Scardamalia & Bereiter, 1985), solve mathematical problems (Schoenfeld, 1985), or ski (Burton, Brown, & Fischer, 1984), for instance. A cognitive apprenticeship is a form of apprenticeship (Rogoff, 1990), which involves modeling and guidance by an experienced and competent person. For example, a journeyman electrician might demonstrate how to strip wires and hang a light fixture or a master plumber might demonstrate how to seal plastic pipes. Those demonstrations and practice with feedback help apprentices learn to perform fundamental skills. Apprenticeships have much to do with social learning, language, and culture (Bandura, 1962, 1977, 1986; Vygotsky, 1962, 1978). Beyond those traditional conceptions of apprenticeship, cognitive apprenticeships emphasize conceptual model building, rather than physical skill, for real world problem solving (Collins et al., 1989). In addition, cognitive apprenticeship attends to metacognition (knowing about knowing). That is, mentors or coaches discuss tacit strategies (heuristics) they use during problem solving and seek to guide their apprentices to reflect and self-correct.

Through behavioral and cognitive instruction, individuals may learn to use a hammer and a saw, to sew and stitch, to swing a tennis racquet to serve and volley, and to hit a forehand and backhand. Given behavioral and cognitive instruction, learners may also form conceptions of nouns, adjectives, verbs, adverbs, phrases, and may compose sentences. In addition, through behavioral and cognitive instruction, learners may acquire knowledge of mathematical concepts, such as place value, integers, rational numbers, irrational numbers, and may simplify arithmetic expressions correctly by following the proper order of operations. Constructivist instruction adds a measure of expertise. After engaging in constructivist instruction, learners would, for instance, draw on mathematical knowledge and skills to solve previously unseen problems. After constructivist instruction, learners would detect weaknesses in an opponent on a tennis court and devise a strategy to defeat the opponent by executing the shot-making skills attained earlier. In Chapter 6, we will create two apps to help learners become more able to perform like educational researchers.

Each learning paradigm is more nuanced and complex than presented in the space available here, but we have established common ground in the three paradigms and have three instructional methods to implement in Part 2.

1.2 Computer-based Instruction

Here we consider the history of computer-based instruction in light of its contextual antecedents. Through the early part of the twentieth century, the distribution of print materials, particularly books and worksheets, was the primary method for disseminating instruction. As discussed earlier, behaviorism offers a stimulus–response method for learning. Thorndike (1912, p. 165) opined:

> If, by a miracle of mechanical ingenuity, a book could be so arranged that only to him who had done what was directed on page one would page two become visible, and so on, much that now requires personal instruction could be managed by print.

Little did Thorndike know that his vision of a mechanical device for automating instruction would come to be implemented by digital computers and his "miracle device" for enabling linear progress upon successful interaction would later be disparaged resolutely. In speaking of the failure of computer-based instruction, Klopfer (1986) concluded that much CBI is "disappointing in quality, pedagogically naïve and mundane." Such a conclusion, though, puts us ahead of the story of computer-based instruction.

There was a brief time in history when instruction was implemented by a mechanical device. Sydney L. Pressey (1926), a professor at The Ohio State University, developed a device capable of providing feedback to the user's response. However, that teaching machine and similar ones were very limited in capability and were not improved much over time. Rather, the development of instructional devices stalled until developers ported *programmed instruction*, which is a form of behavioral instruction from print materials to digital computers in the early 1960s.

One instantiation or implementation of programmed instruction presents a sentence with a blank for a missing word. The missing word often appears in a prior sentence. For example, Joyce, Weil, and Calhoun (2000, p. 333) attribute this prompt for English instruction: Words are divided into classes. We call the largest class nouns. Nouns are a class of _____.

The correct answer, *words*, is derived from the two statements and also appears in close proximity to the blank line. Much of the early computer-assisted instruction (CAI) implemented this type of programmed instruction and other forms of behavioral instruction, but again we are a little ahead of the story.

Prior to developing CAI, educational technologists offered educational programming on radio in the 1920s through 1940s before shifting focus to instructional television in the 1950s. Both instructional radio and TV, new mass media for their times, were initially perceived as highly effective forms of instruction. Further, proponents of instructional radio, such as George Zook, and later advocates of instructional TV claimed that the devices would revolutionize education by solving instructional ills. Among the instructional ills of the early 1940s was the problem of training large numbers of soldiers. Accordingly, the US military was highly receptive to models of systematic processes for the design and development of instruction and invested millions of dollars in training, which catalyzed the educational technology field. Ultimately, radio education came to be regarded as great for distributing information, but not particularly effective for instruction. Similarly, instructional television did not meet expectations. According to Heinich (1991, p. 63), "the television people got caught up in the delivery system and thought all one needed was a dynamic personality and a camera." (Educators ready to whip out their smartphones and tap the video recording button would do well to recall that quotation and also read Section 2.1.1 for helpful tips on the development of instructional video.) Some instructional programming for TV is still created today, so traditional TV (capable of displaying moving images and playing audio) as an instructional medium is not as big a failure as radio. However, traditional TV did not enable interaction; so when computers came around, educational technologists were again quick to fathom that the new device would have to offer effective instruction like no other device ever invented. After all, as the proverb goes: I hear and I forget; I see and I remember; I do and I understand. As the 1950s came to a close, expectations about the potential benefits of instruction by computer grew and the US Military in particular was keen to adopt CAI. As early as 1958, the U.S. Air Force held a conference on the topic of computer instruction at the University of Pennsylvania at which IBM and others presented studies.

In the 1960s, users logged into mainframe computers or minicomputers using so-called *dumb terminals*, which was quite progressive for the time, given that punched cards were in common use through the 1970s. Such a terminal included a keyboard and a black-and-white monitor capable of displaying text. Such a user interface would have sufficed for learners to proceed through programmed instruction in the PLATO (Programmed Logic for Automatic Teaching Operations) system, but Donald Bitzer (the engineering student at the University of Illinois in Champaign-Urbana regarded as the Father of PLATO) realized that for educational purposes the terminal should display graphics as well. PLATO, first available in 1960, was the first CAI system, sporting a keyboard and black-and-orange monitor.[1] PLATO was continually enhanced and functional for four decades, ultimately including the TUTOR programming language, conceived by biology graduate student Paul Tenczar, which was used to create instructional modules. Also, PLATO eventually included a text to speech synthesizer and a music synthesizer. By the late 1970s, PLATO included thousands of terminals worldwide. Eventually, coursework on PLATO offered instruction to learners from elementary school to university.

Following PLATO, and founded on Component Display Theory, instruction was developed over multiple years for a minicomputer system called TICCIT for Time-Shared Interactive Computer-Controlled Information Television. Eventually, TICCIT included lessons to learn algebra, chemistry, physics, English (grammar, mechanics, spelling, and composition), English as a second language (ESL), Danish, French, German, Italian, Japanese, Norwegian, Portuguese, Spanish, Swedish, and Thai. Anastasio and Alderman (1973) conducted a series of evaluations of PLATO and TICCIT. Ultimately, some of the CAI in TICCIT was ported to early microcomputers through projects at Brigham Young University (Merrill, Fletcher, & Schneider, 1980). TICCIT and PLATO benefitted from federal grant funding, which the US government was quick to provide in the post-Sputnik era.

By 1980, hardware had advanced from vacuum tubes through practical transistors to integrated circuits. In 1976, Steve Wozniak created the first Apple microcomputer, a 1MHz 8-bit 6502 CPU with 4K of RAM, expandable to 8K, which Steve Jobs sold for $500. On August 12, 1981, at the Waldorf Astoria in New York City, IBM announced the first IBM PC, which included a 16-bit Intel 8088 CPU with 16K RAM. That computer, with a keyboard and an option for a color/graphics monitor with 16 colors, cost $1,565. In the early 1960s, an IBM computer cost 9 million dollars, required an air-conditioned quarter-acre of space and a staff of 60 people to maintain it.[2] Operating systems were command line interfaces until windows systems replaced them in the late 1980s.

The 1980s was the decade of the standalone computer. Magnetic and optical storage improved throughout the decade. Data were infrequently stored on audio or paper tape. Early microcomputer users typically transported diskettes to move data from one computer to another. Initially, users carried 5.25 inch floppy media until they were replaced by more reliable 3.5 inch magnetic storage media with firm plastic cases. By the middle of the decade, compact discs became available, which made vinyl records of music obsolete and enabled lightweight storage of large data repositories. Grolier's encyclopedia was available in text only form in 1985, which individuals installed on a standalone computer. Without network connectivity readily available, the encyclopedic resource could not be made available instantly for everyone with a computer to use. Compact Discs (CDs) and other storage media were mailed or exchanged in person.

Informed by PLATO and TICCIT, developers in the 1980s created instructional software founded on behaviorist instruction for individual learners using computers with low-resolution monitors and, eventually, graphical user interfaces. Assisted in part by federal grants, educational technologists evaluated the effects of standalone instructional software as the first wave of microcomputers appeared in K-12 classrooms. Conferences focused on computer-assisted instruction. Amid all the hyperbole about the positive and revolutionary impact CAI would have, some subject matter experts found CAI entirely unsatisfactory (Klopfer, 1986) because it was not delivering on its promise to revolutionize learning. As expressed by Walbert (1989, p. 281), the consensus view of educators in science, economics, and other content areas was that "the computer was not the 'dream' teaching tool it was once thought to be." Much software merely displayed text on a screen and urged the learner to "Press spacebar to continue" (Walbert, 1989, p. 282). In addition to subject matter experts, some educational researchers were finding no statistically significant difference in achievement whether learners engaged in CAI or alternative instruction. Two camps had formed with each side holding dearly to their opposing views on the effectiveness of CAI.

Clark debated multiple researchers in seeking to resolve whether media or instructional methods account for learning (Clark, 1983, 1991, 1994, 2005; Kozma, 1991; Kulik, Bangert, & Williams, 1983; Kulik, Kulik, & Bangert-Drowns, 1985; Luterbach, 2005a; 2005b; Petkovich & Tennyson, 1985). Clark realized that many studies were showing no significant difference in learning gains. The Kuliks and others protested. Clark (1983, p. 445) concluded: "The best current evidence is that media are mere vehicles that deliver instruction but do not influence student achievement any more than the truck that delivers our groceries causes changes in our nutrition." Clark was urged by colleagues to soften this strong claim, but he held firm and won that debate. Importantly, instructional app designers and developers need to accept, from an effectiveness perspective, that many instructional methods can be delivered equally well with or without a computer. That does not hold true for the efficiency perspective (Clark, 2005). Returning to the effectiveness claim, Clark argues that since instructional media and method are always separable, all instructional methods can be delivered equally well with or without a computer. I disagree. As I discuss in Section 1.5.1, I claim that computers are unlike "display and play" media and provide learners with unique instructional experiences. The conclusion Clark drew in 1983, which is regarded as valid by many educational technologists today, strikes me as valid only for particularly narrow views of learning and media, as discussed in Section 1.5.1.

Some researchers and developers sought to offer a different form of CAI, called Intelligent Computer Assisted Instruction (ICAI), which, drawing on work in Artificial Intelligence, sought to improve upon standard CAI by modeling instructional activity in a manner similar to a human tutor (Kearsley, 1987; Sleeman & Brown, 1982; Wenger, 1987). ICAI software sought to model the learner, the content, and pedagogical practice, including human–tutor dialog (Duchastel & Imbeau, 1988; Nwana, 1990; Roberts & Park,

1991; Romiszowski, 1987), in order to adapt instruction to the learner's progress. ICAI software may implement an expert system, such as Mycin (1974), which was a rule-based intelligent system and a research project intended to assist physicians in selection of antimicrobial therapies. Mycin was based on a model of imperfect reasoning (Shortliffe & Buchanan, 1975). In addition to describing models of content domains in ICAI systems, Park and Seidel (1989) discussed the pedagogical and learner models. In 1994, Seidel and Park (1994) offered a brief history of ICAI. Work in this field has continued through the decades (Inoue, 2001; Jonassen & Wang, 1993; Merrill, Reiser, Ranney, & Trafton, 1992; Pek & Poh, 2004) and remains active today through research and development (Kulik & Fletcher, 2016), international societies, and conferences (i.e., Artificial Intelligence in Education; and International Conference on Intelligent Tutoring Systems, which are held in alternate years).

While much standalone computer-assisted instruction was developed in the 1980s for individual use, that "Computer as Tutor" perspective on how to utilize computers for learning was just one of three perspectives advanced by Robert P. Taylor (1980) in *The Computer in School: Tutor, Tool, and Tutee*. The "Computer as Tool" perspective promoted the view that students should learn application software, such as word processing, spreadsheets, and slide presentation software, in order to complete practical tasks. Additionally, students may also realize that a computer is a device with a central processing unit (CPU), which draws data from read only memory (ROM) and utilizes random access memory (RAM). Further, students might learn that computers interface with input devices (e.g., keyboard and mouse) and output devices (e.g., monitor and printer). In the 1980s, there was a growing sense that students should become *computer literate*. Indeed, the "Computer as Tool" perspective prompted massive redesigns of curriculum in State Education Agencies. Concomitantly, pre-service teacher preparation and in-service teacher professional development changed considerably in order to foster integration or use of computers in schools for instructional purposes (Nelson, 2008; Roblyer, 2016). That work continues today amidst vastly different notions about how to best utilize computers for learning in schools (Fishman & Dede, 2017).

Throughout the latter part of the 1980s, many users began sending email through university and commercial computer systems using low band-rate modems from their homes. Many computer users also transferred small files and posted information on electronic bulletin board systems, which were the earliest online communities. The latter half of the 1980s also introduced a new technology for information exchange.

In the middle of the 1980s, Bill Atkinson and Dan Winkler developed Hypercard, which favors branching to items of interest over a linear progression through content. That form of branching was achieved through hyperlinks. Ted Nelson (1965) first used the term hyperlink. Previously, Vannevar

Bush (1945) had advanced the concept of a Memex device, which would link between content from multiple sources, particularly the tiny photographs of pages of books, magazines, and newspapers stored on microfiche. In Hypercard, content was arranged in a stack of virtual cards, which is analogous to a stack of cardboard cards, but the hyperlinks on the virtual cards prompted branching. Consequently, in Hypercard stacks developed for instructional purposes, learners pursued content as they wished, rather than in a strict linear manner. In 1987, Apple bundled Hypercard in new Mac computers. Since learners could explore content as they wished, Hypercard stacks enabled guided discovery or constructivist approaches to learning. Had Atkinson enabled access to Hypercard stacks over the Internet, the World Wide Web might have been the World Wide Hypercard Stack (see Atkinson interview in Kahney, 2002).

As interest shifted away from standalone computers to connected computers and educators tired of CAI based on behavioral instruction, attention to computer-assisted instruction waned. For nearly three decades, the World Wide Web, with its hypermedia technology, has been making text, audio, and video content accessible instantly throughout the world. In addition, web browser technologies enabled quick access to email. Greater connection to people and events around the world encourages conceptions of a global village. One of the biggest impacts of the web on education was the change to instructional delivery. Unlike traditional correspondence courses, which provided learners with infrequent feedback due to the pace of postal delivery, learning management systems and other tools on the web enable students to receive feedback from an instructor and peers in a few minutes (or less). The effectiveness and convenience of online courses continue to increase enrollments in online programs (Allen, Seaman, Poulin, & Straut, 2016).

Another fundamental change in education initiated by the web was development of learning experiences appropriate for hypermedia technologies. Thousands of teachers and students shared webquests (Dodge, 1995), which employ a guided discovery instructional method. Opportunities for rapid online collaboration among peers and others accelerated the movement away from CAI. Rather than always consume computer-assisted instruction on a standalone computer, learners engaged in alternative instruction, which sometimes involved guided discovery, as well as online collaboration and feedback. By the end of the 1990s, one rarely heard of CAI, or related forms of instruction, such as computer-aided instruction or computer-managed instruction. Rather, the conversation shifted to technologies for learning. Use of the Internet for email, file transfer, and the web prompted another round of significant revisions to curricula and to teacher preparation and teacher professional development.

In the 2000s, the importance of collaboration and interactivity on the web grew with Web 2.0 technologies, which turned the read only web into the read/write web. That is, on the original web, users browsed relatively static content published on web pages. Users were consumers on the original web. Developers of websites were relatively few. However, with Web 2.0 technologies, users also became producers. Through blogging, individual users posted new content regularly; additionally, those who read the content often posted comments. Also in Web 2.0, a process known as *crowd sourcing*, in which each person in a large group voluntarily makes a relatively small contribution, resulted in the development of large knowledge bases, such as Wikipedia. Unlike traditional encyclopedias, particular experts were not hired to create entries in Wikipedia, but the entries are regarded as sufficiently accurate for many real-world purposes. As Herbert Simon realized, rational agents (people) do not have complete information and consequently must make decisions within a "bounded rationality," which leads to *satisficing* or acceptance of satisfactory if not optimal solutions. (Work along that line earned Herbert Simon the Nobel Prize in Economics in 1978.)

Another key shift in technologies for learning occurred in the late 2000s with the advent of mobile devices. Mobile devices introduced a new app distribution model. With a couple of finger taps on a smartphone or tablet, an app is delivered, installed, and opened, which brings new functionality to the user. In this work, users are learners, and this distribution channel makes possible the delivery of instructional apps to learners with a few finger taps. This distribution channel was also ported to desktop computers, which also makes it possible for learners to obtain instructional apps for desktop computers readily. Development of apps is different from using a computer as a tutor or as a tool, which brings us to the third of Taylor's perspectives on computers in education.

Taylor's (1980) third perspective on uses of computers in education, "Computer as Tutee," encouraged learners to program computers. Seymour Papert, whom some regard as the "Father of Educational Computing" (Stager, 204, p. 56) or the "grandfather of educational computing" (Fluck & Bower, 2015), while others view him as the "Father of the Maker Movement" (Libow Martinez, & Stager, 2013), was especially critical of computer-assisted instruction and banal uses of technology in education (Papert, 1972, 1980; Papert & Solomon, 1971). For Papert, the computer as an instructional device was the "smallest and least important" contribution of the computer to learning. Papert was strongly influenced by Piaget, having worked for him for four years at the University of Geneva, and conceived of children as active agents continually refining their views of the world. For Papert (1980), as expressed in his book, *Mindstorms: Children, Computers and Powerful Ideas*, children ought to construct. Papert provided a programming language, which enabled children to construct. Developed originally in 1968 with Daniel Bobrow, Wallace Feurzeig, Cynthia Solomon, and Richard Grant, and refined by multiple people over time (Papert, 1980), Logo is a complete programming language. Though not mentioned as a direct contributor to the development of Logo, Papert credits Marvin Minsky as the one who most influenced his work during this period. Logo enables children to hypothesize about and then to test possible solutions, such as when constructing and continually refining a program to control a virtual turtle. Soon it will be our turn to build instructional apps and to test hypotheses of primary and immediate interest to us. In particular, will the instruction we conceive be effective and efficient? In the longer run, we may use our programming knowledge and skill for creative expression and other forms of problem solving, perhaps to make instructional apps ubiquitous across diverse digital devices, to enhance instructional development tools, to implement machine learning programs, or to develop a machine tutor capable of real-time dialog, for instance.

Interest in computer programming has been enjoying a surge in popularity through attention to computational thinking (Wing, 2006; Fluck & Bower, 2015) and the hour of code movement (https://hourofcode.com/), as well as advancing to minority groups with respect to technological pursuits in movements such as Girls Who Code (https://girlswhocode.com/) and Black Girls Code (www.blackgirlscode.com/). Learning to create instructional apps offers all the rewards of any computer programming project. One can transfer knowledge of instructional app development to any type of app development.

For additional information on the history of computer-based instruction, you may wish to consider the works of Price (2008) and Sözcü, İpek, & Taşkın, (2013).

1.3 Instructional Simulations and Games

In educational technology, instructional simulations (sims) and games are often discussed together, even though they are distinct and neither requires the other. A simulation is a model of a real world process whereas a game is a competition. Yet simulations and games have much in common. Fundamentally, success in an instructional simulation or game requires learners to continually process multiple stimuli in order to decide which actions will continually advance them toward goal attainment. According to Barsalou (1999, p. 77), "comprehension is grounded in perceptual simulations that prepare agents for situated action." That is, whether engaged in an instructional simulation or game, learners will consider inputs, anticipate consequences of possible actions, and seek to make appropriate decisions. When learners are continually engaged in decision making and taking actions, which they sense are advancing toward ultimate goal attainment, they will enter into what Csikszentmihalyi (2014) calls a state of flow. Importantly, learners will enjoy the experience and persist to goal attainment.

The ability of games and sims to enable learners to enter a state of flow, which has much to do with engagement and persistence, is particularly appealing. Every instructional developer and instructor seeks to engage learners in order for them to attain the learning goals. A key criticism of CAI, rote learning, and programmed instruction is the monotony of the instruction, whether repeatedly filling in a blank, selecting from one of three or four choices, or memorizing definitions, for instance. In contrast, learners engaged in game play are keen to discover methods to overcome challenges resulting in attainment of intermediate goals *en route* to achieving the ultimate goal. When gaming, learners still respond to stimuli, but the experience is perceived much differently due, in part, to encountering animated images and sound effects, as well as controlling their actions.

Of course, there is nothing magical about games and sims. Eventually, learners will become fatigued; the flow state will end after playing any game or sim. Learners engaging in game play until reaching the point of exhaustion is a best-case scenario. There is no guarantee that a game or sim will be optimal. Some games and sims fail. As Homer and Plass (2014) have documented, when inputs confuse or overwhelm the learner, the game is not effective. Another challenge to creating effective instructional games and sims is the need to create the game or sim in a manner that will help learners attain a particular learning goal (Tobias, Fletcher, & Wind, 2014). Through continual refinement, developers can meet those challenges and enable learners to benefit from the effective interactive experiences.

Nearly all children and teenagers in the United States play video games: 99 percent of boys and 94 percent of girls according to Lenhart, Kahne, Middaugh, Macgill, Evans, and Vitak (2008). Video gaming is also popular among adults. According to the Entertainment Software Association (2016), the average video gamer is 35 years old; 56 percent of video gamers are 35 years of age or younger while 44 percent are over 35. Regarding gender, 59 percent of video gamers are male and 41 percent are female. The popularity of games has prompted intensive research into video gaming. Accordingly, research into multiple aspects of sims and games is plentiful (Ferdig, 2009; Gee, 2003; Steinkuehler, Squire, & Barab, 2012; Tobias et al., 2014; Zheng & Gardner, 2017). To prepare for instructional app development, this section considers opposing views on the effects of games. Some researchers regard gaming as beneficial while others find it harmful. Second, we will consider gender and cultural bias in games. Third, we consider game development strategies.

Effects of Video Game Play

Some psychological studies on the effects of playing video games warn of harmful effects. Indeed, decades of research on impacts of video games, including violent games, on aggression, addiction, and depression exist (Anderson, Shibuya, Ihori, Swing, Bushman, Sakamoto, & Saleem, 2010; Ferguson, 2007; Lemola, Brand, Vogler, Perkinson-Gloor, Allemand, & Grob, 2011). Decades of consistent findings constitute important work, which should not be overlooked. In contrast, though, many researchers discovered and documented many benefits to playing video games. Based on empirical studies, Przybylski, Rigby, and Ryan (2010) offer a model of video game engagement founded on self-determination theory. The model asserts that playing video games satisfies fundamental psychological needs, particularly competence, autonomy, and socialization. Multiplayer games are common, as are conversations between video gamers during play, whether in the same room or through headsets in separate locations. According to Granic, Lobel, and Engels (2014), playing video games "may be among the most efficient and effective means by which children and youth generate positive feelings." In addition to social and emotional benefits, many researchers have found cognitive benefits to playing video games. Compared with control groups, participants in video game treatments show significantly better attention allocation (to focus on pertinent information), greater spatial skills, and superior mental rotation abilities (Green & Bavelier, 2012; Uttal, Meadow, Tipton, Hand, Alden, Warren, & Newcombe, 2013; Wai, Lubinski, Benbow, & Steiger, 2010). Video game playing has also been associated with enhanced creativity (Jackson, Witt, Games, Fitzgerald, von Eye, & Zhao, 2012). In something of a contrast, Wouters, van Nimwegen, van Oostendorp, and van der Spek, (2013) found cognitive benefits, but no effects on motivation. Balancing video game play with other activities is important. According to Przybylski (2014), who studied effects based on duration of game play, less than 1 hour of video game play per day was associated with prosocial behavior and life satisfaction. Effects of moderate levels of game play (between 1 and 3 hours per day) were not significantly different from effects for nonplayers. Playing video games more than 3 hours a day (heavy play) was detrimental. The effects of heavy play were opposite to those of the group that played for less than 1 hour per day.

Gender and Cultural Bias in Video Games

Overall, video games display both gender and cultural bias (Carr & Pelletier, 2009; Dietz, 1998; Mou & Peng, 2009). In contrast to the effects of playing video games, there is no disagreement here about the findings. The problem is the striking inequities in frequency of presence, visual appearance, and role. Many games have no female characters. Dietz (1998) found 41 percent of games with no female characters while Beasley and Standley (2002) found female characters in only 14 percent of games. Sampling is critical, as always. Sometimes game researchers select samples from particular types of games, such as popular games. Other times researchers select a sample from among several thousand games. Granic et al. (2014) state that over a million video games exist. In visual comparisons with male characters, female characters were more likely to appear partially nude or in sexually revealing clothing, and were often represented with unrealistic body images (Beasley & Standley, 2002; Downs & Smith, 2010). Regarding roles, Dietz (1998) found that female characters were portrayed as heroines or action characters in 15 percent of the sample as opposed to victims or "damsels in distress" in 21 percent of the sample. There has been some increase in positive portrayal of female characters in games in the past decade, even to the point of declaring the "Lara phenomenon," which is "the appearance of a tough and competent female character in a dominant position" (Jansz & Martis, 2007, p. 142). That the conception of a tough and competent female character was regarded as phenomenal speaks to the level of sexism (Stermer & Burkley, 2015).

As per the research on gender, results pertaining to culture or race are confounded by character representations that make it difficult to discern gender or race. Nevertheless, white characters are more common in video games than characters of other races (Brand, Knight, & Majewski, 2003; Dill, Gentile, Richter, & Dill, 2005). In particular, Downs and Smith (2010) found that 31 percent were minority characters (21 percent black, 7 percent Asian, and 3 percent Hispanic). Interestingly, Mou and Peng (2009) did not find a study in which a minority was likely than a white character to be portrayed negatively. Actually, according to Lachlan, Smith, and Tamborini (2005), 40 percent of most violent characters were white while only 8 percent were Asian/Pacific Islander.

Instructional Sim and Game Development

Games are challenging, yet players persist to goal attainment and enjoy the experience. In such light, we should seek to *excite and engage learners until they master the learning goal.* How might we accomplish that?

In an article titled "Good Video Games and Good Learning," Gee (2005) asserts that effective games for learning incorporate particular learning principles. In the book *What Video Games Have to Teach us About Learning and Literacy,* which was published originally in 2003, Gee (2003) offered 36 learning principles, incorporated into video games, that are good for learning. Upon further reflection, Gee revised and reduced the original set (recognizing in 2005 that some principles address the same theme). In the 2005 article, Gee presented 16 learning principles. Gee makes no claim that the principles are evident in all video games good for learning, but does assert that the potential for learning is enhanced when the principles are incorporated into instruction, whether or not the instruction is a game. The set of 16 principles still seems excessive. I offer the following set of principles, which address similar themes.

Order Practice Tasks from Simple to Complex and Challenge Continually

This may be construed as a matter of common sense. However, it is easy to violate this principle. Seeking relevance to real world application, eager learners want to "run before they can walk." Learners need time to solve simple problems well in order to ultimately transfer knowledge to real world tasks. Research comparing experts and novices has shown that experts devise solutions based on the models they have developed over time. Once the expert has fit the circumstances of the problem to an extant model, the solution follows immediately (Bereiter & Scardamelia, 1987; Chi et al., 1981; Larkin et al., 1980). Simple challenges are appropriate initially. Over time, learners will become more competent and capable of solving complex problems. This principle is consistent with Elaboration Theory (Reigeluth, 1999b) and is similar to Gee's Well-Ordered Problems; Challenge and Consolidation; Performance before Competence; and Pleasantly Frustrating principles.

Interaction and Agency

Learners want to participate and produce; they want to make decisions; they want to take action, and will gladly learn from their mistakes as they progress to successive levels. Accordingly, provide tools to enable participation and construction.

John Keller (1983) spent much of his career studying learner motivation. While researching motivation, Keller realized that building confidence sustains learner motivation. Create instruction that allows learners to gain confidence. Let learners take some risks and learn from their failures and successes. In many instructional cases, the learner will be the only one who realizes that a mistake was made and, once corrected, the learner gains confidence toward real world application. The Interaction and Agency principle combines Gee's principles of Interaction, Production, Risk Taking, Customization, and Agency principles. Gee refers to "smart tools" (quotes are Gee's, p. 36) but he is actually referring to the functionality of game characters and makes a vague reference to other game aspects when elaborating on "smart tools." In my view, when creating an instructional game or sim, provide tools for experimentation and construction. When learners experience the utility of the tools, they will utilize them appropriately.

Encourage Both Individual and Team Play

Each learner wants to participate and to succeed. Each learner needs to overcome the challenges, but need not always do so alone. Learners may converse with peers and teachers. Learning is individual and collaborative. This principle relates to Gee's notions of Distributed Knowledge and, depending on the sim or game design, may also pertain to Cross-Functional Teams.

The importance of challenge, learner engagement, and feedback are also evident in the work of Plass, Homer, and Kinzer (2015), Holman, Aguilar, and Fishman (2013), Rieber (1996), and Betrus and Botturi (2010). Additionally, Plass et al. (2015) discuss elements of instructional game design, which pertain to game mechanics, visual aesthetics, sound effects, subject matter knowledge and skills, narrative storyline, and incentives. Instructional game and sim designers should consider cognitive load, executive function, level of interactivity, and prior knowledge of learners in order to create an effective game or simulation. Csikszentmihalyi (1975, 2014) offers guidance on engagement, or *flow*, which we may regard as an optimal state of concentration and performance, referred to in the vernacular as "in the zone" or "hitting the sweet spot." Hirumi, Appelman, Rieber, and Van Eck (2010) discuss preparation of instructional designers for game-based learning. Ultimately, instructional designers build simulations and games and test them in order to produce effective and engaging instructional simulations, games, and simulation games.

1.4 Virtual Reality, Augmented Reality, Mixed Reality

What is virtual reality (VR)? First, let us consider reality and then address virtual reality. Without getting too deep into ontology (the nature of reality), let's consider the two dominant conceptions of reality, interpretivism and positivism. For interpretivists, reality is internal; it is within each person's mind. Consequently, reality is subjective. Since there are multiple people and reality is unique to each person, there are multiple realities. In such light, reality and virtual reality are the same; reality is conjured up uniquely by each individual. In contrast, positivists regard reality as external; there is a single objective reality. For positivists, then, virtual reality is an imagined reality. There seems to be no middle ground in those positions: Either a single objective reality exists or not. Fortunately for us, we are ultimately seeking to define virtual reality. So even without resolving the ontological question about reality, proceeding from each of the two contrasting ontological ideologies, we uncovered the same conception of virtual reality; that is, virtual reality is imagined reality.

Multiple people listening to *The War of the Worlds* radio broadcast on Sunday, October 30, 1938, which was directed by Orson Welles, conceived of the alien invasion as real. Those people created a virtual reality, which they conceived as real. Perhaps at various times in your life, someone has waved a hand in front of you in hopes that you would return from your virtual world. This notion of *mind-wandering*, during which we become less responsive to external stimuli, may occur 25 percent to 50 percent of the time while awake (Kane, Brown, McVay, Silvia, Myin-Germeys, & Kwapil, 2007; Killingsworth & Gilbert, 2010; Schooler, Mrazek, Franklin, Baird, Mooneyham, Zedelius, & Broadway, 2014). Virtual reality exists in one's mind.

Even though devices are not necessary for entering a virtual reality, they can be used to create various levels of immersive experience. Completely immersive display devices prevent views of the physical world. Flight simulators use display devices and a mock cockpit to immerse pilots in flight training. Commonly, goggles are used to eliminate visual stimuli from the physical world in order to immerse users in a virtual experience. The earliest such goggles were conceived by Ivan Sutherland (1965). If curious about the illusion of depth when using goggles, note that goggles enable viewing of two separate 2D images, which are slightly offset. That is, the two images capture the same scene from slightly different perspectives. Using a process called stereopsis, the human brain automatically combines the images, creating a 3D sense of depth. Instructional apps should take advantage of goggles when circumstances warrant. We might even conceive of creating an instructional app with a device that activates all five senses, which would be similar to Morton Heilig's Sensorama, a device that simulated an experience such as an amusement park ride with sight, scents, wind, and sound (Blascovich & Bailenson, 2011).

Unlike virtual reality, augmented reality (AR) is not completely immersive. In augmented reality, information (symbols, graphics, or text) is displayed in a real scene. For example, information may be displayed in eyeglasses. AR technology is such that the information displayed is collimated (uses parallel light rays) and focused at infinity, which means the user need not refocus to view the scene beyond the information (Aukstakalnis, 2017). Such integration or augmentation makes for augmented reality, a term coined by Tom Caudell (Caudell & Mizell, 1992). Since information appears in the eyeglasses, the user need not look down (or elsewhere) for information about the scene, which leads one to classify the eyeglasses augmented with information as a heads-up display (Previc, 2004). An alternative to eyeglasses for AR is use of a smartphone running an app displaying symbols or a graphic in the real time scene captured by the smartphone's camera. Such technology was utilized in the *Pokeman Go* app.

In a manner of speaking, mixed reality (MR) is a union of VR and AR. According to Rubin (2016), mixed reality is a "blend of reality and illusion." Whereas VR offers no view of the physical world and AR offers no possibility to interact with the augmented objects, mixed reality affords both viewing of physical space and interaction with objects added to the scene. Microsoft's Hololens enables mixed reality, as does Magic Leap's technology.

Importantly, while MR and AR technologies are still growing from infancy, the earliest VR technologies have existed since the 1950s. Consequently, VR technologies have decreased in price considerably and have been distributed widely. Previously, expensive VR technologies were available only to consumers and developers of flight simulators and military simulations, but now VR technology is widely available and growing (Reede & Bailiff, 2016). The market for VR devices and content may be more than $200 billion by 2020. Available since 2015, Samsung Gear VR goggles now retail for $99.99 (and are on sale at times for $69.99). A Google Cardboard kit is approximately $15. With partners, Google has created over 500 VR field trips and experiences (Google, 2017), through which students can take virtual tours of Machu Picchu, Antarctica, Alice Austen House, the Burj Khalifa, and the International Space Station, as well as explore the surface of Mars, for instance. In addition, one can readily find companies focused on developing instruction for VR technology and their products (Burch, 2016; Schaffhauser, 2017). Of course, too, educational technologists and researchers (as well as aspiring educational researchers) throughout the world continue to study the effects of VR.

More than a decade ago, Moore (1995) was speaking of VR and virtual worlds as nascent technologies. Psotka (2013) discussed multiple topics, including the motivation to learn in virtual worlds, such as *SecondLife*, and in Massively Multiplayer Online Games (MMOG), as well as using VR technology. Ghazi Abulrub, Attridge, and Williams (2011) regarded virtual reality as the future of creative learning in engineering education. Psotka (2013) concluded that the technologies were expanding learning environments. Hussein and Nätterdal (2015), undergraduate students, developed an instructional astronomy app, which they implemented using VR and non-VR technologies. Interview data revealed that even though the participants considered the instructional features equivalent in both treatments, participants preferred the immersive VR treatment to the non-VR treatment. Velev and Zlateva (2017) raised some challenges of instructional VR technologies, such as the need for the acquisition of skills to create VR content and apps and incompatibility of VR technology in particular cultures. Yet, Velev and Zlateva (2017) predict that VR apps and services will grow and that the challenges will be overcome, which will create "immense opportunities" in colleges and universities for "real learning processes." Awareness of AR, VR, and MR enables us to conceive of instructional apps deployed on diverse devices.

1.5 Lessons Learned by Educational Technologists

1.5.1 Implications and Limitations of the Media Methods Debate

The strong claim Clark (1983, 1994) makes is that media make no difference in effectiveness of instruction for all learners. Rather, instructional methods account for differences in learning and, according to Clark, instructional methods can be implemented equally well using a variety of media. According to Clark, then, one should expect to attain the same learning outcomes when engaged in the same instructional method using any medium. A key question, then, is whether the same instructional method can be implemented using a variety of media.

The media methods debate (Clark, 1983, 1991, 1994, 2005; Kozma, 1991; Kulik et al., 1983; Kulik et al., 1985) had much to do with comparing computer-assisted instruction with alternative forms of instruction. Hence, the computer was grouped with media, but media (paper, record players, tape players, radios, analog TVs) are delivery mechanisms only. They display images and text (on paper and TV), play sounds (through record players, tape players, radios), or display moving images and play sounds (on analog TVs). A computer can be limited to display and play capabilities (as it was in the media methods studies) but, fundamentally, a computer is a device that processes (alters) inputs to produce some different output. Hence, while it is possible to display still and/or moving text and images on a computer screen and play sounds through a speaker connected to a computer, such uses seriously limit computing capability. When images, text, and sounds are presented for delivery of behavioral instruction, the processing capabilities of a computer are barely utilized.

As stated previously, behavioral instruction involves presenting a stimulus; eliciting a response; and providing feedback commensurate with the response. Presentation of a stimulus requires only display and play capability, which can be done by a computer, but other forms of media (e.g., paper, radios, TVs) do that too. Display and play capability also suffices when eliciting a response because the prompt is (almost always) either visible or audible so something is displayed or some sound played (or both). Lastly, for the behavioral instruction method, we consider computing capability needed to provide feedback. Once the learner has provided the response, whether through the keyboard, mouse, touch screen, touch pad, stylus, voice, or any other input, the response is compared with the correct answer. That's it! One comparison with the correct answer is the only computing capability required to provide feedback. Hence, implementing behavioral instruction requires only display and play capability and one comparison. Since implementation of that instructional method is a matter of displaying and/ or playing stimuli and comparing the expected response with the one the learner provided, there is no difference in achievement gains, whether a computer or a person implements that instructional method. That's fantastic! We can and will create instructional apps that implement behavioral instruction, which are as effective as human tutors and any other implementation of behavioral instruction.

The question now becomes, is there another form of instruction that computers might implement better than people and other instructional implementations? On the surface, instructional methods involving advance organizers, concept mapping, dual coding, coaching, and cognitive apprenticeship, for instance, might also end up in a draw in computer versus human implementations. Why? Advance organizers, concept mapping, and dual coding require display and play capability. In those cases, computers do as well as people. As for coaching and cognitive apprenticeship, computers can immerse learners in simulations and, as per Chapter 6, provide tools for exploration so computers can help learners perform authentic tasks. However, computers have yet to demonstrate the capacity to perform as well as teachers, managers, and physicians, for instance, so we should probably not yet expect our instructional apps to rival human tutors offering complete implementations of constructivist instruction. Now we have compared human and computer implementations of behavioral, cognitivist, and constructivist instruction, partially.

We approached the task of comparing instruction implemented by human beings and computers beginning with the manner in which human beings implement instruction and then sought to determine whether the computer could match the effectiveness of human implementation. Now we consider the converse.

Computers process data accurately and with astonishing speed. Your microcomputer might operate at two billion cycles per second (2 GHz). If it takes one thousand cycles to perform the addition of two integers, which is very likely a considerable overestimate, your computer can perform two million integer additions per second. Hence, in an electronic spreadsheet, a column of ten numbers is summed, in human terms, instantly. Further, the sum is always correct. We know that human beings cannot match that performance, but what do greater speed and accuracy of information processing have to do with instructional effectiveness?

First, when computers provide instruction as effectively as alternative forms of instruction, such as instruction by human tutors, which the media methods debate resolved as true, efficiency and satisfaction are all that matter. So let computers provide instruction in those cases, at least when human beings are satisfied with the instruction. As noted, computers are demonstrably faster and more accurate than people.

Now let us bring emotional gains, as well as cognitive gains, into consideration of the effects of instruction. First, we do this by comparing instruction on use of electronic spreadsheets offered by a computer versus a human tutor.

One could learn to recall that entering the formula =sum(a1:a10) in spreadsheet Cell A11, for instance, would sum the values in cells A1 through A10 whether the instruction were delivered by a computer tutorial, told by a person (live or recorded), or read from a text. Further, multiple media might serve as well to convey knowledge about budgeting and other applications of electronic spreadsheets. However, only an instructional treatment providing the learner with an opportunity to use an electronic spreadsheet would enable the learner to gain personal knowledge of the learner's own ability to use an electronic spreadsheet and then to conceive of how the learner's personal knowledge about entering formulas in spreadsheets could be transferred to other mathematical applications. For example, a learner who made some mistakes when using an electronic spreadsheet and was not able to recover from the errors would know of his or her limitations to use an electronic spreadsheet effectively. In contrast, a learner successfully entering formulae needed to create a budget, for instance, would have different cognitive and emotional gains. Each learner who uses an electronic spreadsheet can fathom the utility of the electronic spreadsheet to herself or himself. That's an increase in *phronesis*, which is an important knowledge gain! Now we contrast that instructional experience to knowledge (cognitive and emotional) gained by a learner visiting a human tutor who teaches use of spreadsheets using video and paper, which are alternative instructional media to a computer.

We might imagine this scenario: The human tutor plays a video about use of spreadsheets and the learner watches as numbers are entered into Cells A1 through A10 and then the formula =sum(a1:a10) is entered into Cell A11. Voila! The sum appears in Cell A11 on the TV screen. Then the tutor or the narrator of the video explains that spreadsheets can be used for budgeting and for other numerical applications, such as loan forecasting. In such a spreadsheet, the user can run "what if" experiments to determine, for instance, how many more months it would take to pay off a loan at 5 percent annual interest versus 4 percent with initial principle and monthly payment held constant. In contrast to the previous scenario, which involved actual practice with a spreadsheet, this learner uses a piece of paper with rows and columns appearing just like an electronic spreadsheet. The learner enters ten numbers in a column and adds them manually. The tutor checks the sum and perhaps provides correct feedback 2 minutes later. The learner and human tutor could also simulate development of a budget or simulate the "what if" exercise pertaining to a loan. In the end, though, even with accurate feedback, which is far from guaranteed, the amount of time taken would far exceed the electronic treatment and, beyond that efficiency, the learner would have no real experience using an electronic spreadsheet.

Someone with personal knowledge of electronic spreadsheets might apply for a job that involves use of electronic spreadsheets, but one who has not used a spreadsheet can only wonder what it must be like. The learner's use or non-use of the computer makes the difference. In this case, the instructional method is inseparable from the medium with respect to known utility of the software to the learner.

Somewhat similar scenarios emerge when those two instructional treatments (actual use of software versus simulated use with paper and/or other media) are considered when learning other computer applications, such as image creation and editing software. For example, a learner can be taught that the eye dropper tool is used to select a color in an extant image equally well, whether told by someone in person or on video or presented with images and text on paper that convey the purpose of the eye dropper tool. Recalling one fact is much easier than application of knowledge and skill to the task of editing an image. While attempting to attain that knowledge and skill, the software provides feedback to the learner's unique inputs, which are a result of the learner's current knowledge and physical dexterity when selecting particular image editing tools and portions of the image displayed on the computer screen. A learner may succeed or fail when attempting to remove the background pixels from an image, for instance. There is also the experience of partial success. The background pixels may have been removed for the most part, but some of them may remain and some pixels in the foreground image may have been deleted. In those cases, the learner needs to recover from the error, whether deciding to repair the image by restoring incorrectly deleted pixels and removing the remaining background pixels, or undoing the background deletion and being more precise when reselecting the background pixels. As in the previous scenario, the learner's personal experience using the software matters because the feedback received leads to learning gains in both the cognitive and affective domains. It is not entirely clear how one simulates deletion of background pixels with paper, but conceivably, a paper palette of tools could be presented and the tutor could watch the learner tap the "magic wand tool" on paper and then tap a part of the background image on a piece of paper. The tutor might then draw a dotted line around a portion of the background and explain that the software deleted some pixels from the foreground in error and that some background pixels remain. The simulation might continue in that manner, even though the tutor would be challenged to simulate the selection of background pixels accurately based on a finger press on paper. As in the previous instructional scenario with the spreadsheet, the learner simulating the image editing task on paper would be unsure about actual performance with the software, having not used it.

In the final case here, we contrast implementation of the instructional method for learning to write a computer program on a computer versus on paper with a tutor. On a computer, the compiler would provide accurate feedback about each and every error in the learner's source code; the learner would then seek to fix the errors in light of the feedback; and then launch the program to find any run-time errors; and seek to fix any of those errors in order to perceive the resulting output. In contrast, a learner using paper would hand the source code to a human tutor who would try to provide accurate feedback about source code errors. Assuming that went well, the tutor would ask the learner to fix the errors on paper. Then the tutor must try to determine whether there would be any run-time errors and, once discerned, must explain them to the learner. Again, even if the tutor and learner performed optimally, the source code would not really be translated into machine code and, consequently, the program would not actually execute. The learner would not really know what it is like to debug a program. Would Clark claim that those two instructional methods would be equally effective or would he claim that the instructional methods are different? If the latter, then we must conclude that the instructional method is inseparable from the computer (which Clark has denied for the past 35 years). If the former, then Clark would have only beliefs, rather than data, to support his claim. In that case, Clark should experience empiricism envy, which Clark (1994, p. 24) noted was an issue with Cunningham.

In my view, not all instructional goals can be decomposed and captured in a Mager objective. Yet, for those who may have a contrasting view, do they claim that engagement in a whole task is never greater than the sum of the parts of the task? Further, as discussed, sometimes multiple learning objectives are pursued at once and sometimes knowledge gains are personal. Knowledge of personal achievement or failure matters, as does perception of utility of a software tool based on prior experience. Learners with experience can be asked about their confidence to perform, which would yield self-report data, and those data could be compared with data based on observations of actual performance. On the other hand, learners simulating experiences would have only their beliefs about actual performance to report and no observations of performance of the actual task would be available.

Would Clark accept inclusion of learning objectives in the affective domain in comparisons of the effects of instructional methods? Would Clark claim that these two contrasting instructional treatments (actual use of software versus simulated use with paper and/or other media) in the three scenarios (spreadsheet, image editing, and computer programming) would be equally effective for all learners with respect to knowledge gained in the cognitive and affective domains? Would Clark want to conduct empirical tests of the two contrasting instructional methods in all three scenarios? Why or why not?

1.5.2 Exhibit Excitement Judiciously

Many educators have overstated the potential benefits of technological advances (Saettler, 2004). The invention of new technologies, and even their widespread distribution, does not ensure radical improvements in education. An educational technologist should not promise, nor even believe, that radical improvements to instructional delivery will enhance learning. Keep in mind the colossal error of George Zook, who spoke of the *inevitable* benefits of radio education, even before instructional methods for radio programming had been much contemplated.

According to Zook, "Education is concerned with the transmission of knowledge to individuals. Any modern device, therefore, which reaches such a large proportion of our population so speedily and so effectively as does radio, will inevitably affect educational practice vitally."

Zook further asserted, "It is a fact that, notwithstanding considerable attention to the new situation created by the advent of radio, possible uses of this new medium for educational purposes have not been at all adequately explored or fully considered" (George Zook in Marsh, 1937; Saettler, 2004).

History has taught us that despite US Department of Education funding and some early success, instructional radio programming largely ceased in 1940 when Congress eliminated funding. Some work continued through the 1940s, but many realized that instructional radio had much greater potential to motivate students than to teach them (Saettler, 1990). When history lessons are dismissed, errors will be repeated, which is precisely what happened in the following two decades.

Excitement over instructional television was massive, as was the spending to develop instructional programming for television. U.S. States created public TV stations in order to create and deliver instructional TV. Many expected such programming to solve the problem of teacher shortages and overcrowded classrooms of that time period. Moreover, instructional TV was expected to reduce the cost of instructional services (Saettler, 1990). Again, developers did not adequately consider challenges that come with implementing instructional methods in TV programs. As a result, some "instructional" TV programs provided only a "talking head." One can find some interesting educational programs on TV today, but relative to expectations, analysts were expressing their disappointment with instructional programming using terms such as "disaster" and "enormous failure." We have already heard from Heinich (1991, p. 63) on this matter: "the television people got caught up in the delivery system and thought all one needed was a dynamic personality and a camera."

Advocates of technologies for learning continued to promise enhanced learning and radical improvements for learners, even after the first two waves of the media methods debate (Clark, 1983, 1991, 1994, 2005; Kozma, 1991; Kulik et al., 1983; Kulik et al., 1985). For example, electronic classrooms with multimedia devices used for demonstration, rather than hands–on work by learners, were going to revolutionize learning, according to Chambers, Mullins, Boccard, and Burrows (1992). In another case of multimedia infatuation, Mydlarski (1993) expressed disappointment when a student, once captivated by the text and graphics in a program, withdrew from the class before she had used a laserdisc. Mydlarski (1993) asserted that without use of sophisticated multimedia systems (i.e., the laserdisc), the student was never empowered to learn.

As discussed above, CAI came to be regarded by many as having failed to deliver on the promise to radically improve instruction. Learners continue to benefit from CAI today so CAI is not even close to a complete failure. The problem arises with the onset of grandiose expectations. Unlike the prior lessons, which focus on the delivery devices, developers of CAI can implement a variety of instructional methods. Yet even that does not guarantee instructional benefits, never mind a revolution in learning.

It is very easy to get overly excited about the potential benefits of instructional technologies and the instruction one creates or encounters, which is recognized in the Gartner Hype Cycle (Gartner, 2017). Go ahead and

develop great instructional apps. Remain excited about the learning journey ahead and take pride in providing learners with effective instruction.
At the same time, try to recall these lessons evident in the history of educational technology. Try not to be overzealous about the potential impact
of instructional technologies. Learners will need time to process whatever
instruction you create, even if you should develop an instructional robot.

1.5.3 Importance of Safety, Privacy, Informed Consent, and Equity

As you gain knowledge and skills necessary to develop and distribute instructional apps, you will face multiple ethical questions. For instance, you may
want to use an image or a sound file you downloaded from a website. Use
and distribution of media that you have not developed may be absolutely
fine or absolutely criminal. Some images, sounds, and videos available to
download are free to use without attribution, even for commercial purposes.
On the other hand, other images, sounds, and videos require permission
and payment of fees to use and distribute. Another possibility grants free use
with attribution, provided the use is non-commercial. Whether use of an
image, sound, or video is acceptable depends on the terms set by the copy-
right holder. Read the terms before using and distributing media owned by
others. Abide by the terms, just as others should abide by your terms when
distributing your property.

The issue of informed consent includes consideration of safety and privacy.
Imagine a couple of months from now when you're working on Chapter 7
and you have developed an instructional app capable of responding to spoken
words. Once the user grants permission to your app to access input conveyed
through the microphone, make sure your app treats the input appropriately.
That is, use the microphone input only for the instructional purpose conveyed
explicitly to the user and disable microphone input when the instructional
purpose is complete. Such practice honors the notion of informed consent.
The app informs the user of the intended purpose; seeks permission to access
the needed resource; and uses the resource as stipulated. The app keeps the
learner's input private. This notion of informed consent extends beyond use
of hardware to any and all forms of human participation. For example, apps
should inform learners about the use of information they provide. Will the
data be stored? If so, where? Who might access the data? How will the data be
secured? For apps seeking to store user input, answers to all of those questions
should be revealed before the learner interacts with the app. When designing and developing apps for human use, the word *beneficence* should come to
mind, reminding us to support the welfare of each human participant.

With respect to equity, the cost of digital technologies favors people
with financial resources (money). The cost of hardware has decreased considerably over time, which diminishes the digital divide and invites some

reconsideration of the nature of the divide based on economic status. The 2017 update to the National Educational Technology Plan, produced by the Office of Educational Technology (2017) in the U.S. Department of Education, discusses a *digital use divide* (p. 7). The *digital use divide* is based on the manner in which digital technologies are used, whether the tools are used to perpetuate past educational practice (e.g., electronic page turning, rote learning) or to transform learning through creativity. Mention of past educational practice recalls this lament: "the computers-in-education community seems remarkably reluctant to use the computer for any purpose that fails to look very much like something that has been taught in schools for the past century" (Papert & Solomon, 1971, p. 1). Further, given the profound impact of digital technologies on society, Papert and Solomon (1971, p. 2) continue: "How strange, then, that 'computers in education' should so often reduce to 'using bright new gadgets to teach the same old stuff in thinly disguised versions of the same old way.'" The *digital use divide* is not income based; the *digital use divide* is present in low-poverty and high-poverty schools, as well as in formal and informal learning environments.

While it is important to acknowledge the most unfavorable views on CAI and instructional technologies more generally, we must recognize the diversity of instructional circumstances and seek to provide effective, efficient, and, hopefully, inspiring instruction across the spectrum of instructional circumstances. There are many types of learners seeking to attain numerous distinct learning goals, which call for multiple instructional methods. Through the design and development of robust instructional apps, we will do our best to provide instruction for the widest variety of learners.

Notes

1 There is an authentic image of a late model PLATO terminal at the following URL:
    https://en.wikipedia.org/w/index.php?title=File%3APlatovterm1981.jpg
2 See: https://www-03.ibm.com/ibm/history/exhibits/pc25/pc25_birth.html

References

Allen, I. E., Seaman, J., Poulin, R., & Straut, T. T. (2016). Online report card: Tracking online education in the United States. Online Learning Corsortium. http://onlinelearningsurvey.com/reports/onlinereportcard.pdf

Anastasio, E. J. & Alderman, D. L. (1973). *Evaluation of the educational effectiveness of PLATO and TICCIT*. Princeton, NJ: Educational Testing Service. http://files.eric.ed.gov/fulltext/ED088934.pdf

Anderson, L. W. & Krathwohl, D. R. (Eds) (2001). *A taxonomy for learning, teaching, and assessing: A revision of Bloom's Taxonomy of educational objectives*. New York, NY: Longman.

Anderson, C. A., Shibuya, A., Ihori, N., Swing, E. L., Bushman, B. J., Sakamoto, A., Rothstein, H. R., & Saleem, M. (2010). Violent video game effects on aggression, empathy, and prosocial behavior in eastern and western countries: A meta-analytic review. *Psychological Bulletin, 136*(2), 151–173.

Atkinson, R. & Shiffrin, R. (1968). Human memory: A proposed system and its control processes. In K. Spence & J. Spence (Eds), *The psychology of learning and motivation* (Vol. 2, 89–195). New York, NY: Academic Press.

Aukstakalnis, S. (2017). *Practical Augmented Reality: A guide to the technologies, applications, and human factors for AR and VR.* Boston, MA: Pearson Education.

Ausubel, D. P. (1960). The use of advance organizers in the learning and retention of meaningful verbal material. *Journal of Educational Psychology, 51,* 267–272.

Ausubel, D. P. (1963). *The psychology of meaningful verbal learning.* New York, NY: Grune and Stratton.

Baddeley, A.D. & Hitch, G. (1974). Working memory. In G.H. Bower (Ed.), *The psychology of learning and motivation: Advances in research and theory* (Vol. 8, pp. 47–89). New York, NY: Academic Press.

Bandura, A. (1962). *Social learning through imitation.* Lincoln, NE: University of Nebraska Press.

Bandura, A. (1977). *Social learning theory.* Englewood Cliffs, NJ: Prentice Hall.

Bandura, A. (1986). *Social foundations of thought and action: A social cognitive theory.* Englewood Cliffs, NJ: Prentice-Hall.

Barrows, H. S. & Tamblyn, R. M. (1980). *Problem-based learning: An approach to medical education.* New York, NY: Springer.

Barsalou, L. W. (1999). Language comprehension: Archival memory or preparation for situated action. *Discourse Processes, 28*(1), 61 80.

Baumard, P. (1999). *Tacit knowledge in organizations.* Thousand Oaks, CA: Sage. Translated by Samantha Wauchope.

Beasley, B. & Standley, T. C. (2002). Shirts vs. skins: Clothing as an indicator of gender role stereotyping in video games. *Mass Communication & Society, 5*(3), 279–293.

Bednar, A. K., Cunningham, D., Duffy, T. M., & Perry, J. D. (1991). Theory into practice: How do we link? In G. J. Anglin (Ed.), *Instructional technology: Past, present, and future* (pp. 17–35). Englewood, CO: Libraries Unlimited.

Bereiter, C. & Scardamelia, M. (1987). *The psychology of written composition.* Mahwah, NJ: Lawrence Erlbaum Associates.

Betrus, A. K. & Botturi, L. (2010). Principles of using simulations and games for teaching. In A. Hirumi (Ed.), *Playing games in schools: Engaging Learners through interactive entertainment* (pp. 33–56). Arlington, VA: International Society for Technology in Education.

Blascovich, J. & Bailenson, J. (2011). *Infinite reality: Avatars, eternal life, new worlds, and the dawn of the virtual revolution.* New York, NY: HarperCollins.

Brand, J. E., Knight, S., & Majewski, J. (2003). The diverse worlds of computer games: A content analysis of spaces, populations, styles and narratives. In M. Copier & J. Raessens (Eds), *Level up: Digital games research conference* [CD-ROM]. Utrecht: Faculty of Arts, Utrecht University.

Bransford, J. D., Franks, J. J., Morris, C.D., & Stein, B.S. (1979). Some general constraints on learning and memory research. In L. S. Cermak & F. I. M. Craik (Eds), *Levels of processing in human memory* (pp. 331–354). Hillsdale, NJ: Lawrence Erlbaum Associates.

Bransford, J. D., Sherwood, R. D., Hasselbring, T. S., Kinzer, C. K., & Williams, S. M. (1990). Anchored instruction: Why we need it and how technology can help. In D.

Nix & R. Spiro (Eds), *Cognition, education, and multi-media: Exploring ideas in high technology* (pp. 115–141). Hillsdale, NJ: Lawrence Erlbaum Associates.

Broadbent, D. (1958). *Perception and communication*. London: Pergamon Press.

Burch, A. (2016). *The top 10 companies working on education in virtual reality and augmented reality*. Branford, CT: Touchstone Research. https://touchstoneresearch.com/the-top-10-companies-working-on-education-in-virtual-reality-and-augmented-reality/

Burton, R. R., Brown, J. S., & Fischer, G. (1984). Skiing as a model of instruction. In B. Rogoff & J. Lave (Eds), *Everyday cognition: Its development in social context* (pp. 139–150). Cambridge, MA: Harvard University Press.

Bush, V. (1945). As we may think. *The Atlantic*, 1–8. www.theatlantic.com/magazine/archive/1945/07/as-we-may-think/303881/

Carr, D. & Pelletier, C. (2009). Gamers, gender, and representation. In R. E. Ferdig (Ed.), *Handbook of research on effective electronic gaming in education* (pp. 911–921). Hershey, PA: Information Science Reference, IGI Global.

Caudell, T. P. & Mizell, D. W. (1992). Augmented reality: An application of heads-up display technology to manual manufacturing processes. *IEEE System Sciences*, 2, 659–669.

Chambers, J. A., Mullins, J. Q., Boccard, B., & Burrows, D. (1992). Electronic classrooms: The learning revolution. *Interactive Learning International*, 8(4), 291–295.

Chi, M. T. H., Feltovich, P. J., & Glaser, R. (1981). Categorization and representation of physics problems by experts and novices, *Cognitive Science*, 5, 121–152.

Clark, R. E. (1983). Reconsidering research on learning from media. *Review of Educational Research*, 53(4), 445–459.

Clark, R. E. (1991). When researchers swim upstream: Reflections on an unpopular argument about learning from media. *Educational Technology*, 31(2), 34–40.

Clark, R. E. (1994). Media will never influence learning. *Educational Technology Research and Development*, 42(2), 21–29.

Clark, R. E. (2005). Flying planes can be expensive (and dangerous): Do media cause learning, or sometimes make it less expensive (and safer)? *Educational Technology*, 45(4), 52–53.

Cognition and Technology Group at Vanderbilt (1990). Anchored instructional and its relationship to situated cognition. *Educational Researcher*, 19, 2–10.

Collins, A., Brown, J. S., & Newman, S. E. (1989). Cognitive apprenticeship: Teaching the crafts of reading, writing, and mathematics. In L. B. Resnick (Ed.), *Knowing, learning, and instruction: Essays in honor of Robert Glaser* (pp. 453–494). Hillsdale, NJ: Lawrence Erlbaum Associates.

Craik, F. I. M. & Lockhart, R. S. (1972). Levels of processing: A framework for memory research. *Journal of Verbal Learning and Verbal Behavior*, 11, 671–684.

Csikszentmihalyi, M. (1975). *Beyond boredom and anxiety: Experiencing flow in work and play*. San Francisco, CA: Jossey-Bass.

Csikszentmihalyi, M. (2014). *Applications of flow in human development and education: The collected works of Mihaly Csikszentmihalyi*. Dordrecht, Netherlands: Springer.

Dietz, T. L. (1998). An examination of violence and gender role portrayals in video games: Implications for gender socialization and aggressive behavior. *Sex Roles*, 38, 425–441.

Dill, K. E., Gentile, D. A., Richter, W. A., & Dill, J. C. (2005). Violence, sex, race and age in popular video games: A content analysis. In E. Cole & J. Henderson Daniel (Eds), *Featuring females: Feminist analyses of the media*. Washington, DC: American Psychological Association.

Dodge, B. (1995). *Some thoughts about webquests*. http://webquest.org/sdsu/about_webquests.html

Domingues, T., Lima, L., & Chong, R. (2014). *Move a toy car with your mind*. Armonk, NY: International Business Machines (IBM). www.ibm.com/developerworks/library/ba-muse-toycar-app/index.html

Downs, E. & Smith, S. (2010). Keeping abreast of hypersexuality: A video game character content analysis. *Sex Roles, 62*(11), 721–733.

Duchastel, P. & Imbeau, J. (1988). Intelligent computer-assisted instruction (ICAI): Flexible learning through better student-computer interaction. *Journal of Information Technology, 3*(2), 102–105.

Duffy, T. M. & Jonassen, D. H. (1992). *Constructivism and the technology of instruction: A conversation*. Mahwah, NJ: Lawrence Erlbaum Associates.

Entertainment Software Association (2016). *Essential facts about the computer and video game industry*. Washington, DC: Author.

Ferdig, R. E. (2009) (Ed.). *Handbook of research on effective electronic gaming in education*. Hershey, PA: IGI Global.

Ferguson, C. J. (2007). The good, the bad and the ugly: A meta-analytic review of positive and negative effects of violent video games. *Psychiatric Quarterly, 78*, 309–316.

Fishman, B. & Dede, C. (2017). Teaching and technology: New tools for new times. In D. Gitomer & C. Bell (Eds), *Handbook of research on teaching* (5th ed.) (pp. 1269–1334). Washington, DC: American Educational Research Association.

Fluck, A. & Bower, M. (2015). Computational thinking: Philosophy and practice. In Michael Henderson & Geoff Romeo (Eds), *Teaching and digital technologies: Big issues and critical questions* (pp. 73–88). Port Melbourne, Australia: Cambridge University Press.

Gagné, R. M. (1965). *The conditions of learning*. New York, NY: Holt, Rinehart and Winston.

Gagné, R. M. (1985). *The conditions of learning and theory of instruction* (4th ed.). New York, NY: Holt, Rinehart and Winston.

Gardner, H. (1985). *The mind's new science: A history of the cognitive revolution*. New York, NY: Basic Books.

Gartner (2017). *Gartner hype cycle*. Stamford, CT: Gartner. www.gartner.com/technology/research/methodologies/hype-cycle.jsp

Gee, J. P. (2003). *What video games have to teach us about learning and literacy*. New York, NY: Palgrave Macmillan.

Gee, J. P. (2005). Good video games and good learning. *Phi Kappa Phi Forum, 85*(2), 33–37.

Ghazi Abulrub, A-H., Attridge, A., & Williams, M. A. (2011). Virtual reality in engineering education: The future of creative learning. *International Journal of Emerging Technologies in Education, 6*(4), 4–11.

Google (2017). Google expeditions. https://docs.google.com/spreadsheets/d/1uwWvA zAiQDueKXkxvqF6rS84oae2AU7eD8bhxzJ9SdY/edit#gid=0

Granic, I., Lobel, A., & Engels, R. C. M. E. (2014). The benefits of playing video games. *American Psychologist, 69*(1), 66–78.

Green, C. S. & Bavelier, D. (2012). Action-video-game experience alters the spatial resolution of vision. *Psychological Science, 18*(1), 88–94.

Hannafin, M. J., Hannafin, K. M., Land, S. M., & Oliver, K. (1997). Grounded practice and the design of constructivist learning environments. *Educational Technology Research and Development, 45*(3), 101–117.

Heinich, R. (1991). The proper study of instructional technology. In G. J. Anglin (Ed.), *Instructional technology: Past, present, and future* (pp. 59–81). Englewood, CO: Libraries Unlimited.

Hirumi, A., Appelman, B., Rieber, L., & Van Eck, R. (2010). Preparing instructional designers for game-based learning: Part 1. *Tech Trends, 54*(3), 27–37.

Holman, C., Aguilar, S., & Fishman, B. (2013). Designing a game-inspired learning management system (pp. 189–194). Proceedings of the 9th international conference on Games + Learning + Society. Madison, WI.

Homer, B. D. & Plass, J. L. (2014). Level of interactivity and executive functions as predictors of learning in computer-based chemistry simulations. *Computers in Human Behavior, 36*, 365–375.

Hussein, M. & Nätterdal, C. (2015). The benefits of using virtual reality in education: A comparison study. Bachelor of Science Thesis in Software Engineering and Management. Göteborg, Sweden: Department of Computer Science and Engineering, Chalmers University of Technology, University of Gothenburg. https://gupea.ub.gu.se/bitstream/2077/39977/1/gupea_2077_39977_1.pdf

Inoue, Y. (2001). Methodological issues in the evaluation of intelligent tutoring systems. *Journal of Educational Technology Systems, 29*(3), 251–258.

Jackson, L. A., Witt, E. A., Games, A. I., Fitzgerald, H. E., von Eye, A., & Zhao, Y. (2012). Information technology use and creativity: Findings from the Children and Technology Project. *Computers in Human Behavior, 28*, 370–376.

Jansz, J. & Martis, R. G. (2007). The Lara phenomenon: Powerful female characters in video games, *Sex Roles, 56*(3–4), 141–148.

Jonassen, D. H. (1991). Objectivism versus constructivism: Do we need a new philosophical paradigm? *Educational Technology Research and Development, 39*(3), 5–14.

Jonassen, D. H. & Land, S. M. (2000) (Eds). *Theoretical foundations of learning environments*. New York, NY: Routledge.

Jonassen, D. H. & Wang, S. (1993). The physics tutor: Integrating hypertext and expert systems. *Journal of Educational Technology Systems, 22*(1), 19–28.

Joyce, B., R., Weil, M., & Calhoun, E. (2000). *Models of teaching* (6th ed.). New York, NY: Pearson.

Kahney, L. (2002). HyperCard: What Could Have Been. *Wired*, www.wired.com/2002/08/hypercard-what-could-have-been/

Kane, M. J., Brown, L. H., McVay, J. C., Silvia, P. J., Myin-Germeys, I., & Kwapil, T. R. (2007). For whom the mind wanders, and when: An experience-sampling study of working memory and executive control in daily life. *Psychological Science, 18*(7), 614–621.

Kearsley G. P. (1987). *Artificial Intelligence and instruction: Applications and methods*. Reading, MA: Addison-Wesley.

Keller, J. M. (1983). Motivational design of instruction. In C. M. Reigeluth (Ed.), *Instructional design theories and models: An overview of their current status* (pp. 383–434). Hillsdale, NJ: Lawrence Erlbaum Associates.

Killingsworth, M. A. & Gilbert, D. T. (2010). A wandering mind is an unhappy mind. *Science, 330*, 932.

Klopfer, L. E. (1986). Intelligent tutoring systems in science education: The coming generation of computer-based instructional programs. *Journal of Computers in Mathematics and Science Teaching, 5*(4), 16–32.

Kozma, R. B. (1991). Learning with media. *Review of Educational Research, 61*(2), 179–211.

Kulik, J. A., Bangert, R. L, & Williams, G. W. (1983). Effects of computer-based teaching on secondary school students. *Journal of Educational Psychology, 75*(1), 19–26.

Kulik, J. A. & Fletcher, J. D. (2016). Effectiveness of intelligent tutoring systems: A meta-analytic review. *Review of Educational Research, 86*(1), 42–78.

Kulik, J. A., Kulik, C. C., & Bangert-Drowns, R. L. (1985). The importance of outcome studies: A reply to Clark. *Journal of Educational Computing Research, 1*(4), 381–387.

Lachlan, K. A., Smith, S. L., & Tamborini, R. (2005). Models for aggressive behavior: The attributes of violent characters in popular video games. *Communication Studies, 56,* 313–329.

Larkin, J. H., McDermott, J., Simon, D. P., & Simon, H. A. (1980). Models of competence in solving physics problems. *Cognitive Science, 4,* 317–345.

Lave, J. & Wenger, E. (1990). *Situated learning: Legitimate peripheral participation*. Cambridge: Cambridge University Press.

Lemola, S., Brand, S., Vogler, N., Perkinson-Gloor, N., Allemand, M., & Grob, A. (2011). Habitual computer game playing at night is related to depressive symptoms. *Personality and Individual Differences, 51*(2), 117–122.

Lenhart, A., Kahne, J., Middaugh, E., Macgill, A., Evans, C., & Vitak, J. (2008). *Teens, video games, and civics*. Washington, DC: Pew Research Center.

Libow Martinez, S. & Stager, G. S. (2013). *Invent to learn: Making, tinkering, and engineering in the classroom*. Torrance, CA: Constructing Modern Knowledge Press.

Luterbach, K. J. (2005a). On media and learning: When learners need instant feedback, only a computer can implement the requisite instructional method. *Educational Technology, 45*(2), 50–55.

Luterbach, K. J. (2005b). From two opposing perspectives on instructional media come two views on the inseparability of instructional media and methods. *Educational Technology, 45*(4), 53–56.

Marsh, C. S. (Ed.) (1937). *Educational broadcasting. Proceedings of the First National Conference on Educational Broadcasting*. Chicago, IL: The University of Chicago Press.

Mayer, R. E. (1982). Learning. In H. E. Mitzel, J. H. Best, W. Rabinowitz, & A. E. R. Association (Eds), *Encyclopedia of educational research* (5th ed., pp. 1040–1058). New York, NY: Free Press.

Mayer, R. E. (2009). *Multimedia learning* (2nd ed.). New York, NY: Cambridge University Press.

McCulloch, W. S. & Pitts, W. H. (1943). A logical calculus of the ideas imminent in nervous activity. *Bulletin of Mathematical Biophysics, 5,* 115–133.

McLellan, H. (Ed.) (1996). *Situated learning perspectives*. Englewood Cliffs, NJ: Educational Technology Publications.

Merleau-Ponty, M. (1963). *The structure of behaviour*, trans. A. Fisher. Boston, MA: Beacon Press.

Merrill, D. C., Reiser, B. J., Ranney, M., & Trafton, J. G. (1992). Effective tutoring techniques: A comparison of human tutors and intelligent tutoring systems. *Journal of the Learning Sciences, 2*(3), 277–305.

Merrill, M. D. (1983). Component display theory. In C. M. Reigeluth (Ed.), *Instructional design theories and models: An overview of their current status*. Hillsdale, NJ: Lawrence Erlbaum Associates.

Merrill, M. D. (1994). *Instructional design theory*. Englewood Cliffs, NJ: Educational Technology Publications.

Merrill, M. D. (2002). First principles of instruction. *Educational Technology Research & Development, 50*(3), 43–59.

Merrill, M. D., Fletcher, K., & Schneider, E. (1980). *Ticcit* (The Instructional Design Library, v. 40). Englewood Cliffs, NJ: Educational Technology Publications.

Miller, G. A. (2003). The cognitive revolution: A historical perspective. *Trends in Cognitive Sciences, 7*(3), 141–144.

Moore, P. (1995). Learning and teaching in virtual worlds: Implications of virtual reality for education. *Australian Journal of Educational Technology, 11*(2), 91–102.

Mou, Y. & Peng, W. (2009). Gender and racial stereotypes in popular video games. In R. E. Ferdig (Ed.), *Handbook of research on effective electronic gaming in education* (pp. 922–937). Hershey, PA: Information Science Reference, IGI Global.

Mydlarski, D. (1993). Multimedia in the teaching and learning of French as a second language. In P. Liddell (Ed.), *Proceedings of the Second Canadian CALL Conference* (pp. 89–98). Victoria, British Columbia, Canada: The University of Victoria.

Neisser, U. (1967). *Cognitive psychology*. Englewood Cliffs, NJ: Prentice-Hall.

Nelson, K. J. (2008). *Using the Internet to increase student engagement and understanding*. Thousand Oaks, CA: Corwin Press.

Nelson, T. H. (1965). Complex information processing: A file structure for the complex, the changing, and the indeterminate. *Proceedings of the Association for Computing Machinery (ACM)*, 84–100.

Newell, A. & Simon, H. A. (1972). *Human problem solving*. Englewood Cliffs, NJ: Prentice-Hall.

Novak, J. D. & Gowin, D. B. (1984). *Learning how to learn*. New York, NY: Cambridge University Press.

Nwana, H. S. (1990). Intelligent tutoring systems: An overview. *Artificial Intelligence Review, 4*, 251–277.

Office of Educational Technology (2017). National education technology plan update. Washington, DC: U.S. Department of Education. https://tech.ed.gov/netp/

Paivio, A. (1971). *Imagery and verbal processes*. New York, NY: Holt, Rinehart & Winston.

Paivio, A. (1986). *Mental representations*. New York, NY: Oxford University Press.

Palincsar, A. S. & Brown, A. L. (1984). Reciprocal teaching of comprehension-fostering and monitoring activities. *Cognition and Instruction, 1*, 117–175.

Park, O. & Seidel, R. J. (1989). A multidisciplinary model for development of intelligent computer-assisted instruction. *Educational Technology Research and Development, 37*(3), 72–80.

Papert, S. (1972). Teaching children thinking. *Programmed Learning and Educational Technology, 9*(5), 245–255.

Papert, S. (1980). *Mindstorms: Children, computers, and powerful ideas*. Hemel Hempstead, UK: Harvester Press.

Papert, S. & Solomon (1971). Twenty things to do with a computer. MIT Laboratory Report. www.stager.org/articles/twentythings.pdf

Pek, P.-K. & Poh, K.-L. (2004). A Bayesian tutoring system for Newtonian mechanics: Can it adapt to different learners? *Journal of Educational Computing Research, 31*(3), 281–307.

Petkovich, M. D. & Tennyson, R. D. (1985). Clark's "Learning from Media": A critique. *Educational Communications and Technology Journal, 32*(4), 233–241.

Phillips, D. C. (1995). The good, the bad, and the ugly: The many faces of constructivism. *Educational Researcher, 24*(7), 5–12.

Piaget, J. (1936). *Origins of intelligence in the child*. London: Routledge & Kegan Paul.

Plass, J. L., Homer, B. D., & Kinzer, C. K. (2015). Foundations of game-based learning. *Educational Psychologist*, *50*(4), 258–283.

Previc, F. H. (2004). Visual orientation mechanisms. In Fred H. Previc & William R. Ercoline (Eds), *Progress in astronautics and aeronautics: Spatial disorientation in aviation* (pp. 95–144). Reston, VA: American Institute of Aeronautics and Astronautics.

Price, R.V. (2008). An historical perspective on the design of computer-based instruction: Lessons from the past. *Computers in the Schools*, *6*(1–2), 145–158.

Pressey, S. L. (1926). A simple apparatus which gives tests and scores – and teaches. *School and Society*, *23*(586), 373–376.

Przybylski, A. K. (2014). Electronic gaming and psychosocial adjustment. *Pediatrics*, *134*, 1–7.

Przybylski, A. K., Rigby, C. S., & Ryan, R. M. (2010). A motivational model of video game engagement. *Review of General Psychology*, *14*(2), 154–166.

Psotka, J. (2013). Educational games and virtual reality as disruptive technologies. *Educational Technology & Society*, *16*(2), 69–80.

Reede, E. & Bailiff, L. (2016). When virtual reality meets education. *TechCrunch*. https://techcrunch.com/2016/01/23/when-virtual-reality-meets-education/

Reigeluth, C. M. (Ed.) (1983). *Instructional-design theories and models: An overview of their current status*. Hillsdale, NJ: Lawrence Erlbaum Associates.

Reigeluth, C. M. (Ed.) (1999a). *Instructional-design theories and models: A new paradigm of instructional theory (Vol. II)*. Mahwah, NJ: Lawrence Erlbaum Associates.

Reigeluth, C. M. (1999b). The elaboration theory: Guidance for scope and sequence decisions. In C. M. Reigeluth (Ed.), *Instructional-design theories and models: A new paradigm of instructional theory, Volume II* (pp. 425–454). Mahwah, NJ: Lawrence Erlbaum Associates.

Reigeluth, C. M., & Carr-Chellman, A. (Eds) (2009). *Instructional design theories and models, Volume III: Building a common knowledge base*. New York, NY: Routledge.

Rieber, L. P. (1996). Seriously considering play: Designing interactive learning environments based on the blending of microworlds, simulations, and games. *Educational Technology Research & Development*, *44*(2), 43–58.

Roblyer, M. D. (2016). *Integrating educational technology into teaching* (7th ed.). New York, NY: Pearson.

Rogoff, B. (1990). *Apprenticeship in thinking: Cognitive development in social context*. New York, NY: Oxford University Press.

Roberts, F. C. & Park, O. (1991). Intelligent computer-assisted instruction: An explanation and overview. In *Expert systems and intelligent computer-aided instruction* (pp. 131–136). Englewood Cliffs, NJ: Educational Technology.

Romiszowski, A. J. (1981). *Designing instructional systems: Decision making in course planning and curriculum design*. New York, NY: Falmer Press.

Romiszowski, A. J. (1987). Artificial intelligence and expert systems in education: Progress, promise, and problems. *Australian Journal of Educational Technology*, *3*(1), 6–24.

Rubin, P. (2016). AR, VR, MR: Making sense of magic leap and the future of reality. Wired. www.wired.com/2016/04/differences-between-vr-mr-ar/

Saettler, P. (1990). *The evolution of American educational technology*. Englewood, CO: Libraries Unlimited.

Saettler, P. (2004). *The evolution of American educational technology*. Charlotte, NC: Information Age Publishing.

Scardamalia, M. & Bereiter, C. (1985). Fostering the development of self-regulation in children's knowledge processing. In S. F. Chipman, J. W. Segal, & R. Glaser (Eds), *Thinking and learning skills: Research and open questions* (pp. 563–578). Mahwah, NJ: Lawrence Erlbaum Associates.

Schaffhauser, D. (2017). Immersive education: VR comes of age. Chatsworth, CA: *THE Journal*.https://thejournal.com/articles/2017/02/27/immersive-education-vr-comes-of-age.aspx

Schoenfeld, A. H. (1985). *Mathematical problem solving*. New York, NY: Academic Press.

Schooler, J. W., Mrazek, M. D., Franklin, M. S., Baird, B., Mooneyham, B. W., Zedelius, C., & Broadway, J. M. (2014). The middle way: Finding the balance between mindfulness and mind-wandering. In B. H. Ross (Ed.), *The psychology of learning and motivation* (pp. 1–33), vol. 60. Burlington, MA: Academic Press.

Seidel, R. J. & Park, O. (1994). An historical perspective and a model for evaluation of intelligent tutoring systems. *Journal of Educational Computing Research, 10* (2), 103–128.

Shortliffe, E. H. & Buchanan, B. G. (1975). A model of inexact reasoning in medicine. *Mathematical Biosciences, 23*, 351–379.

Skinner, B. F. (1974). *About behaviorism*. New York, NY: Knopf.

Sleeman, D. & Brown, J. S. (1982). *Intelligent tutoring systems*. New York, NY: Academic Press.

Sözcü, Ö. F., İpek, İ., Taşkın, E. (2013). A history of computer-based instruction and its effects on developing instructional technologies. *European Researcher, 59*(9–2), 2341–2347.

Spiro, R. J., Feltovich, P. J., Jacobson, M. J., & Coulson, R. L. (1991). Cognitive flexibility, constructivism, and hypertext: Random access instruction for advanced knowledge acquisition in ill-structured domains. *Educational Technology, 31*(5), 24–33.

Stager, G. S. (2004). The educational technology canon. *District Administration*, 56–60. http://stager.org/articles/edtechcanon.pdf

Steinkuehler, C., Squire, K., & Barab, S. (2012) (Eds). *Games, learning, and society: Learning and meaning in the digital age*. New York, NY: Cambridge University Press.

Stermer, S. P. & Burkley, M. (2015). SeX-Box: Exposure to sexist video games predicts benevolent sexism. *Psychology of Popular Media Culture, 4*(1), 47–55.

Stewart, D. (1994). *Herbert Simon on the mind in the machine*. Interview transcript available at www.omnimagazine.com/archives/interviews/simon/index.html

Sutherland, I. E. (1965). The ultimate display. In W. A. Kalenich (Ed.), *Proceedings of the International Federation for Information Processing. Congress 65*, (pp. 506–508). London: Macmillan.

Taylor, R. P. (Ed.) (1980). *The computer in school: Tutor, tool, and tutee*. New York, NY: Teachers College Press.

Thompson, M. (2017). Announcing the world's first brain-computer interface for virtual reality. *Medium*, July 30, 2017. https://medium.com/neurable/announcing-the-worlds-first-brain-computer-interface-for-virtual-reality-a3110db62607

Thorndike, E. L. (1912). *Education: A first book*. New York, NY: Macmillan.

Tobias, S. & Duffy, T. M. (Eds) (2009). *Constructivist instruction: Success or failure?* New York, NY: Routledge.

Tobias, S., Fletcher, J. D., & Wind, A. P. (2014). Game-based learning. In M. Spector, M. D. Merrill, J. Elen, & M. J. Bishop (Eds), *Handbook of research on educational communications and technology* (pp. 485–503). New York, NY: Springer Science and Business Media.

Treisman, A. (1964). Selective attention in man. *British Medical Bulletin, 20*, 12–16.

Uttal, D. H., Meadow, N. G., Tipton, E., Hand, L. L., Alden, A. R., Warren, C., & Newcombe, N. S. (2013). The malleability of spatial skills: A meta-analysis of training studies. *Psychological Bulletin, 139*, 352–402.

Velev, D. & Zlateva, P. (2017). Virtual reality challenges in education and training. *International Journal of Learning and Teaching, 3*(1), 33–37.

von Glasersfeld, E. (1989). Cognition, construction of knowledge, and teaching. *Synthese, 80*(1), 121–140.

von Glasersfeld, E. (1995). *Radical constructivism: A way of knowing and learning.* London: The Falmer Press.

Vygotsky, L. S. (1962). *Thought and language.* Cambridge MA: The MIT Press.

Vygotsky, L. S. (1978). *Mind in society: The development of higher psychological processes.* Cambridge, MA: Harvard University Press.

Walbert, M. S. (1989). Writing better software for economics principles textbooks. *Journal of Economic Education, 20*(3), 281–289.

Wai, J., Lubinski, D., Benbow, C. P., & Steiger, J. H. (2010). Accomplishment in science, technology, engineering, and mathematics (STEM) and its relation to STEM educational dose: A 25-year longitudinal study. *Journal of Educational Psychology, 102*, 860–871.

Watson, J. B. (1913). Psychology as the behaviorist views it. *Psychological Review, 20*(2), 158–177.

Watson, J. B., Tolman, E. C., Titchener, E. B., Lashley, K. S., & Thorndike, E. L. (2009). *Behaviorism: Classic studies.* Scotts Valley, CA: Information Age Publishing.

Wenger, E. (1987). *Artificial intelligence and tutoring systems: Computational and cognitive approaches to the communication of knowledge.* Los Altos, CA: Morgan Kaufmann.

Whitehead, A. N. (1929). *The aims of education.* New York, NY: Macmillan.

Wilson, B. & Cole, P. (1991). A review of cognitive teaching models. *Educational Technology Research and Development, 39*(4), 47–64.

Wing, J. M. (2006). Computational thinking. *Communications of the ACM, 49*(3), 33–35.

Wouters, P., van Nimwegen, C., van Oostendorp, H., & van der Spek, E. D. (2013). A meta-analysis of the cognitive and motivational effects of serious games. *Journal of Educational Psychology, 105*(2), 249–265.

Zheng, R. & Gardner, M. K. (2017). *Handbook of research on serious games for educational applications.* Hershey, PA: IGI Global.

Chapter 2

Instructional Design for App Development

One may refer to any of several resources (books, articles, and videos) when seeking information about how to design and develop instruction. There are numerous resources dedicated to collaborative learning while other materials guide the development of instruction for individual learners. Some resources discuss online learning while others address teaching in a classroom. There are resources on developing instruction for various subjects, such as anthropology, sociology, philosophy, law, medicine, music, dance, sculpting, cinematography, mathematics, astronomy, botany, chemistry, computer science, architecture, building construction, and project management, for instance. There are resources discussing formal and informal learning. Some resources consider instruction for skills, while others consider instruction for gaining conceptual knowledge or attitudes. Some resources consider behavioral instruction, cognitive instruction, or constructivist instruction. In addition, there are resources informing the development of instruction for all combinations of the categories above (e.g., online instruction for groups of learners interested in real estate law; online instruction for individuals learning to become notaries; instruction for individuals to learn particular strokes in swimming; classroom instruction for learners to gain skill in drawing). The number of resources that provide guidance on instructional development continues to grow. With so many resources offering information about the design and development of instruction, where should one begin? Due to its focus on the study of Instructional Design (ID), we will turn to the field of educational technology. According to Smith and Ragan (2005, p. 4), ID is "the systematic and reflective process of translating principles of learning and instruction into plans for instructional materials, activities, information resources, and evaluation." Gibbons (2014) conceives of instructional design layers but, historically, emphasis has been on ID models, and that focus remains today. ID models describe instructional design processes (Gibbons, Boling, & Smith, 2014; Gustafson & Branch, 1997, 2002; Richey, Klein, & Tracey, 2011).

2.1 ID Models and Processes

Educational technologists focus on the design and development of instruction. They regard technologies as composed of both devices (e.g., projectors, computers) and systematic methods. Such methods include ID models, which is the focus of this section.

2.1.1 Systematic Design of Instruction

One starting place for considering ID models is the ADDIE model (Branch, 2009; Molenda, 2003; Tracey & Boling, 2014). Though criticized as too general to offer prescriptions for the creation of instruction and hence too general to be regarded as an ID model, the ADDIE approach does offer an overview of the phases typically included in systematic models of instructional design. ADDIE is the acronym for Analysis, Design, Development, Implementation, and Evaluation. In essence, instructional designers assert that one may create effective instruction by engaging first in front-end analyses, then by designing the instruction, followed by development, implementation, and evaluation of the instruction. Instructional design is perceived as an iterative process. Indeed, according to Branch and Kopcha (2014, p. 77): "Instructional design is intended to be an iterative process of planning outcomes, selecting effective strategies for teaching and learning, choosing relevant technologies, identifying educational media, and measuring performance." A description of each phase of the ADDIE model follows. Entire books dedicated to instructional design offer more detailed treatments (Brown & Green, 2016; Dick, Carey, & Carey, 2015; Morrison, Ross, Kalman, & Kemp, 2013; Smaldino, Lowther, Mims, & Russell, 2015).

Front-end Analyses

Instructional designers begin the process of creating instruction by gathering information about the instructional context, including details about program, course, and lesson objectives, the target learners, and the environments in which the instruction occurs. Such information is collected through learner analysis, content/task analysis, and context analysis. Needs analysis is also important for real world implementation. Further, each type of analysis may be considered in detail, which may involve description of the functions of task analysis, classification of task analysis procedures, or discussion of steps to perform when conducting a task analysis (Gagné, 1974; Foshay, 1983; Jonassen & Hannum, 1986). Alternative terms are possible for these types of analyses, such as goal analysis for needs analysis. Front-end analyses provide information used to plan the instruction. For example, a needs analysis identifies statements of learning objectives (Davies, 1976; Mager, 1962, 1997). Learning objectives identify an observable act, the conditions for performance, and a mastery criterion. Since instruction is goal directed, learning objectives are crucial, both for planning and assessment. This is consistent with *Backward Design* (Wiggins & McTighe, 2005), which begins with the end in mind and continually works toward attainment of the final goal.

In systematic approaches to the design of instruction, learning objectives are necessary, but not sufficient. Knowledge of the learners, motivation of the learners (Keller, 1983, 1987a, 1987b), knowledge of the subject matter (content), and familiarity with the instructional setting are also important for selecting an effective instructional method. Regarding the importance of knowing the learners, which is obtained during learner analysis, Ausubel (1968, p. vi) stated: "The most important single factor influencing learning is what the learner already knows. Ascertain this and teach him accordingly." Beyond knowledge of learners, Cook-Sather (2003, 2014), Fishman (2014), and Könings, Seidel, and van Merriënboer (2014) call for involvement of learners in the design of instruction. To stimulate motivation to learn, Keller's (1987a) ARCS (Attention, Relevance, Confidence, Satisfaction) model calls for: piquing interest to gain attention; ensuring the relevance of the learning outcomes; sequencing tasks to build learner confidence; and seeking to provide clear, focused instruction to promote satisfaction with the instructional experience. Keller (1983) regards stimulating learner motivation to be a design activity. Just as one plans to create instruction, one can plan to foster the motivation to learn. With knowledge of the learners, the instructional task, the instruction objective, and instructional setting, one may draw on instructional design theories to prescribe an instructional method for a particular learning outcome (Merrill, 1983, 1994; Reigeluth, 1983, 1999a; van Merriënboer & de Bruin, 2014).

While some instructional designers regard comprehensive analyses as a great strength, others view front-end analyses as a great weakness. The argument in favor of front-end analyses is that knowledge of the objectives, learners, content, and context are necessary to create suitable instruction. After all, one cannot expect to arrive at a destination without knowing the goal. The argument against conducting front-end analyses is that real world circumstances rarely provide sufficient time and funding to conduct all of the analyses. Extensive front-end analyses may even lead to "paralysis by analysis" (Hites Anderson, 2010, p. 139). Practically, the one designing the instruction often has a personal stake in the matter and hence has some prior knowledge of the learners, the subject matter, or the instructional setting. In such cases, the instructional designer may draw on personal knowledge to some extent and seek others, such as a subject matter expert, for additional information.

Design

During this phase, the instructional designer selects an instructional method and plans the instruction. First, the instructional designer needs to answer this question for each instructional objective: What instructional presentations and activities will help learners attain the instructional objective? Second, the instructional designer needs to resolve this question about the availability of instructional resources. What instructional materials exist or need to be created that will enable the learner to view and/or listen to any instructional presentations and to engage in the instructional activities?

SELECTING THE INSTRUCTIONAL METHOD

Over time, multiple researchers have offered prescriptions for selecting an instructional method. In the cognitive domain, Bloom (1956) described instructional methods for recalling and comprehending knowledge, as well as for gaining skill to apply, analyze, synthesize, and evaluate. Gagné (1965) described instructional methods for helping learners acquire learning outcomes classified as perceptual motor skills, attitudes, verbal information, cognitive strategies, and intellectual skills. The intellectual skills are further subdivided into discrimination, concrete concepts, defined concepts, rules, and higher order rules. According to elaboration theory, instruction ought to begin by teaching an epitome and refining learner conceptions with increasingly complex treatments of the topic (Reigeluth, 1979; Reigeluth & Stein, 1983, Reigeluth, 1999b). Merrill's (1983, 1994) Component Display Theory prescribes instructional methods for recall, application, and discovery of facts, concepts, procedures, and principles. Those four ID theories are not nearly exhaustive of prescriptions for selecting an instructional method suitable for attaining a particular learning outcome, but provide a starting place for considering how to design (plan) instructional events for learners seeking to attain particular knowledge, skills, and dispositions. For additional information, Dick, Carey, & Carey (2015) and Smith and Ragan (2005) offer comprehensive discussions of instructional methods or, as they are often called, *instructional strategies*, which foster attainment of particular learning outcomes.

In light of the learning paradigms and examples described in Chapter 1, Table 2.1 prescribes an instructional method for attainment of particular learning outcomes. The first section of the table pertains to association learning, which enables rapid responses to stimuli. Through association learning, people can identify objects, as well as recall facts and definitions. The lowest two levels of Bloom's revised taxonomy of the cognitive domain (Krathwohl, 2002) require recollection of facts and definitions, or what Gagné (1965) referred to as verbal information. In addition, Gagné (1965) addressed motor skills. Learning to grip a tool and make basic motions with it would also be acquired through stimulus–response associations.

Table 2.1 Selecting an Instructional Method

Learning Outcome	Instructional Method	Example
Rapid response to a stimulus	Present stimulus; Elicit response; Provide feedback to convey whether the learner provided the expected response	Identify words, phrases, and sentences Identify hammer, nail, saw, sandpaper, wood, and chair; hold hammer; raise and lower forearm to move hammer up and down; hold saw; move saw forward and backward; hold sandpaper and move forward and backward Identify tennis ball and tennis racquet; hold tennis racquet and swing at ball Identify and label countries on a map Recall a definition of instructional design
Application of concepts Analysis of conditions Performance of basic procedure	To improve mental models, introduce variability through analogy, metaphor, and diverse examples; May use an advance organizer or concept map	Form sentences Pound nail into wood; Assemble a chair, given parts and instructions Return tennis ball on the move, adjusting for variations in height of the ball from ankles, to hip, to shoulder Follow framework to assess political risk of investment in a particular country after reading a specific chapter about the banking system in the country Follow visual design principles to create step by step instructions for multiplying two-digit integers (assume learners have mastered one digit multiplication)
Build; construct; synthesize; engage in real world performance	Engage learners in authentic tasks; encourage reflection; and require justification; May use cognitive apprenticeship	Write paragraphs, essays, newspaper columns, book reports, manuscripts, theses, novels Build custom cabinets and furniture Defeat opponents in tennis matches Become a geopolitical risk consultant; become foreign policy advisor and Secretary of State Become an instructional designer

The second section of Table 2.1 prescribes an instructional method to enable application, analysis, and evaluation. Those capabilities occupy the third, fourth, and fifth layers of Bloom's revised taxonomy (Krathwohl, 2002). Since those capabilities are acquired through consideration of variable inputs, prompting refinement of mental models through cognitive instruction is appropriate. This recalls Gagné's (1965) notion of cognitive strategies. For example, a learner might form a sentence by replacing a noun, verb, or adjective in a model sentence. If the model sentence is "The small dog jumps," the learner might write "The small cat jumps," or "The small dog barks," or "The large cat eats."

Motor tasks may also improve through variability of practice, which requires some refinement of mental models. For example, switching from a forehand to a backhand shot in tennis requires different racquet preparation (at least a different wrist position if not also a different grip) and different timing (the tennis ball can be struck later on the forehand). Given the variability in the forehand and backhand strokes, through practice, the learner may refine her or his mental model of shot making in tennis. For example, the learner's model of the racquet face making contact with the ball, and where and when that should occur, is likely to become more sophisticated. That increase in sophistication of the mental model should result in better performance of both the backhand and forehand strokes, assuming physical condition remains relatively constant.

Attaining learning outcomes in the third section of Table 2.1, which is also the top level of Bloom's revised taxonomy (Krathwohl, 2002), enables one to create, build, develop, or construct. In this case, constructivist instruction is prescribed for attaining real world performance. Many authentic or real world tasks are complex and there is no single correct answer or best way to proceed. Carpenters build cabinets uniquely to suit the dimensions of the space and the customer's budget. Tennis players adjust their game plans and tactics based on unanticipated events that occur during the match. In these cases, learning can become indistinguishable from performance.

Learning is not only cerebral or not only physical; learning involves mental activity in conjunction with physical acts and feelings. Hence, selection of an instructional method is a starting place in the planning (design) of instruction. Once the instructional method has been selected, more planning ensues.

PREPARING INSTRUCTIONAL DESIGN DOCUMENTS AND PROTOTYPES

To convey a design for a building, architects use drawings (formerly rendered in blue ink and called blueprints). Instructional designers do not have a standard document to convey plans for instruction. Perhaps the closest type of document would be a lesson plan, which is useful for identifying instructional objectives and may also contain information about the learners, the instructional setting, the instructional methods, the assessment, and perhaps a scoring rubric.

When developing an instructional app, it is helpful initially to create a lesson plan and at least one sketch. The lesson plan need not be elaborate; it might contain the following elements:

1. Description of the target learners, including specification of prerequisite knowledge
2. Specification of the instructional objective
3. Description of the instructional method, particularly what the learners will do during the instruction
4. Estimated duration of the instruction.

The sketch should convey the structure of the app, as in Figure 2.1. An instructional designer might also create a paper prototype (Snyder, 2003) to help convey how the learner would navigate through the app and use various features of the app. Since instructional apps engage or prompt the learner to take multiple actions, a functional prototype should be created to reify the instructional design. With a prototype (Coleman & Goodwin, 2017; McElroy, 2017), the user can become aware of the app's features and may be able to test the features, at least to some extent, even if the prototype contains little content in early stages of development. The extent to which features can be tested depends upon the fidelity of the prototype to the fully functioning app. If the instructional app includes a video, a storyboard is often used to convey the types of shots to record. See Figure 2.2 for sample frames of a storyboard, which may be used to guide the development of an instructional video on job interviewing. Some scripting for audio segments may be incorporated into the storyboard. For longer segments of audio in an instructional video and for any instruction including audio, an outline should be created during this design step, prior to writing the complete script.

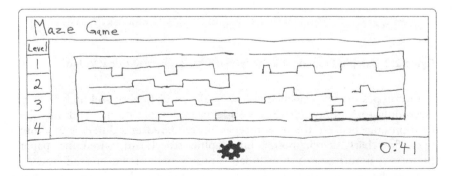

Figure 2.1 Sketch of an Instructional App.

Figure 2.2 Sample Frames of a Storyboard for an Instructional Video.

Prototypes may be classified as low fidelity, mid–fidelity, and high fidelity. According to McElroy (2017) low-fidelity prototypes do not look like the final product because these prototypes are rendered in a different medium (e.g., flowchart, sketch, poster, infographic, storyboard, wireframe, paper prototype, mood board). Low–fidelity prototypes can be created quickly because the graphics are crude sketches (e.g., stick people). The goal is to test core concepts, rework problem areas, and gain confidence in the main ideas.

Mid-fidelity prototypes begin to appear like the final product. In the case of mobile app development, one might use a prototype tool such as Invision (www.invisionapp.com/), Marvel (https://marvelapp.com/features/), MockingBot (https://mockingbot.com/), or proto.io. Also consider creating a mid-fidelity prototype for a wearable or any other instruction. Feedback on prototypes of instructional apps provides insights into the mental, physical, and emotional requirements of the instruction. Approval to proceed beyond the mid-level prototype is important because high-fidelity prototypes will include actual images, icons, and sounds. Further, the interactions and user flow will all be implemented in a high-fidelity prototype.

After the lesson plan, instructional design documents vary according to the type of instruction to be created. Additionally, instructional design documents may include sketches, outlines for audio to be scripted, storyboards, paper prototypes, or other low-fidelity prototypes. In the case of instructional apps, an experienced instructional designer may spend 5-10 hours creating a mid-fidelity prototype.

Development

To avoid duplication of effort, instructional designers generally seek first to select instructional materials from available sources. When that is not possible, instruction must be created and then distributed. This immediately gives rise to questions about the development medium and distribution options. Instruction can be created on print materials and handed to students. It is also possible to send instruction on paper through mail services, but sending digital versions of the materials is usually much faster and may be less expensive.

Instructional developers attend to both form and content issues. The content must be accurate and the form at least satisfying. Unsatisfactory form may diminish learner motivation, decrease efficiency, and could even reduce effectiveness. When creating instructional materials on paper or computer screen, following visual design principles helps to organize the materials and convey professionalism in form. Guidance from Williams (2015) regarding the visual design principles of *proximity* (positioning related items close together), *alignment* (arranging lines of text with edges of images), *consistency* (called *repetition* by Williams), and *contrast* (be bold in making contrasts) is critical. All books, magazines, and newsprint implement those visual design principles. In this book, text is aligned on the left and right; there is consistency in the font type and size for all headings (chapter, section, and subsection); the large difference in font size and weight (thickness of characters) for text in the headings and text in the body draws a stark contrast between those elements. Lastly, proximity is also apparent, for instance, in the close positioning of the first line of text in a section to the section heading.

In addition to layout issues, Williams (2015) offers tips on color selection. A novice might put blue text on a red background, for instance. However, to make viewing easy for readers, the blue text could appear against a yellow background. Generally speaking, complementary colors make for appropriate contrasts. While it is helpful to explain where analogous and complementary colors appear on a color wheel, it is particularly beneficial to see why analogous color combinations are avoided in favor of complementary color combinations. Be sure to view the examples of color combinations in the eResources for this book. The visual design principles apply to print materials and to electronic displays, which means we will implement the visual design principles in our instructional apps. Occasionally one may violate a visual design principle, which might be acceptable, depending on the strength of the justification. For additional information about message design, you may wish to see work by Bishop (2014), for instance.

When not creating print materials, instruction may be created in an audible form or on video. Just as one creates visual materials in accordance with visual design principles, one also does well to follow guidelines for audio and video production. When planning to use only audio for instructional delivery, Carter (2012) offers four design principles, which pertain to narrative format, the environmental soundscape, the fleeting nature of spoken words, and the difference between listening and hearing. In light of those principles, an important first step is selection of the narrative style, which may be informational, personal, or dramatic. The information format sounds like a person delivering facts on the news. The personal narrative format often acknowledges the listener's presence in order to seemingly engage the listener in a conversation. The dramatic or poetic narrative format evokes and appeals to emotion. Once the narrative style has been selected, a script is written. Then the voice or voices are recorded. Portions of the audio may be recorded multiple times and editing software used to alter sound qualities. For additional information about the audio production path (planning, recording, editing), consider Sauls and Stark (2016) and for technical aspects of audio production, consider work by Corey (2017). In addition, the Audio Engineering Society (www.aes.org/standards/) and the Producers and Engineers Wing of the Recording Academy (www.grammy.org/recording-academy/producers-and-engineers/guidelines) develop and publish audio recording standards.

The production path for instructional video is complex. In the instructional video design process, professionals first create a storyboard and write a script. They also consider the recording environment. To begin, professionals plan the actions and movements of the people in the video (a process called blocking) and select appropriate attire for them. Further, video professionals select a high-definition video camera or cameras and choose particular lighting arrangements for different shots (long shot, medium shot, close up), as well as vary camera angles appropriately. Professionals also use high-quality microphones and may include a voice coach. Once recording has been completed, the video is edited to enhance production quality. Editing is often time consuming because numerous adjustments can be made, each of which improves the quality of the video. To create effective instructional video, Heinich (1991) was right; one needs more than a camera and a dynamic personality. Generally speaking, one needs to plan extensively, rehearse with the talent, and record and edit the video with a team of production assistants. A decent budget is helpful. For additional information about video production, consider the work of Musburger and Ogden (2014) and Sweetow (2017), as well as work by Halls (2012) who describes a rapid development process for creating instructional video.

For details pertaining to the development of instructional apps, see Chapters 3–7.

Implementation and Evaluation

To implement instruction is to put it into use in its intended environment. Once implemented, stakeholders can evaluate the instruction. *Evaluation* is intended to convey judgment relative to purposes and values, whereas *measurement* is a neutral term (Cronbach, 1975). Pace and Friedlander (1978, p. 9) describe the relationship between evaluation and measurement as follows: "Good evaluation, like good science, utilizes measurement and observations that are accurate, reliable, and valid, gathers evidence systematically, and analyzes results objectively." Evaluation for the purpose of refinement is called *formative evaluation*. Scriven (1967) distinguished *formative evaluation* from *summative evaluation*, which occurs after implementation and provides an overall assessment of the effectiveness of the innovation, which for educators is typically the instruction. There are numerous resources for planning and conducting evaluations (e.g., Stake, 1973; Tessmer, 1993), which involve data collection to inform decision making. Many organizations still utilize Kirkpatrick's (1959) four levels of evaluation training, which involve learner reactions (opinions regarding the utility of and satisfaction with the instruction), learning (attainment of the learning objectives), workplace behavior (use of new knowledge and skills on the job), and return on investment, which might be evident in increased sales, employee retention, and reduced waste, for instance. In practice, summative evaluation may be relatively infrequent, but continual improvement through formative evaluation is considered frequently.

Additional perspectives on teaching and learning are available in Skinner (1991), Foshay, Silber, and Stelnicki (2003), Jonassen (1997), and Steffe and Thompson (2000), for instance. Further information about systematic approaches to instructional design is available in descriptions of specific models, such as the Dick and Carey model (Dick, Carey, & Carey, 2015), the ASSURE model (Smaldino et al., 2015), the Kemp model (Morrison et al., 2013), and the Smith and Ragan (2005) model, for instance. Brown and Green (2016) offer an overview of multiple instructional design models and elaborate on fundamental components of instructional design and development. Sugar and Betrus (2002) discuss multiple roles played by instructional designers. The *Educational Media and Technology Yearbook* (Orey & Branch, 2015) contains additional information about programs of study in educational technology and organizations through-out the world involved in technologies for learning.

In summary, the systematic design of instruction begins with front-end analyses. Information collected during the various analyses is used to plan and develop effective instruction. During the task analysis, instructional content is analyzed, which involves breaking down broad learning goals into clear and specific learning objectives. Once the analysis phase has been completed, an instructional method is selected prior to developing, imple-menting, and evaluating the instruction. Some instructional designers favor this systematic, mechanistic, deductive, reductionist approach to developing instruction. In contrast, others prefer Gestalt design, which favors a holistic, inductive, constructive approach.

2.1.2 Gestalt Design

Silber (2007) asks what if instructional design is not a systematic process. Well, in that case, one dismisses the previous section and proceeds along an alternative path. When circumstances warrant, such as when guiding learners to solve authentic problems in a discipline, constructivists eschew traditional systematic approaches to the design of instruction in favor of holistic design.

In traditional systematic approaches, an instructional designer would conduct a content analysis to determine the facts, concepts, principles, and procedures to teach. However, for constructivists, content cannot be specified before the instruction. Learners must determine relevant con-tent for themselves in light of authentic tasks. Hence, in gestalt design, identification of actual tasks performed by practitioners is an important first step. The instruction will guide learners to engage in those tasks. For complete novices, the tasks are simplified (Bednar, Cunningham, Duffy, & Perry, 1991). With respect to learner analysis, rather than identify content deficiencies, a constructivist is focused on knowledge construction and seeks to determine each learner's unique preparation for reflection, which Bednar et al. (1991) refer to as reflexivity awareness of knowledge con-struction. Constructivists perceive processes uniquely and some envision a more thorough learner analysis. For example, van Merriënboer, Clark, and de Crook (2002) identify particular skills as necessary for conduct-ing a search for literature, which learners should seemingly possess before attempting that task.

An outcome of traditional front-end analyses is specification of perfor-mance objectives, but constructivists have no such statements of objectives.

While performing an authentic task, specific objectives may emerge. Indeed, while engaged in the instruction, the learner is free to create any such objectives *en route* to solving the task.

With no *a priori* performance objectives, there is no selection of an instructional strategy to help learners attain a particular fact, concept, principle, or procedure. Rather, the instructional environment ensures that the learner is situated in a real-world context in order to pursue an authentic task (Lave & Wenger, 1990; McLellan, 1996). The authenticity and complexity of the real-world context are modulated in accordance with each learner's unique knowledge and experience (Bednar et al., 1991). Further, consistent with cognitive apprenticeship (Collins, Brown, & Newman, 1989), a competent performer or expert guides students and models problem solving suitable for the task. Such coaching also ensures that learners consider the task from multiple perspectives.

With respect to evaluation, traditional ID would have created an assessment aligned with the performance objective, but the absence of such an objective renders that approach impossible in gestalt design. Rather than test for acquisition of a particular fact, concept, principle, or procedure, learners can be assessed on their performance of the task (Bednar et al., 1991). To what extent were the actions taken effective? Also, learners should be able to defend their decisions. Learners may benefit from mentor, peer, and self-assessment.

2.1.3 Rapid Prototyping

The systematic design of instruction begins with front-end analyses and proceeds through design and development before implementation and evaluation. Accordingly, the instructional designer gets ready to create instruction by performing the front-end analyses and then plans or designs the instruction in light of information about the learners, the content, and the instructional context. Once the instruction is created, it is implemented. One might characterize that systematic instructional design process as following this pattern: "Ready, Aim, Fire," though Makhlouf (2016) would use: "Ready, aim, aim, aim, fire."

Similarly, in gestalt design, the instructional designer selects an authentic task. In this way the instructional designer gets ready to offer instruction. Further, with the target learner in mind, the instructional designer may calibrate the task, perhaps by simplifying the task for a novice learner. Even if not simplified, the task must be communicated to the learner, which involves calibrating the task description for the learner. Instruction begins with delivery of the task description and proceeds with modeling and coaching. Once again, we find the familiar pattern: "Ready, Aim, Fire."

Rapid prototyping is different (Tripp & Bichelmeyer, 1990). The approach is actually akin to: "Ready, Fire, Aim." Rapid prototyping does uphold the *minimum commitment* principle of design (Asimow, 1962; Chitale & Gupta, 2013).That is, at each design stage, expend the fewest resources possible to get the job done. In such light, and with an experienced instructor, front-end analyses can occur rapidly. An experienced instructor knows the subject matter and is aware of common characteristics of the target learners. Further, in light of the instructional objective (e.g., the learner will identify the verb in a sentence), the instructor might create the initial version of the instruction in 30 minutes.

In many cases of rapid prototyping, creating the instruction with a computer is helpful. Paper will work at times, but prototyping environments favor *modularity* and *plasticity*. Ink on a page may be difficult to alter and revision is what prototyping is largely about. Modularity enables components of work to be altered quickly. In desktop publishing an image can be exchanged for another. Plasticity concerns the rate at which changes can be made. Again, with respect to desktop publishing, text can be modified quickly. In contrast, even though one might readily draw a diagram and write facts on paper, when it comes time to modify the diagram or words, the page gets messy. Ink on a page is neither modular nor plastic. Digital audio and video can be treated as modular. For example, with common editing software, sections of audio and video can be selected, treated, or replaced. Replacement does require selecting from multiple recordings, which might become time consuming, especially with video. Hence, the plasticity of audio and video varies. In both cases, though, the digital forms of audio and video are much more plastic than the old tape formats, which are not plastic. Of course, too, in the case of video, the film format is not plastic.

With a computer and digital media production skills, initial versions of instruction can be created rapidly, in some circumstances. Rapid prototyping is a viable instructional development technique (Desrosier, 2011), which was evident to Markle (1967) half a century ago. Markle (1967) promoted iterative development and testing in order to verify the effectiveness of instructional materials. According to Peters (1999, p. 97), "an iterative/prototyping approach beats a meticulous (Ready. Aim. Aim. Aim. Aim ...) approach." Based on observations of work at the Massachusetts Institute of Technology Media Lab and products produced in multiple corporations, Schrage (2000) regards prototyping as critical to innovation.

2.2 User Experience Design

The field of user experience design draws on studies in ergonomics. The scientific study of ergonomics began around the middle of the twentieth century, but ancient Greeks also sought to develop principles for increasing efficiency and improving working conditions. Hippocrates, for instance, described an optimal surgical space (Marmaras, Poulakakis, & Papakosto-poulosas, 1999).We may regard those efforts of ancient Greeks as the roots of ergonomic design. The word, ergonomics is a combination of ergon (ἔργον), meaning work; and nomoi (νόμος), meaning natural laws.

The scientific study of ergonomics accelerated when human beings needed to simplify complex machines (Hill, 2000). For example, before all motor vehicles had steering wheels, foot pedals controlled the vehicles. That might have been satisfactory if all manufacturers had implemented the pedal controls in the same manner. Automobile design evolved to simplify controls for "typical" users. In the 1940s, the designs of early aircraft challenged human sensory systems, which prompted development of new techniques for successful operation. In a book about how to design products for people, Henry Dreyfuss (1955) describes the evolution of Industrial Design. For Dreyfuss (1955, p. 15), an industrial designer is a "liaison linking management, engineering, and the consumer and cooperates with all three."

Around the middle of the twentieth century, developed by engineers for engineers, the earliest digital computers were exceedingly complex. However, as computers became more reliable and smaller, people other than engineers sought to use them. Though many readers may not recall vacuum tubes in devices or computers occupying a considerable portion of a room, some may recall command line interfaces, which have largely been superseded by graphical user interfaces. That change in computer technology owes much to studies of the relationship between computers and human factors, such as those conducted at Xerox Parc, Lincoln Labs, and the Stanford Research Institute (Hill, 2000). Even though the characterization of the field has changed from Human–Computer Interaction (HCI) to User Experience (UX) or User Experience Design (UXD), work in the discipline pertaining to the interactions of human beings with computers remains strong today.

Like Dreyfuss, Don Norman (1988, 2013) advanced the UXD discipline by writing a book about designing things for people. Regarding the design of computer programs, Norman recognized that satisfaction with software involved more than the human–computer interface. For example, a database query that unexpectedly returns no results is unsatisfying, even when the user interface (e.g., entering a single search term) is entirely satisfying. In such light, *Human–Computer Interaction* (HCI) is too narrow a term to convey a person's entire experience with a computer system. Norman (1995) offered *User Experience* (UX) as an alternative, which has remained with the discipline.

Among the major contributions of the user experience discipline is attention to the user. Engage in User-Centered Design (UCD) or what is sometimes called Human-Centered Design. Learn about the users and get their feedback before, during, and after product development ("early and often"). The importance of user feedback gives rise to the notions of *usability* (Gould & Lewis, 1985), *design heuristics* (Nielsen & Molich, 1990), and *usability testing* (Hartson & Pyla, 2012; Sauro & Lewis, 2012).

2.2.1 Usability

The International Standards Organization (ISO 9241–11, 1998) defines usability as "The extent to which a product can be used by specified users to achieve specified goals with effectiveness, efficiency, and satisfaction." In computing, *usability* pertains to the utility of a user interface. *Usability* replaced the expression "user friendly," which was popular in the 1980s. User interfaces should be easy to use. Nielsen (1993) regards usability as a multidimensional property of user interfaces, which includes the following five attributes: Learnability, Memorability, Efficiency, Errors, and Satisfaction. Computer systems should provide an interface that is easy to learn, which will enable the user to accomplish actual tasks quickly. Further, the interface should be memorable so that even after non-use, the user should readily regain proficiency. With respect to efficiency, the interface should enable users to be highly productive. The interface should reduce errors and enable users to recover from errors.

User-centered design insists on testing with users to ensure that a computer interface is easy to use. To create the first prototype, UX Designers draw on guidelines for making effective user interfaces (Allen & Chudley, 2012; Hartson & Pyla, 2012; Nielsen, 1993; Shneiderman, 1986; Shneiderman, Plaisant, Cohen, Jacobs, Elmqvist, & Diakopoulos, 2017; Tognazzini, 1992). In various circles, those guidelines may be called "best practices" or *design heuristics*. Since users are diverse, one cannot be certain that they will find the design of a new computer interface effective, efficient, and satisfying. To increase the likelihood of success, UX Designers draw on design heuristics ("rules of thumb"), which are guidelines generally applicable and beneficial to users. These have been established by UX researchers and practitioners (Hartson & Pyla, 2012; Nielsen, 1993; Weinschenk & Barker, 2000). Researchers use somewhat different terminology and have derived different numbers of guidelines, but the following are common.

- Language: Use terms familiar to users; use simple phrasing
- System Status: Interface should inform users of current state; (e.g., in instructional apps, display percent of lesson completed)
- User Control: Enable users to maintain control; interfaces should respond to users and, to the extent possible, permit users to undo prior actions
- Simple/Minimalist: Use uncluttered dialogs; exclude rarely used features in main dialogs
- Consistency: Use the same font size, weight, and type for headings; use menus, dialogs, and fields consistently; incorporate conventions of the distribution platform
- Aesthetics: Create a pleasing and appropriate visual design

- Effectiveness and efficiency: The interface needs to work well; minimize user time and errors
- Flexibility: To the extent possible, aim for universality; try to incorporate natural interactions, whether audible, visual, or physical.

The byline of the Center for Universal Design in the College of Design at North Carolina State University is "Environments and Products for All People." Ron Mace (2008) offers a formal definition: "Universal design is the design of products and environments to be usable by all people, to the greatest extent possible, without the need for adaptation or specialized design." A wide door that opens automatically when someone approaches enhances access for everyone. Similarly, curb cuts and ramps enhance access. Awareness of accessibility guidelines for people with disabilities can help app designers create human–computer interfaces for diverse people. The World Wide Web consortium has a Web Accessibility Initiative (www.w3.org/WAI/), which offers guidelines for making content on the web accessible (www.w3.org/WAI/gettingstarted/tips/designing). Many of the guidelines transfer to content beyond the web, such as providing sufficient contrast between foreground and background; create responsive designs for different viewport sizes; present content using multiple media. Since people are diverse, one of the key principles to universality is flexibility. To the extent possible, enable users to adjust font size and the level of contrast between foreground and background, for instance. We will return to the notion of universality in a subsequent discussion about universal design for learning. At this time, make note of this key point: App designers can save everyone on the production team the pain of retrofitting (reworking a completed product) by designing human–computer interfaces for all people from the start of the project.

2.2.2 Usability Testing

There are some rapid inspection methods (Hartson & Pyla, 2012; Nielsen, 1989), such as cognitive walkthrough (Wharton, Rieman, Lewis, & Polson, 1994) and heuristic evaluation (Nielsen & Molich, 1990; User Experience Professionals' Association, 2012), which designers and developers can use to improve the user experience. A cognitive walkthrough is rather similar to heuristic evaluation. In the case of an instructional app, an expert or person with experience in UX proceeds through the app identifying and documenting features that do not conform to the list of design principles. In light of the documentation and consultation with the designer and UX reviewer, the developer improves the app.

Expert review does not replace testing with users (Hartson & Pyla, 2012; Sauro, 2015; Tan, Liu, & Bishu, 2009). Observing users engaged in completing tasks with the interface is important. Such observation sessions may be called *user testing*, which is intended to convey that the user is doing the testing rather than the user is being tested. Even though the testing does reveal some insights into the user's capabilities, the testing is focused on collecting data to improve the interface. Hartson and Pyla (2012) regard usability testing with users as rigorous empirical evaluation. Indeed, like all serious evaluation, considerable time is spent planning and conducting usability sessions, as well as analyzing and reporting on the data collected. When usability sessions are conducted daily, or at least weekly, an organization may allocate space to a usability lab. A usability lab offers convenience because recording equipment is already in place and set to use. Without such a lab, a reasonably quiet office space is generally quite sufficient.

Early in the planning stage, the UX Designer selects a range of tasks that participants will attempt during the usability session. The UX Designer also selects and recruits participants. It is helpful to conduct a pilot study to ensure that the system is functioning as expected and that all materials for the participants are finalized. If the UX Designer or UX Design Team conducting a rigorous empirical evaluation seeks to advance the UX knowledge base by publishing results in a journal or presenting the study at a conference, a study protocol is submitted to the Internal Review Board at the primary investigator's institution. Data collection would not begin unless and until the protocol was approved.

During each usability session, the UX Designer follows a protocol to collect data consistently. Once a participant has arrived and is ready to begin the session, the UX Designer will explain that the purpose of the session is to improve the user experience of the system and that the participant's role is to proceed through particular tasks. Verbal or written consent may be required to begin the session if the data will be used for research purposes. The UX Designer may ask the participant to "think aloud" while completing tasks and, throughout the session, may need to remind the participant to "think aloud," which means to provide continual commentary explaining why the participant is taking particular actions. Data may be collected through a combination of video recordings, audio recordings, recordings of computer screen activity, and note taking. After task completion, participants may be asked to complete a survey or reply to interview questions. As each session comes to a close, participants are thanked and in some cases may even be paid.

When all participants have finished, the quantitative and qualitative data are analyzed. An important step is to prioritize the order in which problems will be resolved. Hartson and Pyla (2012) recommend conducting a cost–importance analysis in order to prioritize the problems. Devise solutions to the problems and report results to the stakeholders. Offer the solutions you identified and seek the assistance of the stakeholders while prioritizing the problems to be fixed. Of course, one seeks first to resolve big problems that cost little to fix. Subsequently, other problems with quick fixes can be resolved readily. Then the stakeholders can help prioritize the remaining problems. Sauro and Lewis (2012) provide comprehensive discussions about data analysis, including the number of participants to recruit, which varies according to the purpose of the study. According to Nielsen (1989), usability testing with five users will reveal sufficient information to improve the interface. When seeking to generalize results to a large population, research studies may include 30, 100, or more participants.

2.2.3 UX Design Process

The UX Design discipline, like the field of instructional design, includes both practitioners and researchers. Further, UX professionals have developed a systematic process for designing user experiences, which includes stages similar to the traditional ID process. According to the User Experience Professionals Association (UXPA), a typical UX project includes these four phases: *Analysis, Design, Implementation*, and *Deployment* (https://uxpa.org/resources/about-ux). During the Analysis Phase, the UX Designer meets with the stakeholders to establish the project vision and to identify particular performance requirements and usability tasks. Also during this phase, the UX Designer performs a task analysis and conducts field studies, which lead to user personas and use cases. When budgets warrant, a multidisciplinary team is assembled prior to engagement in the Design Phase.

In the Design Phase, the UX Designer (or UX team) brainstorms ideas and considers metaphors that may lead to an interface and user experience that meet the performance requirements. A low-fidelity prototype is created, which may include a sketch, flowchart, wireframe, activity diagram, storyboard, mood board, poster, or site map, for instance. The goal is to create a low-cost prototype that conveys the core ideas of the project. Once the low-fidelity prototype has been created, usability testing commences. The initial prototype is either improved or abandoned in light of feedback from the UX reviewers and target users. When the results of usability testing indicate that the low-fidelity prototype is viable, the designer or design team creates a high-fidelity design, which may include a style guide and documentation. More usability testing ensues. Data collected are analyzed and reported to the stakeholders. Final revisions are made prior to the design documents.

During the Implementation Phase, the UX Designer or UX team works closely with the developers who reify the design. Usability testing is conducted as soon as possible. Lastly, the functioning system is deployed and field tests are conducted to determine effectiveness, efficiency, and satisfaction with the product in actual use.

The four phases may include over 40 steps (as depicted in a poster available for purchase through the Usability Professionals Association), which make for a complex process. Not surprisingly, then, actual engagement in a pristine implementation of the 40-step UX Design process is rare (Treder, 2017).

UX design guidelines are helpful for developing effective, efficient, and satisfying interfaces. Like visual design principles, a designer will encounter circumstances when it is appropriate to deviate from the guidelines. For example, Apple Computer (1992) provided explicit recommendations for going beyond interface design guidelines for the Macintosh computer. The key is to know the guidelines and their suitability for particular purposes. When you are seeking to create an atypical user experience or encounter a unique circumstance, you may deviate from UX guidelines. Rationales for deviating from guidelines may be justifiable in various circumstances.

UX design guidelines (Gothelf & Seiden, 2013; Hartson & Pyla, 2012; Levy, 2015) are readily available to inform instructional designers and developers when creating instructional apps, whether the app is deployed on the web (Krug, 2014), includes a voice interface (Pearl, 2017), or is deployed across multiple devices (Levin, 2014), for instance. Some instructional designers may also seek to contribute to the UX knowledge base (Sauro & Lewis, 2012). Consistent with the mission of UXD, seek to make instructional apps usable. When designing a new instructional app, draw on UX design guidelines and involve learners continually in order to make the app effective, efficient, and at least satisfying, if not a joy to use.

2.3 Real World Design and Implementation

Context is critical. Resources allocated to projects depend entirely on real world circumstances. For example, if you are working on an audio production assignment for a school project with no budget, no teammates, no coaching, no time for scripting, you may need to pick a familiar topic; turn on the recording app on your smartphone; and go for it. Good luck with that production path. Results will depend on your experience with audio recording. At the other extreme, a corporate sponsor may fund an instructional development project for one million dollars, which will include a team of specialists and a production studio. Yet even in such favorable conditions, results would be imperfect. After all, instructional design is a rather complex undertaking.

Also consider the work of K–12 teachers. They design and deliver instruction daily, to approximately 25 students per hour for 5 hours. Perhaps at the beginning of a school year or semester, some K–12 teachers distribute a combination pretest and questionnaire to gain insights into the prior knowledge and interests of their students. That would constitute the entire learner analysis and not every teacher does that. Some teachers draw on their experience and provide nearly the same lesson year after year. After all, experienced teachers are familiar with their classroom and the subject matter, which eliminates the need for a task or content analysis and a context analysis. Further, a government agency has provided statements of learning objectives or standards, as they are often called, so given time constraints and experience, K–12 teachers (except first-year teachers) are ready for instructional delivery on Day 1. Rather than fully implement a systematic ID model, such as the Dick and Carey model (Dick, Carey, & Carey, 2015), K–12 teachers need to design instruction for multiple lessons per day. The ASSURE model (Smaldino et al., 2015) might work for them. On the other hand, a company rolling out instruction to a few thousand employees, perhaps to introduce new software for managing clients, can spend the money and time necessary to conduct learner and task analyses prior to designing and developing the instruction, plus pilot test and revise it before engaging the entire work force in the instruction. That sounds ideal but, in reality, there will be time and cost constraints. Everything is contextual.

2.3.1 Project Management

The design and development of instruction for real world implementation often requires multiple people and materials. Resources are used in both planning and production phases. Materials may include a questionnaire, computer hardware and software, and digital images and sounds, for instance. The acquisition of the materials, as well as the hiring and monitoring of personnel, is a substantial undertaking.

Classic project management (Kerzner, 2013) takes a systematic approach to initiating, planning, managing, and completing a project. To outline project management practices, Kerzner (2013) draws on the Project Management Body of Knowledge, which has been accrued over time by the Project Management Institute (2013). Rather than identify phases in the life cycle of a project, which could imply that projects always proceed in a linear manner, the Project Management Institute (2013) offers these five process groups: Initiating; planning; executing; monitoring and controlling; and closing.

Initially, the Project Sponsor appoints a Project Manager and conveys the project goal, expectations for quality, and stipulates the budget. During planning, the Project Manager accomplishes the following.

- Clarifies the scope of work and work requirements
- Identifies activities necessary to meet work requirements, which clarifies personnel requirements
- Estimates costs
- Conducts an assessment of risks
- Communicates with the sponsor.

During project execution, the project team is assembled. Team members become aware of their work requirements and target dates for completing work. In addition, team members may engage in training. The Project Manager communicates with team members and the sponsor.

While monitoring and controlling the project, the Project Manager tracks progress and adapts processes as necessary to achieve the desired outcome. The team continually adapts processes in light of the current state of the project with respect to the desired outcome. Communication continues between the Project Manager and the Sponsor and the Project Manager and Team Members (one hopes). At closing, the sponsor verifies that the outcomes have been achieved satisfactorily and final payments are made (in general).

Speaking of project management overall is much easier than implementing the processes, which will surely deviate in some manner from the plans. Nontrivial real world projects always do. Classic project management has its critics (Lechler, Edington, & Gao, 2012). Also noteworthy is that there are many variations on the project management processes, which go variously by labels such as lean, agile, waterfall, scrum, kanban (Highsmith, 2010; Rubin, 2013; Sims & Johnson, 2012; Wysocki, 2014). There are also combinations of those approaches, such as agile and scrum, lean and agile, kanban and agile, and lean Six sigma (Brechner, 2015; Davis, 2012; Furterer, 2009; Schwaber, 2004). Further, project management methods can be incorporated into organizational development methods, which add to management complexity. Perhaps in response to this complexity, the first of Kerzner's 16 Points to Project Management Maturity (2013, p. 2) advises one to select a project management method and use it consistently.

Briefly, a project is an effort intended to accomplish a particular goal. Each project is unique and transient. The Project Management Institute (2013) offers a systematic project management process, developed in consensus with multiple Project Managers over time, which applies across many industries to "most projects most of the time." Many fields refer to such practices as "best practices," but the Project Management Institute (2013) calls them "Good practices." When an instructional design project is sustained over time, the instruction will need to be maintained with respect to content and delivery.

2.3.2 Diffusion of Innovations

In the mid-1900s, Everett Rogers conducted seminal studies on the diffusion of innovations. To present lessons learned from that work, Rogers (2003) began with three case studies documenting reluctance to boil water in order to stay healthy, as well as reluctance to consume citrus fruit to prevent scurvy, and reluctance to reject the QWERTY keyboard, which intentionally inhibits typing speed. Why are we so slow to accept particular innovations, at least some innovations?

One reason for rejecting an innovation pertains to perception of its advantage relative to alternatives. No one would reject citrus fruit to prevent scurvy today, but in the mid-nineteenth century, it was not obvious that consumption of citrus fruit would have helped maintain good health. When hearing of an innovation's benefits, the message must be regarded as valid. Dr. Lind's message to consume citrus fruit to maintain good health was rejected by the British Navy because he was not prominent in naval medicine (Rogers, 2003). Accordingly, change agents promoting an innovation do well to persuade influential people of the innovation's benefits. More than a change agent of unknown character, when people perceived as credible communicate the benefits of the innovation, the likelihood of accepting it increases. In general, early adopters of an innovation are often perceived as capable leaders, skilled at implementing new ideas (Rogers, 2003). Change agents do well to engage early adopters in order to accelerate the diffusion process. Acceptance of an innovation also increases when one has the opportunity to observe the innovation and try it out at low risk. In such light, some companies make software or other products available at no cost for a trial period, such as 7, 14, or 30 days. Another factor affecting the acceptance of an innovation is its perceived complexity. The simpler an innovation is conceived to be, the more likely its acceptance. In addition to *relative advantage, observability, trialability,* and *complexity,* Rogers (2003) has established the influence of values on decisions to accept or reject an innovation. Many Peruvian villagers who rejected water boiling, which would have eliminated harmful bacteria, did so because they may have been ostracized for using heat to boil water. When promoting an innovation, clearly communicate (especially to credible people who network with many others) its benefits relative to alternatives; enable observation and low risk trials to the extent possible; keep it simple; and ensure that the innovation is compatible with the values of the target audience.

With respect to implementing change, Hall and Hord (2015) note that individuals proceed through seven stages of concern: (0) Unconcerned; (1) Informational; (2) Personal; (3) Management; (4) Consequence; (5) Collaboration; and (6) Refocusing. Those promoting change may assist each decision maker as she or he contemplates the following: (1) initial information about the innovation; (2) how will my practices change? (3) how much time will it take to learn how to use the innovation? and (4) how will others be affected by the innovation? After accepting an innovation, attention turns to sharing information about personal experiences with the innovation and finally making changes to enhance use of the innovation.

Wejnert (2002) integrates three types of diffusion variables into a framework for comprehending the spread of innovations. The three components pertain to characteristics of the innovation, characteristics of decision makers, and environmental factors. With respect to characteristics of innovations, Wejnert (2002) considers scope and costs/benefits of the innovation, which is considerably different from Rogers (2003). Regarding scope, Wejnert compares innovations for individuals versus innovations for groups. For example, the diffusion process for citizens of a country determining whether to accept or reject new laws to protect natural ecosystems is much different from one person's decision about the type of tennis racquet to purchase. Interestingly, observability is a factor in both cases. Formerly, many individual tennis players switched from a wooden to a light-weight metal tennis racquet after observing (and trying out) a metal racquet. Democracies also serve as a model for governing. Sometimes the behavior of politicians may lead one to question the effectiveness, or even viability, of a democracy, but democracies often survive tumultuous times (e.g., Argentina during 2001–2002; Brazil during 2016–2017). For Wejnert (2002), the second key factor of an innovation influencing diffusion is cost, monetary and otherwise (e.g., time and effort). Cost is also a factor in comparisons of relative advantage.

Moving to characteristics of people deciding whether to accept or reject an innovation, Wejnert (2002) speaks of decision makers as actors. In this sense, each of us plays a role in determining whether to accept or reject innovations. We do this on an individual basis for personal choices and on a collective basis for civic (societal) innovations. According to Wejnert (2002), the following characteristics of actors influence the diffusion of innovations: (1) societal entity; (2) familiarity with the innovation; (3) status factors; (4) socioeconomic factors; (5) position in social networks; and (6) personal factors. Although a complete discussion of all of those factors is beyond the scope of this book, it is possible to draw some parallels between the work of Rogers (2003) and Wejnert (2002). For example, a change agent does well to influence actors perceived as credible by others and actors with large social networks. Perceptions of credibility and influence are based on a combination of status factors (e.g., level of education, financial well-being, cosmopolitanism) and position in social network (number of people in social network). The third category of factors influencing the diffusion of an innovation pertains to environmental factors, including geography, culture, political conditions and global uniformity. Within global uniformity are factors such as global standardization, global technologies, including both devices and practices (e.g., agricultural and manufacturing practices), and mass media, which enables universal communication. In addition to the influence of factors within each category (innovation, actor, environment), there are effects between categories. For example, an individual actor can influence the perception of costs and benefits of an innovation.

Creating the instructional apps in this book may have modest effects on societies, but after gaining instructional app development knowledge and skills and experience diffusing instructional apps, whatever your impact may be, enjoy the ride.

2.4 The Grand Synthesis

One draws on knowledge in multiple disciplines when designing, developing, and providing instruction. Building on Shulman's (1986) notion that teachers draw on pedagogical knowledge and content knowledge (PCK) to provide instruction, Mishra and Koehler (2006) added technological knowledge to PCK, forming Technological Pedagogical Content Knowledge (TPCK), which applies to teachers integrating technology into their instruction.

Chapter 1 and this chapter confirm the necessity of pedagogical knowledge and content knowledge, plus technological knowledge for instruction deployed or created on computers. More specifically, Chapters 1 and 2 discuss the importance of synthesizing knowledge and skills in the following disciplines in order to design and develop instruction:

- Instructional design and development
  - Front-end analyses
  - Instructional planning (design)
    - Selection of instructional method
    - Motivational design
    - Preparation of design documents and prototypes
  - Instructional development
  - Implementation and evaluation
- User experience design
- Diffusion of innovations
- Subject matter (content)
- Project management (at least for paid work).

As discussed previously in this chapter, front-end analyses may involve developing and distributing questionnaire to learners, as well as conducting task, needs, and context analyses. Those analyses begin the ID process. After those analyses, instructional planning, development, and evaluation follow. Each of those specialties requires knowledge and skills; plus, for instructional development with computers, knowledge and skills in user experience design will improve the quality of the instruction. Then, to diffuse the instructional innovation, one draws on knowledge of effective change agent practices. Of course, too, content knowledge is required to create instruction.

Given the breadth and depth of knowledge and skills needed to master those disciplines, instruction in the real world is often designed and developed by teams supervised by a Project Manager. Individual team members specialize in any one of the key disciplines or any one specialty within the disciplines. In the remaining chapters of this book we focus on the instructional development specialty. Pursuing our goal to create instructional apps, we will develop computer programming skills and multimedia development skills. "Lone Ranger" scenarios, in which one person completes tasks in all of the disciplines, might be feasible after prolonged study in an instructional technology program or position, even if working on a complex problem alone is not advisable. On the other hand, it is certainly possible to pursue instructional design and development projects individually in simplified contexts. For example, this book reduces the complexity of instructional app design and development by providing the instructional goal, the instructional method, and an image of the interface for each instructional app created in Chapters 4–7. This will enable you to focus on app development.

Instructional design and development may be regarded as a complex or ill-structured problem (Branch & Kopcha, 2014), rather than a wicked problem (Conklin, 2006; Kolko, 2012), the difficulty of defining a problem notwithstanding (Rittel & Webber, 1973). Whereas wicked problems involve societal and cultural reckoning to resolve problems of poverty and equality, for instance, a merely complex problem, like creating effective instruction, has a much more limited scope. Creating instruction requires one to synthesize a variety of knowledge and skills. As noted in Section 2.1.1, synthesizing and creating are at the top of Bloom's Taxonomy (Krathwohl, 2002), which is the pinnacle of complexity in the cognitive domain. Further, the ID process is dynamic and some decisions must be made in light of uncertainty. Moreover, once testing begins with actual target learners, the instruction created may work well for some learners and not well for others. Such vagaries, fluctuations, and oddities encountered during the design and development of instruction make the endeavor at least somewhat complex. Resolving such complexity may lead one to question whether the design of instruction is a scientific undertaking, if not questioned already. We are free to perceive this matter as we wish; the study of instructional design and the work of an instructional designer may be perceived as science, art, or a combination of the two (Rieber in Hirumi, Appelman, Rieber, & Van Eck, 2010, p. 23).

2.4.1 Epitome of Instructional Design Process

This chapter has discussed multiple design processes, including a systematic instructional design process, gestalt design, and rapid prototyping, along with a user experience design process and a video design process. Design processes seek novelty and functionality—some new way to make life easier. With contributions from Dreyfuss (1955), Simon (1969, 1996), Lawson (1980, 2005), Cross (2011), and many others, design has emerged as a discipline. The design field offers a general design process, which Hasso Plattner (n.d.) conceives as including the following elements.

Empathize—Define—Ideate—Prototype—Test

Meinel and Leifer (2011) offer minor modifications to the language and representation of the Plattner sequence, as noted below.

* (re)Define the problem
* Needfinding and benchmarking (understanding the users)

- Bodystorm (ideate)
- Prototype (build)
- Test (learn).

In essence, Meinel and Leifer (2011) have reversed the first two stages of the process advanced by Plattner, while retaining the order of the final three stages. Whichever of those two processes one prefers, note that actual design practice would not necessarily follow the stages in pristine fashion (Meinel & Leifer, 2011). For example, idea generation in the Ideate Stage might reveal some information missing about the users so the next step would be to return to Needfinding. Uncovering the missing information might lead to either redefinition of the problem or a return to idea generation.

Design thinking involves interviews and observations of target users. Further, design thinking involves communication and collaboration with target users throughout the design process to refine prototypes. That is consistent with the notion of user-centered design in the UX field. Plattner (2017a) regards continuous collaboration between designers and users as contrasting engineering and scientific approaches. In the design thinking mindset, failure is regarded as a natural occurrence in the design process. Though failure creates short-term challenges, in the long run it advances the design process by informing the next iteration (Plattner, 2017b).

In addition to ID, UXD, and video design processes, we have also considered project management processes and the work of change agents. Further, front-end analyses (task analysis, learner analysis, context analysis) and evaluation work require planning, instrument selection or development, and data collection processes. In one respect, each of the processes considered in this chapter can be regarded as a problem, which makes addressing each one a problem-solving venture. Polya (1945, 2004), who sought not only to solve mathematics problems but also to gain insights into how to invent solutions to problems, offered this problem-solving strategy (Polya, 2004).

1. Understand the problem
2. Devise a plan
3. Carry out the plan
4. Look back.

Adding "Empathize" ahead of Polya's first step would bring us back to Plattner's design process. Having considered different formulations of design and problem-solving processes, I have come to epitomize instructional design as depicted in Figure 2.3.

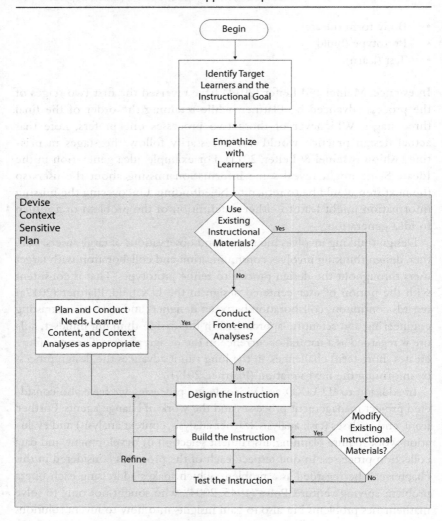

Figure 2.3 Epitome of Instructional Design Process.

1. Identify Target Learners and the Instructional Goal

Instruction is intended to increase the learner's knowledge (*episteme, techne, phronesis,* and *mètis*). Begin instructional planning knowing who will engage in the instruction and what they will learn. Consistent with the backward design process of Wiggins and McTighe (2005), begin with the end in mind.

Many instructional designers are most comfortable when the instructional goal is stated as a performance objective. When circumstances warrant, state the behavior, the conditions under which the behavior will be performed, and the mastery criterion (Mager, 1962). When the goal is to increase problem-solving capabilities (e.g., reading, writing, solving math problems), for instance, such a statement of the instructional objective may be challenging. Instructional designers who favor the systematic approach to instructional design will seek to reduce that goal to observable subordinate goals, which might focus the learner's attention on character or plot development, for instance. Alternatively, the goal might focus on succinct expression for business writing. Even with the focus on a particular aspect of writing, a Mager objective might be difficult to provide. One might offer: The learner will write three paragraphs, each of which clearly reveals attributes of a character's personality. Such a statement is missing the mastery criterion. After all, there is no single correct manner in which an author can reveal traits of a character. Further, assessing the quality of such writing is context dependent. For instance, in revealing a trait of a character, the author might also seek to advance the plot. This should remind us of Gestalt design, which seeks to retain complexity because simplification inhibits authenticity of practice. In many cases, scoring rubrics can be helpful for referencing mastery criteria in a statement of an objective. For example, the prior objective might become: The learner will write three paragraphs, each of which clearly reveals a character trait, and attain at least a score of four on the following rubric.

RUBRIC

1. No character traits revealed
2. Imprecise expression leaves reader somewhat uncertain about the character's traits
3. Character traits revealed in one paragraph
4. Character traits revealed in two paragraphs
5. Character traits revealed in three paragraphs.

Yet, even with the inclusion of a mastery criterion, the quality of the scoring rubric could be questioned and raters would score performance differently. The same rater might even score the same performance differently if rated more than once. In any case, it is not always important to produce a Mager objective. For the purposes of creating instruction, when completion of a task does not yield a correct answer, it will suffice to write a clear statement of the goal (e.g., learners will improve the clarity of their writing). The learners and raters will be able to reflect on writing samples over time and assess improvement relative to prior performance. At the conclusion of this first stage of the ID process, it is important to be able to state who is going to learn what. The more precise the specification of what is to be learned, the easier it will be to determine the extent to which it was learned.

2. Empathize with Learners

Instructional designers care about learners. Prior to designing instruction, become aware of the conditions in which the learners will engage in the instruction. Conceivably, instruction could be designed and developed for one learner, but engagement in a systematic process to design and develop instruction is more likely to occur when multiple learners will engage in the instruction. Will the learners meet in a classroom? If so, will the students be seated in rows of desks or will they be seated in groups around a table? Can the seating arrangement be adjusted? Will any equipment be used and, if so, does the equipment reside in the classroom? Do students like the learning environment? If engagement in the instruction will not occur in a classroom, will the instruction take place in a park, at a lake, or on a mountain, for instance, or will learners use a microcomputer at home? Will learners using a computer have access to the Internet? What motivates the students to learn? Of course, students may be motivated for a variety of reasons. Our job at this stage is to imagine ourselves in the learning environment; as instructional designers, we should come to recognize the diversity of the learners and what it is like to function in the learning environment.

3. Devise Context-Sensitive Plan

The plan for the design and development of instruction emerges in accordance with decisions made at key points. Decisions made depend upon the unique context or circumstances. Some ID projects use existing instructional materials and the lone instructional designer moves forward quickly to implementation and testing. In contrast, some ID projects involve million dollar budgets, multiple instructional designers, subject matter experts, and production teams. Many ID projects fall within those extremes. For example, one instructional designer with a modest budget may work with another instructional developer to create a new instructional manual, perhaps receiving tips and feedback from a subject matter expert (SME).

An important consideration in creating the context-sensitive plan is the expected compensation for time spent. When the stakes are low, little time is likely to be expended on the effort and few new instructional materials are likely to be created.

3A. WILL EXISTING INSTRUCTIONAL MATERIALS BE USED?

If existing instructional materials will be used, they may need to be modified. If so, some instructional development will occur before the instructional materials are tested.

If existing materials will not be used, context-sensitive planning proceeds to the next decision point (3b).

3B. WILL FRONT-END ANALYSES BE CONDUCTED?

When time is of the essence, the budget is minimal, and the instructional designer is working with a SME, front-end analyses are unlikely. The SME is expected to convey to the instructional designer sufficient information about the learners, the instructional content and context, and the need for the instruction.

On the other hand, when the budget and time permit, front-end analyses may be planned and conducted in order to collect information needed to design the instruction. For example, an instructional designer may develop a questionnaire for target learners, as well as observe them in the learning environment or environments. Some information about the learners will have been gained during the empathy step, but key information may be missing. Perhaps the project sponsor has limited knowledge about the learners and the learning environment enjoyed or endured by the learners. The instructional designer or designers may also conduct content/tasks analyses, perhaps by interviewing subject matter experts. The need for the instruction should also be confirmed and there may be some additional information to collect about the learning environment (context) that did not become evident during the empathy step.

At this point in an ID project, commonly, a Project Manager is monitoring progress, allocating resources as necessary, informing stakeholders of progress and expenditures, and making adjustments in personnel and acquisition of resources as necessary. The work of the Project Manager continues through the remaining steps.

3C. DESIGN THE INSTRUCTION

Taking into account learner motivation and other characteristics of the learners, especially their prior knowledge and skills, along with knowledge of the instructional goal, the instructional designer selects an instructional method. When designing (planning) instruction, seek to make the instruction effective, efficient, and at least satisfying, though inspiring is preferable.

First, the instruction that implements the instructional method should be effective. That is, learners should attain the instructional goal or goals through engagement in the instruction. In addition, the instruction should be efficient, enabling the learners to attain the instructional goal or goals with minimal resources, especially time. Moreover, the instruction should at least satisfy learners, if not inspire them. When designing instruction, seek to inspire learners to apply what they learn and to learn more. Perhaps the best we can do as instructional designers and developers is to create effective, efficient, and inspiring instruction, which I call *elegant instruction* (Luterbach, 2013).

In this work, the instructional method derives from behaviorism, cognitivism, or constructivism. Once the instructional method is selected, the instructional designer draws on pedagogical knowledge, content knowledge, technological knowledge, user experience design knowledge, and psychological knowledge to design an instructional experience appropriate for attainment of the instructional goal. As noted, the instruction should also be efficient and hopefully inspiring, though sometimes we create (merely) satisfying instruction. With information about the learners and the instructional goal, the instructional designer is prepared to create an instructional experience that implements the instructional method effectively and efficiently. Further, having reflected on the diversity of the learners and the learning environment (in accordance with the empathy step), the instructional designer is prepared to create a satisfying or even inspiring instructional experience.

As a designer planning an instructional experience, ask yourself these three questions for each instructional goal: What instructional presentations and activities will increase the confidence of the learners and ultimately enable them to attain the instructional goal? Why is the instructional goal relevant to the learners? Why would learners want to engage in the instruction?

As mentioned previously, answers to those questions require application of pedagogical knowledge, content knowledge, technological knowledge, user experience design knowledge, and psychological knowledge. Given the diversity of learners, awareness of universal design for learning principles is helpful. That is, provide multiple representations (text, symbols, images, audio, video) and multiple means for action, expression, and engagement (Meyer, Rose, & Gordon, 2014; Rao & Meo, 2016). A key lesson in the design of instruction for culturally and linguistically diverse learners is to use culturally responsive pedagogy (Gay, 2000; Ladson-Billings, 1994) and to use both the learner's native language and the second language (Rodriguez, Carrasquillo, & Soon Lee, 2014).

Both parenting and designing instruction are complex endeavors, which involve people and multiple dynamic factors. In parenting, there is no single correct way to raise a child, but there is variability in the effectiveness and suitability of particular parenting methods for particular children seeking to attain specific goals. In ID, there is no single correct instructional method, but there is variability in the effectiveness and suitability of particular instructional methods for particular learners seeking to attain specific instructional goals. Once the instructional designer has conceived of the instructional presentations and activities that will help particular learners attain a specific instructional goal or goals, the instructional designer produces design documents (e.g., lesson plan, sketch, flowchart, storyboard) and prototypes to convey the plan to developers and other stakeholders.

3D. BUILD THE INSTRUCTION

Developers turn design plans, conveyed through sketches, flowcharts, storyboards, prose, and prototypes, into functioning products (instruction in our case). Since instruction often includes text, images, sounds, and video, instructional developers need multimedia development skills. With multimedia development skills, developers create images, combine text and images, scale (resize) images, record and edit audio, and record and edit video, for instance.

One of the challenges of multimedia development is that software tools change continuously. Consequently, developers need to engage in continuous professional development in order to capitalize on the latest features available for image processing (e.g., in GIMP for 2D images and Blender for 3D image processing). Of course, too, sound editing and video editing tools advance all the time, as do commercial tools for instructional development (e.g., Adobe Captivate, Articulate Studio, Advantis Lectora). As noted in Chapter 1, we should seek to create instructional development tools superior to existing ones. Until we create those superior tools, we must work with software available today. In addition to continually honing multimedia development skills to capitalize on the latest capabilities of the tools, developers are challenged by asset maintenance. After developing and editing multimedia assets, each of which is stored in a separate and potentially large (say 500 MB or more) file, the developer must organize and backup the files. A well-conceived hierarchical folder structure is important for asset management.

In addition to multimedia development and management skills, instructional app developers need computer programming skills. We gain those in Chapter 3 and draw on them to create the instructional apps in Chapters 4–7. New computer programming languages do emerge over time, such as Lua and Swift, and we instructional developers do well to learn them when necessary or advantageous. However, since core components of computer programming languages, such as JavaScript and C, have been stable for more than three decades, the skills learned in Chapter 3 will serve us for some time. Yet even if work in computer science in some future decade might reduce the need for those computer programming skills, we will always be well served by the logical thought processes sharpened while learning and using computer programming skills.

3E. TEST THE INSTRUCTION

Since implementation must occur in order to test instruction, we can dispense with the term *implementation* and speak only of testing the instruction. As noted in the UXD section, usability testing may first involve discount methods, such as expert review. At some point, though, we need to test the instruction with actual target learners. Initially the testing is formative. Instructional designers/developers seek information to improve the effectiveness, efficiency, and appeal of the instruction.

This implies collecting data to determine whether learners attained the instructional goal. As early as the conclusion of the first step in this ID process, immediately after identifying the target learners and the instructional goal, an assessment could be developed, which would be consistent with the ID process advocated by Dick, Carey, and Carey (2015). However, in some cases, assessment will occur over time as the learners create artifacts (e.g., writings, drawings). Further, provided the instructional goal is clear at the conclusion of the first step, one ought to be able to create instruction to help learners attain the goal. If not created sooner, instructional assessment and any scoring rubrics will need to be created prior to testing the instruction. Analysis of data collected during this step will determine which revisions should be made to the instruction. In some cases, feedback might suggest that the design of the instruction be revised.

Some paths through the ID process depicted in Figure 2.3 require multiple personnel, while other paths can be pursued by individuals. An individual instructional designer will need analytical skills, evaluation skills, and design skills, as well as multimedia development skills to create and edit images, audio, and video; additionally, the instructional designer will need computer programming skills in the case of instructional app development. Moreover, anyone pursuing an instructional design and development project individually, which is common in low-stakes projects, will also need sufficient "people" skills to persuade others to join the project for the joy of working with the individual, at least to provide some feedback and encouragement along the way.

2.4.2 Creativity Conquers Complexity

Formerly, creativity was regarded as a rare talent exhibited by the likes of Sofonisba Anguissola, Filippo Brunelleschi, Leonardo da Vinci, Michelangelo di Lodovico Buonarroti Simoni, Artemisia Gentileschi, and Frida Kahlo, for instance. Today, we celebrate creativity in everyone, including artists. At the core of creativity is the generation of new and useful ideas (Clinton & Hokanson, 2012). Commonly, ideas are generated to solve problems, which is consistent with the adage "Necessity is the mother of invention." Yet necessity is just one source of creativity. We also wonder how phenomena work. We need not know about the properties of stars, but we might make our world more comprehensible and predictable if we discover more about stars. So astronomers generate hypotheses about stars and test their hypotheses. Einstein wondered about the sun and, after pondering light and physics for a couple of decades, he solved multiple mysteries about atoms and light, publishing five journal articles in one year, 1905. Creativity conquered complexity.

We, too, use creativity to conquer complexity. Every decision we make is based on a particular set of circumstances (a particular context). Each of us draws on personal knowledge to devise a solution to the problems we encounter in our unique circumstances. Sometimes implementation of the solution goes well and other times not so well. Reflecting on the outcomes, whatever they are, results in accumulation of knowledge, particularly *phronesis*.

In the case of ID projects, we solve one problem after another as we proceed through the analysis, design, development, and testing phases. Per Clinton and Hokanson (2012, p. 112): "an instructional designer is routinely confronted with the next task or design problem in a project, these tasks or problems spawn iterative mental excursions that are opportunities for creative thinking." The Design Phase yields design documents, which depict the instruction believed appropriate for enabling target learners to attain the instructional goal or goals. We will create instructional apps in Chapters 4–7 in light of the target learners, the instructional goal, the instructional method, and with a particular design in mind. From that point, we build, test, and refine.

References

Allen, J. J. & Chudley, J. J. (2012). *Smashing UX design: Foundations for designing online user experiences.* Chichester, UK: John Wiley & Sons.

Apple Computer (1992). Macintosh human interface guidelines. Reading, MA: Addison-Wesley.

Asimow, M. (1962). *Introduction to design.* Englewood Cliffs, NJ: Prentice-Hall.

Ausubel, D. P. (1968). *Educational psychology: A cognitive view.* New York, NY: Holt, Rinehart & Winston.

Bednar, A. K., Cunningham, D., Duffy, T. M., & Perry, J. D. (1991). Theory into practice: How do we link? In G. J. Anglin (Ed.), *Instructional technology: Past, present, and future* (pp. 17–35). Englewood, CO: Libraries Unlimited.

Bishop, M. J. (2014). Instructional message design: Past, present, and future relevance. In M. Spector, M. D. Merrill, J. Elen, & M. J. Bishop (Eds), *Handbook of Research on Educational Communications and Technology* (pp. 373–383). New York, NY: Springer Science and Business Media.

Bloom, B. (1956). *Taxonomy of educational objectives, Book 1: Cognitive Domain.* New York, NY: Longman.

Branch, R. M. (2009). *Instructional design: The ADDIE approach.* New York, NY: Springer.

Branch, R. M. & Kopcha, T. J. (2014). Instructional design models. In M. Spector, M. D. Merrill, J. Elen, & M. J. Bishop (Eds), *Handbook of research on educational communications and technology* (pp. 77–87). New York, NY: Springer Science and Business Media.

Brechner, E. (2015). *Agile project management with kanban.* Redmond, WA: Microsoft Press.

Brown, A. & Green, T. D. (2016). *The essentials of instructional design: Connecting fundamental principles with process and practice* (3rd ed.). New York, NY: Routledge.

Carter, C. W. (2012). Instructional audio guidelines: Four design principles to consider for every instructional audio design effort. *TechTrends, 56*(6), 54–58.

Chitale, A. K. & Gupta, R. C. (2013). *Product design and manufacturing* (6th ed.). Delhi, India: PHI Learning.

Clinton, G. & Hokanson, B. (2012). Creativity in the training and practice of instructional designers: The design/creativity loops model. *Educational Technology Research and Development, 60*(1), 111–130.

Collins, A., Brown, J. S., & Newman, S. E. (1989). Cognitive apprenticeship: Teaching the crafts of reading, writing, and mathematics. In L. B. Resnick (Ed.), *Knowing, learning, and instruction: Essays in honor of Robert Glaser* (pp. 453–494). Hillsdale, NJ: Lawrence Erlbaum Associates.

Coleman, B. & Goodwin, D. (2017). *Designing UX: Prototyping.* Collingwood, Victoria, Australia: Sitepoint Pty.

Conklin, J. (2006). *Dialogue mapping: Building shared understanding of wicked problems.* Chichester, UK: John Wiley & Sons.

Cook-Sather, A. (2003). Listening to students about learning differences. *Teaching Exceptional Children, 35*(4), 22–26.

Cook-Sather, A. (2014). Multiplying perspectives and improving practice: What can happen when undergraduate students collaborate with college faculty to explore teaching and learning. *Instructional Science, 42*(1), 31–46.

Corey, J. (2017). *Audio production and critical listening: Technical ear training.* New York, NY: Routledge.

Cronbach, L. J. (1975). Course improvement through evaluation. In D. A. Payne & R. F. Macmorris (Eds), *Educational and psychological measurement: Contributions to theory and practice* (2nd ed., pp. 243–256). Morristown, NJ: General Learning Press.

Cross, N. (2011). *Design thinking: Understanding how designers think and work.* New York, NY: Bloomsbury.

Davies, I. K. (1976). *Objectives in curriculum design.* New York, NY: McGraw Hill.

Davis, B. (2012). *Agile practices for waterfall projects: Shifting processes for competitive advantage.* Plantation, FL: J. Ross Publishing.

Desrosier, J. (2011). Rapid prototyping reconsidered. *The Journal of Continuing Higher Education, 59*, 135–145.

Dick, W., Carey, L., & Carey, J. O. (2015). *The systematic design of instruction* (8th ed.). New York, NY: Pearson Higher Education.

Dreyfuss, H. (1955). *Designing for people.* New York, NY: Allworth Press.

Fishman, B. (2014). Designing usable interventions: Bringing student perspectives to the table. *Instructional Science, 42*(1), 115–121.

Foshay, W. R. (1983). Alternative methods of task analysis: A comparison of three methods. *Journal of Instructional Development, 6*(4), 2–9.

Foshay, W. R., Silber, K. H., & Stelnicki, M. B. (2003). *Writing training materials that work: How to train anyone to do anything.* San Francisco, CA: Jossey-Bass/Pfeiffer.

Furterer, S. L. (2009) (Ed.). *Lean Six Sigma in service: Applications and case studies.* Boca Raton, FL: CRC press.

Gagné, R. M. (1965). *The conditions of learning.* New York, NY: Holt, Rinehart and Winston.

Gagné, R. M. (1974). Task analysis: Its relation to content analysis. *Educational Psychology, 11*(1), 11–18.

Gay, G. (2000). *Culturally responsive teaching: Theory, research, and practice.* New York, NY: Teachers College Press.

Gibbons, A. S. (2014). *An architectural approach to instructional design.* New York, NY: Routledge.

Gibbons, A. S., Boling, E., & Smith, K. M. (2014). Instructional design models. In M. Spector, M. D. Merrill, J. Elen, & M. J. Bishop (Eds), *Handbook of research on educational communications and technology* (pp. 607–615). New York, NY: Springer Science and Business Media.

Gothelf, J. & Seiden, J. (2013). *Lean UX: Applying lean principles to improve user experience.* Sebastopol, CA: O'Reilly Media.

Gould, J. D. & Lewis, C. (1985). Designing for usability: Key principles and what designers think. *Communications of the ACM (Association for Computing Machinery), 28*(3), 300–311.

Gustafson, K. L. & Branch, R. M. (1997). Revisioning models of instructional development. *Educational Technology Research & Development, 45*(3), 73–89.

Gustafson, K. L. & Branch, R. M. (2002). *Survey of instructional development models* (4th ed.). Syracuse, NY: ERIC Clearinghouse on Information & Technology.

Hall, G. E. & Hord, S. M. (2015). *Implementing change: Patterns, principles and potholes* (4th ed.). Upper Saddle River, NJ: Pearson.

Halls, J. (2012). *Rapid video development for trainers: How to create learning videos fast and affordably.* Alexandria, VA: American Society for Training and Development.

Hartson, R. & Pyla, P. S. (2012). *The UX book: Process and guidelines for ensuring a quality user experience.* Waltham, MA: Morgan Kaufmann.

Heinich, R. (1991). The proper study of instructional technology. In G. J. Anglin (Ed.), *Instructional technology: Past, present, and future* (pp. 59–81). Englewood, CO: Libraries Unlimited.

Highsmith, J. (2010). *Agile project management: Creating innovative products* (2nd ed.). Boston, MA: Pearson.

Hill, D. R. (2000). Give us the tools: A personal view of multi-modal computer-human dialogue. In M. M. Taylor, F. Néel, & D. G. Bouwhuis (Eds), *The structure of multimodal dialogue II* (pp. 25–62). Philadelphia, PA: John Benjamins Publishing.

Hirumi, A., Appelman, B., Rieber, L., & Van Eck, R. (2010). Preparing instructional designers for game-based learning: Part 2. *TechTrends, 54*(4), 19–27.

Hites Anderson, J. (2010). Collecting analysis data. In K. H. Silber & W. R. Foshay (Eds), *Handbook of improving performance in the workplace* (vol. 1, instructional design and training delivery, pp. 95–143). San Francisco, CA: Pfeiffer.

International Standards Organization (1998). ISO 9241–11, 1998. Available at: www.iso.org/standard/16883.html

Jonassen, D. H. (1997). Instructional design models for well-structured and ill-structured problem-solving learning outcomes. *Educational Technology Research & Development, 45*(1), 65–94.

Jonassen, D. H. & Hannum, W. H. (1986). Analysis of task analysis procedures. *Journal of Instructional Development, 9*(2), 2–12.

Keller, J. M. (1983). Motivational design of instruction. In C. M. Reigeluth (Ed.), *Instructional design theories and models: An overview of their current status* (pp. 383–434). Hillsdale, NJ: Lawrence Erlbaum Associates.

Keller, J. M. (1987a). Strategies for stimulating the motivation to learn. *Performance & Improvement, 26*(8), 1–7.

Keller, J. M. (1987b). The systematic process of motivational design. *Performance & Improvement, 26*(9/10), 1–8.

Kerzner, H. (2013). *Project management: A systems approach to planning, scheduling, and controlling* (11th ed.). Hoboken, NJ: John Wiley & Sons.

Kirkpatrick, D. L. (1959). Techniques for evaluating training programs. *Journal of American Society of Training Directors, 13*(3), 21–26.

Kolko, J. (2012). *Wicked problems: Problems worth solving.* Austin, TX: Austin Center for Design.

Könings, K. D., Seidel, T., & van Merriënboer, J. J. G. (2014). Participatory design of learning environments: Integrating perspectives of students, teachers, and designers. *Instructional Science, 42*(1), 1–9.

Krathwohl, D. R. (2002). A revision of Bloom's taxonomy: An overview. *Theory into Practice, 41*(4), 212–218.

Krug, S. (2014). *Don't make me think: A common sense approach to web usability* (3rd ed.). San Francisco, CA: New Riders.

Ladson-Billings, G. (1994). T*he dreamkeepers: Successful teachers of African American children.* San Francisco, CA: Jossey-Bass.

Lave, J. & Wenger, E. (1990). *Situated learning: Legitimate peripheral participation.* Cambridge: Cambridge University Press.

Lawson, B. (1980). *How designers think.* London: Architectural Press.

Lawson, B. (2005). *How designers think: The design process demystified.* New York, NY: Routledge.

Lechler, T. G., Edington, B. H., & Gao, T. (2012). Challenging classic project management: Turning project uncertainties into business opportunities. *Project Management Journal, 43*(6), 59–69.

Levin, M. (2014). *Designing multi-device experiences.* Sebastopol, CA: O'Reilly Media.

Levy, J. (2015). *UX strategy: How to devise innovative digital products that people want.* Sebastopol, CA: O'Reilly Media.

Luterbach, K. J. (2013). Elegant Instruction. *Journal of Educational Technology Systems. 41*(2), 183–204.

Mace, R. (2008). About UD. https://projects.ncsu.edu/www/ncsu/design/sod5/cud/about_ud/about_ud.htm

Mager, R. F. (1962). *Preparing objectives for programmed instruction.* Belmont, CA: Fearon Publishers.

Mager, R. F. (1997). *Preparing instructional objectives* (3rd ed.). Atlanta, GA: The Center for Effective Performance.

Makhlouf, J. (2016). Iterative design models: ADDIE vs SAM. http://elearningmind.com/iterative-design-different-strokes-different-folks/

Markle, S. M. (1967). Empirical testing of programs. In P.C. Lange (Ed.), *Programmed instruction. The sixty-sixth yearbook of the national society for the study of education, part II* (pp. 104–138). Chicago, IL: The University of Chicago Press.

Marmaras, N., Poulakakis, G., & Papakostopoulos, V. (1999). Ergonomic design in ancient Greece. *Applied Ergonomics, 30*(4), 361–368.

McElroy, K. (2017). *Prototyping for designers.* Sebastopol, CA: O'Reilly Media.

McLellan, H. (Ed.) (1996). *Situated learning perspectives.* Englewood Cliffs, NJ: Educational Technology Publications.

Meinel, C. & Leifer, L. (2011). Design thinking research. In H. Plattner, C. Meinel, & L. Leifer (Eds), *Design thinking: Understand, improve, apply* (pp. xiii–xv). Berlin, Germany: Springer-Verlag.

Merrill, M. D. (1983). Component display theory. In C. Reigeluth (Ed.), *Instructional design theories and models* (pp. 279–333). Hillsdale, NJ: Erlbaum Associates.

Merrill, M. D. (1994). *Instructional design theory.* Englewood Cliffs, NJ: Educational Technology Publications.

Meyer, A., Rose, D. H., & Gordon, D. (2014). *Universal design for learning: Theory and practice.* Wakefield, MA: CAST Professional Publishing.

Mishra, P. & Koehler, M. J. (2006). Technological pedagogical content knowledge: A framework for teacher knowledge. *Teachers College Record, 108*(6), 1017–1054.

Molenda, M. (2003). In search of the elusive ADDIE model. *Performance Improvement, 42*(5), 34–36.

Morrison, G. R., Ross, S. M., Kalman, H. K., & Kemp, J. E. (2013). Designing effective instruction (7th ed.). Hoboken, NJ: Wiley.

Musburger, R. B. & Ogden, M. R. (2014). *Single-camera video production.* Burlington, MA: Focal Press.

Nielsen, J. (1989). *Usability engineering at a discount.* Third International Conference of Human-Computer Interaction. Boston, MA.

www.nngroup.com/articles/discount-usability-20-years/

Nielsen, J. & Molich, R. (1990). Heuristic evaluation of user interfaces. *Proceedings of the conference on Computer Human Interaction,* 249–256.

Nielsen, J. (1993). *Usability engineering.* Cambridge, MA: Academic Press.

Norman, D. (1988). *The psychology of everyday things.* New York, NY: Basic Books.

Norman, D. (1995). What you see, some of what's in the future, and how we go about doing it: HI at Apple Computer. Proceedings of the CHI '95, 155.

Norman, D. (2013). *The design of everyday things: Revised and expanded edition.* New York, NY: Basic Books.

Orey, M. & Branch, R. M. (2015) (Eds). *Educational media and technology yearbook.* Cham, Switzerland: Springer.

Pace, C. R. & Friedlander, J. (1978). Approaches to evaluation: Models and perspectives. In G. R. Hanson (Ed.), *New directions for student services* (pp. 1–17). San Francisco, CA: Jossey-Bass.

Pearl, C. (2017). *Designing voice user interfaces.* Sebastopol, CA: O'Reilly Media.

Peters, T. (1999). *The circle of innovation: You can't shrink your way to greatness.* New York, NY: Vintage Books.

Plattner, H. (n.d.). An introduction to design thinking: Process guide. Stanford, CA: Institute of Design at Stanford. https://dschool-old.stanford.edu/sandbox/groups/design-resources/wiki/36873/attachments/74b3d/ModeGuideBOOTCAMP2010L.pdf?sessionID=1b6a96f1e2a50a3b1b7c3f09e58c40a062d7d553

Plattner, H. (2017a). What is design thinking? https://hpi-academy.de/en/design-thinking/what-is-design-thinking.html

Plattner, H. (2017b). What is design thinking? Retrieved June 14, 2017 from https://hpi.de/en/school-of-design-thinking/design-thinking/mindset.html

Polya, G. (1945). *How to solve it: A new aspect of mathematical method.* Princeton, NJ: Princeton University Press.

Polya, G. (2004). *How to solve it: A new aspect of mathematical method.* Princeton, NJ: Princeton University Press.

Project Management Institute (2013). *A guide to the project management body of knowledge* (5th ed.). Newtown Square, PA: Author.

Rao, K. & Meo, G. (2016). Using universal design for learning to design standards-based lessons, *SAGE Open, 6*(4). http://journals.sagepub.com/doi/pdf/10.1177/2158244016680688

Reigeluth, C. M. (1979). In search of a better way to organize instruction: The elaboration theory. *Journal of Instructional Development, 2*(3), 8–15.

Reigeluth, C. M. (Ed.). (1983). *Instructional design theories and models: An overview of their current status*. Hillsdale, NJ: Lawrence Erlbaum Associates.

Reigeluth, C. M. (Ed.) (1999a). *Instructional-design theories and models: A new paradigm of instructional theory, Volume II*. Mahwah, NJ: Lawrence Erlbaum Associates.

Reigeluth, C. M. (1999b). The elaboration theory: Guidance for scope and sequence decisions. In C. M. Reigeluth (Ed.), *Instructional-design theories and models: A new paradigm of instructional theory, Volume II* (pp. 425–454). Mahwah, NJ: Lawrence Erlbaum Associates.

Reigeluth, C. M. & Stein, F. S. (1983). The elaboration theory of instruction. In C. M. Reigeluth (Ed.), *Instructional design theories and models: An overview of their current status* (pp. 335–382). Hillsdale, NJ: Lawrence Erlbaum Associates.

Richey, R. C., Klein, J. D., & Tracey, M. W. (2011). *The instructional design knowledge base: Theory, research, and practice*. New York, NY: Routledge.

Rittel, H. W. J. & Webber, M. M. (1973). Dilemmas in a general theory of planning. *Policy Sciences, 4*, 155–169.

Rodriguez, D., Carrasquillo, A., & Soon Lee, K. (2014). *The bilingual advantage: Promoting academic development, biliteracy, and native language in the classroom*. New York, NY: Teachers College Press.

Rogers, E. (2003). *Diffusion of innovations* (5th ed.). New York, NY: Free Press.

Rubin, K. S. (2013). *Essential scrum: A practical guide to the most popular agile process*. Boston, MA: Pearson.

Sauls, S. J. & Stark, C. A. (2016). Audio production worktext: Concepts, techniques, and equipment (8th ed.). New York, NY: Routledge.

Sauro, J. (2015). The expert review is more than a second-rate usability test. https://measuringu.com/expert-review/

Sauro, J. & Lewis, J. R. (2012). *Quantifying the user experience: Practical statistics for user research*. Waltham, MA: Morgan Kaufmann.

Schrage, M. (2000). *Serious play: How the world's best companies simulate to innovate*. Brighton, MA: Harvard Business School Press.

Schwaber, K. (2004). *Agile project management with scrum*. Redmond, WA: Microsoft Press.

Scriven, M. (1967). The methodology of evaluation. In R. W. Tyler, R. M. Gagné, & M. Scriven (Eds), *Perspectives of curriculum evaluation* (pp. 39–83). Chicago, IL: Rand McNally.

Shneiderman, B. (1986). *Designing the user interface: Strategies for effective human-computer interaction*. Reading, MA: Addison-Wesley.

Shneiderman, B., Plaisant, C., Cohen, M., Jacobs, S., Elmqvist, N., & Diakopoulos, N. (2017). *Designing the user interface: Strategies for effective human-computer interaction* (6th ed.). Boston, MA: Addison-Wesley.

Shulman, L. S. (1986). Those who understand: Knowledge growth in teaching. *Educational Researcher, 15*(2), 4–14.

Skinner, B. F. (1991). *Verbal behavior*. Brattleboro, VT: Echo Point Books & Media.

Silber, K. H. (2007). A principle-based model of instructional design: A new way of thinking about and teaching ID. *Educational Technology, 47*(5), 5–19.

Simon, H. A. (1969). *The sciences of the artificial*. Cambridge, MA: The MIT Press.

Simon, H. A. (1996). *The sciences of the artificial* (3rd ed.). Cambridge, MA: The MIT Press.

Sims, C. & Johnson, M. L. (2012). *Scrum: A breathtakingly brief and agile introduction*. CA: Dymaxicon.

Smaldino, S. E., Lowther, D. L, Mims, C., & Russell, J. D. (2015). *Instructional technology and media for learning* (11th ed.). Boston, MA: Pearson.

Smith, P. L. & Ragan, T. J. (2005). *Instructional design* (3rd ed.). Hoboken, NJ: John Wiley & Sons.

Snyder, C. (2003). *Paper prototyping: The fast and easy way to design and refine user interfaces.* San Francisco, CA: Morgan Kaufmann.

Stake, R. E. (1973). The countenance of educational evaluation. In B. R. Worthen & J. R. Sanders (Eds), *Educational evaluation: Theory and practice* (pp. 106–127). Belmont, CA: Wadsworth Publishing.

Steffe, L. P. & Thompson, P. W. (2000). *Radical constructivism in action: Building on the pioneering work of Ernst von Glasersfeld.* New York, NY: Routledge.

Sugar, W. & Betrus, A. (2002). The many hats of an instructional designer: The development of an instructional card game. *Educational Technology, 42*(1), 45–51.

Sweetow, S. (2017). *Corporate video production* (2nd ed.). New York, NY: Routledge.

Tan, W-s, Liu, D., & Bishu, R. (2009). Web evaluation: Heuristic evaluation vs. user testing. *International Journal of Industrial Ergonomics, 39*(4), 621–627.

Tessmer, M. (1993). *Planning and conducting formative evaluations.* London: Kogan Page.

Tognazzini, B. (1992). *Tog on interface.* Reading, MA: Addison-Wesley.

Tracey, M. W. & Boling, E. (2014). Preparing instructional designers: Traditional and emerging perspectives. In M. Spector, M. D. Merrill, J. Elen, & M. J. Bishop (Eds), *Handbook of research on educational communications and technology* (pp. 653–660). New York, NY: Springer Science and Business Media.

Treder, M. (2017). *Beyond wireframing: The real-life UX design process.* www.ceros.com/blog/beyond-wireframing-real-life-ux-design-process/

Tripp, S. & Bichelmeyer, B. (1990). Rapid prototyping: An alternative ID strategy. *Educational Technology Research & Development, 38*(1), 31–44.

User Experience Professionals' Association (2012). Usability body of knowledge: Usability evaluation methods. www.usabilitybok.org/usability-evaluation-methods.

van Merriënboer, J. J. G., Clark, R. E., & de Crook, M. B. M. (2002). Blueprints for complex learning: The 4C/ID-Model. *Educational Technology Research & Development, 50*(2), 39–64.

van Merriënboer, J. J. G. & de Bruin, A. B. H. (2014). Research paradigms and perspectives on learning. In M. Spector, M. D. Merrill, J. Elen, & M. J. Bishop (Eds), *Handbook of research on educational communications and technology* (pp. 21–29), New York, NY: Springer Science and Business Media.

Weinschenk, S. & Barker, D. T. (2000). *Designing effective speech interfaces.* Hoboken, NJ: John Wiley & Sons.

Wejnert, B. (2002). Integrating models of diffusion of innovations: A conceptual framework. *Annual Review of Sociology, 28*, 297–326.

Wharton, C., Rieman, J., Lewis, C., & Polson, P. (1994). The Cognitive Walkthrough: A practitioner's guide. In J. Nielsen & R. L. Mack (Eds), *Usability inspection methods* (pp. 105–140). Hoboken, NJ: John Wiley & Sons.

Wiggins, G. J. & McTighe, J. (2005). *Understanding by design.* Alexandria, VA: Association for Supervision and Curriculum Development.

Williams, R. (2015). *The non-designer's design book* (4th ed.). Hoboken, NJ: Peachpit Press.

Wysocki, R. K. (2014). *Effective project management: Traditional, agile, extreme* (4th ed.). Indianapolis, IN: John Wiley & Sons.

Chapter 3
Computer Programming

Computer programming languages are tools for problem solving and creative expression. Indeed, people engaged in creative problem solving with computer programming languages developed technologies that resulted in the epochal transformation of the past half century. This information era is marked by computer programs (software) that implement the communication protocols enabling the Internet and the web; software enabling mobile communications; software enabling email and other messaging; software for shopping; software for creating 2D images and 3D models; animation software; office productivity software; voice recognition software, and software for learning, for instance. Learning a computer programming language is extremely beneficial as an outlet for creative expression and problem solving.

One selects a particular programming language to fit a variety of circumstances. When it is necessary to receive and respond to data at particular microsecond intervals, one writes code in a low-level programming language using the CPU's instruction set, which addresses memory and input ports directly. Commonly, though, application software is written in a high-level computer programming language, which eliminates the need to consider the computer's architecture. After distinguishing between low-level and high-level computer programming languages, it is helpful to recognize four main programming paradigms: imperative (procedural/ structural); object-oriented; functional; and logical. Each paradigm has something to offer problem solvers (Kedar, 2011). In this book, we will not be using Haskell (Thompson, 2011) or any functional programming language (so no f(g(x)) for us in this work). Also, we do not consider a logic programming language, such as Prolog. We will consider object-oriented concepts, as necessary. Object-oriented languages, such as C++, C# (C sharp), Objective-C, and Java include imperative language components. Indeed, C++, C#, and Objective-C are implementations of C with objects. C, like JavaScript, Perl, Lua, Swift, Java, and Python, all have imperative (procedural) language components, which enable input/output, and solve problems using the following core elements:

1. Variables in one of three data types (character, numeric, or Boolean);
2. Three types of statements (i.e., assignment, conditional, iterative);
3. Data structures (arrays and files); and
4. Decomposition (subroutines, variably called procedures, functions, or methods).

We focus on those core elements in this chapter and throughout the book. Even if you have never written a computer program before, you will write an interactive program in JavaScript in the first section of this chapter. By the end of the third section of this chapter (3.1.3), you will write a program in JavaScript to solve an instructional problem. You will also use JavaScript to create the apps in Chapters 4 and 7. In Chapters 5 and 6, you will transfer your knowledge of JavaScript to C# (C Sharp) and Python, respectively. Transferring your knowledge and skills to C# and Python will enable you to learn other computer programming languages, as well as to gain confidence in the extensibility of your knowledge. Extending knowledge across multiple development environments increases your capabilities and favors efforts to make instructional apps ubiquitous across multiple digital devices.

3.1 Procedural Programming

JavaScript is both a procedural programming language and object oriented. We begin with procedural programming features and then proceed to objective-oriented techniques, which arise in the section on Software Development Kits (Section 3.2.2). Using a procedural programming language, you can solve problems and express yourself creatively.

3.1.1 Input and Output

To convey the effects of data processing to users, computer programs output results, which may be numeric or alphabetic. A series of alphabetic characters, such as "Hello, World," is called a string. Our first JavaScript program will display "Hello, World!" and will run in either the Google Chrome or Firefox web browser.[1]

To begin, open the JavaScript Console in Google Chrome by pressing Option-Command-J on a Mac or Control-Shift-I on a Windows PC (or you could drop down the View menu and select Developer; JavaScript Console). Alternatively, open the JavaScript Console in Firefox by pressing Option-Command-K on a Mac or Control-Shift-K on a Windows PC (or you could drop down the Tools menu and select Web Developer; Web Console). On a Windows PC, whether using Google Chrome or Firefox, make sure the Console tab is selected. Whether using a Mac or a Windows PC, in the JavaScript Console, type the following line of JavaScript code and press the Enter or Return key.

```
console.log("Hello, World");
```

Do not be concerned that the word, *undefined* appears below "Hello, World." Also in the JavaScript Console, enter a few arithmetic expressions, such as the following, and press the Enter or Return key after each expression.

```
3 + 8
28 * 2 + 1
(4 - 20) / 8
6
```

It is helpful to know that one can run JavaScript code within popular web browsers, but we will use SpiderMonkey JavaScript because it has several advantages. First, SpiderMonkey JavaScript enables data to be entered from the keyboard, which is critical because learners need to respond to prompts and receive feedback. Second, SpiderMonkey JavaScript uses `print`, rather than `console.log`, to display information on the screen. Third, SpiderMonkey JavaScript does not display undefined. Fourth, SpiderMonkey JavaScript permits programs to read data from a file. Like the JavaScript interpreter in web browsers, SpiderMonkey JavaScript is free of monetary cost.

Installing SpiderMonkey JavaScript on a Mac

1. Open a terminal window (Applications; Utilities; Terminal.app).
2. Run the following command (entire command is one line):

```
ruby -e "$(curl -fsSL
https://raw.githubusercontent.com/Homebrew/install/
master/install)" < /dev/null 2> /dev/null
```

3. Run the following command:

```
brew install spidermonkey
```

Installing SpiderMonkey JavaScript on a PC

The Mozilla Developer Network enables one to build SpiderMonkey from source code (https://developer.mozilla.org/en-US/docs/Mozilla/Projects/ SpiderMonkey/Getting_SpiderMonkey_source_code#Getting_the_latest_ SpiderMonkey_source_code). In order to do that, however, one must compile the source using a C++ complier (and perhaps spending hours contemplating build settings). The straightforward approach is to obtain a pre-built version, which you can do at www.kahusecurity.com/2010/spidermonkey-1-8-5-for-windows/

Just click the spidermonkey-1.8.5.zip link. Once downloaded, unpack the .zip file, which will create a folder that contains three files. (If you wish, you can move the folder to any location on your hard drive.) One of the files is the executable file, js.exe.

Running SpiderMonkey Javascript

After installation of SpiderMonkey JavaScript, as described above, follow either the Apple Mac or Windows PC instructions below to open the JavaScript environment (shell), which enables you to enter and run Java-Script statements one at a time.

APPLE MAC

On a Mac, open a Terminal Window (Applications; Utilities; Terminal.app). In the Terminal Window, enter js and the js> prompt will be displayed, which indicates that the JavaScript shell is open and ready to process Java-Script statements and expressions.

WINDOWS PC

On a Windows PC, double-click the js.exe file, which will open a Command window and the js> prompt will be displayed, which indicates that the JavaScript shell is open and ready to process JavaScript statements and expressions.

Type the following command and run it by pressing the Enter or Return key.

```
print("Hello, World");
```

As before, run some arithmetic expressions, such as the following, pressing the Enter or Return key after each one.

```
8 + 3
1 + 2 * 28
-6
(4 - 20) / 8
4 - 20 / 8
```

If you tried an expression resulting in an infinitely repeating decimal, such as 10 / 3, you would have discovered that computers have finite representations of numbers. Consequently, the result of 10 / 3 appears as 3.3333333333333335. At some point, no matter how many bits are used to represent numbers, the fixed number of bits results in a rounding error for infinitely repeating decimals. Practically, such a small rounding error has no noticeable effect on the vast majority of apps, including the instructional apps we will create.

When you have finished entering arithmetic expressions, close JavaScript by pressing Ctrl-C, whether you're running the JavaScript interpreter on a Mac or a Windows PC.

At times we run code one line at a time in order to get immediate feedback, but computer programs almost always contain more than one line of code. Hence, we often write and edit code in a text editor, such as TextEdit on a Mac or NotePad on a PC. Then we save the file and run the program. Upon running a program, you may discover that an error needs to be corrected or that you want to enhance the functionality of the program in some manner. This will lead you to edit the code, which will necessitate that the file be saved and the program run again. This Program Development Cycle consists of editing, saving, and running code, as depicted in Figure 3.1.

We will engage in the program development cycle to write a program that will obtain the user's name and greet the user.

Open TextEdit on a Mac or NotePad on a PC. If using TextEdit, make sure that Plain Text is selected in the Format section of the Preferences dialog. Enter the following single line of code into your text editor.

```
print("Hello, World");
```

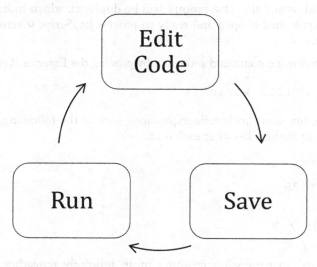

Figure 3.1 Program Development Cycle.

Save the file as *firstProgram.js*. Ensure that your text editor has not saved the file as firstProgram.js.txt. Rename the file to *firstProgram.js* if `.txt` was appended to the file name.

Run *firstProgram.js* through the JavaScript interpreter using the following command.

```
js firstProgram.js
```

Debug if necessary by editing *firstProgram.js*; save; and then run the program again. It is very important to be precise in computer programming. A missing semicolon or a quotation mark, or a mistyped command (e.g., `printt` instead of `print`) will produce an error. Edit, save, and run your programs until they are free of errors. Interpreters and compliers often identify the line number containing a syntax error so you know where to focus your attention. Once you have *firstProgram.js* working, copy the file to *secondProgram.js* and edit the code so the program contains the following two lines.

```
print("Enter your name");
userName = readline();
```

Save and run. The second line in the program introduces a variable, which in this case is called `userName`. The second line also includes the command, `readline()`, which SpiderMonkey JavaScript recognizes as a function call to retrieve user input from the keyboard. We will discuss the need for the parentheses in `readline()` in Section 3.1.4. Just be sure to include them. The `readline` function captures the characters the user types on the keyboard until the user presses the Enter/Return key. When the user presses the Enter or Return key, the value of the `userName` variable is set to the string of characters typed by the user, which could be 0, 1, or more characters. Since the program does not output the user's name, or whatever characters the user entered after being prompted to enter her or his name, you might not be convinced that the program is working. To ensure that the variable `userName` actually contains the input characters, echo the user's input by adding a print statement that displays the value of `userName`, as shown below.

```
print("Enter your name");
userName = readline();
print(userName);
```

Save and run. Debug as necessary.
One more tweak; modify the print statement, as shown below.

```
print("Enter your name");
userName = readline();
print ("Hi, " + userName);
```

Save and run. Notice that the + in the final print statement is used to combine the string "Hi, " with the string of characters in the userName variable, which was obtained from the user. Combining characters in this manner is called *string concatenation*.

Create a new document in your text editor. Enter the code below and save the program as *practiceAdding.js*. Run the program; debug as necessary.

```
print("What is 6 + 8?");
userResponse = readline();
print("You replied that 6 + 8 = " + userResponse);
```

Writing programs containing one to three lines of code is a fine starting place. Given that approach, you have already learned vital JavaScript commands (print and readline) for communicating with the user. Technically, as discussed in Section 3.1.4, such commands are calls to *subroutines*, which many programmers also refer to as *functions* or *methods*. In the Spider-Monkey version of JavaScript, we use print for output and readline for input. Other programming languages are similar in this regard. For example, the Pascal programming language uses write for output and readln for input; Perl uses print for output and <stdin> for input; BASIC and Python use print for output and input for input.

To summarize this section, we have written interactive programs in Java-Script to obtain the user's name and the user's response to a question. Those programs have revealed that computer programs contain variables and statements. The fundamental building blocks of computer programs are *variables, statements*, and *data structures*. Once you know those fundamental building blocks, you can combine them in unique ways to express yourself creatively and to engage in problem solving. Note that variables contain information, which we generally refer to as data. Each variable contains one particular type of data. With knowledge of three data types and the skill to use three types of statements, three data structures, and one technique, you will be able to program a computer for general purpose problem solving and creative expression.

3.1.2 Three Data Types

In JavaScript programming, a variable can be a *number*, a *character string*, or a *Boolean value*. A Boolean value is either true or false. The Boolean type is named after George Boole, an early nineteenth-century mathematician and philosopher, who developed Boolean algebra or Boolean logic. As an aside, Boolean algebra offers a set of 16 propositions based on two variables (x and y), each of which is either true or false. If one depicts true as 1 and false as 0, the 16 propositions can be expressed as per Table 3.1.

Table 3.1 Propositions in Boolean Algebra

x	y																
0	0	0	0	0	0	0	0	0	0	I	I	I	I	I	I	I	I
0	I	0	0	0	0	I	I	I	I	0	0	0	0	I	I	I	I
I	0	0	0	I	I	0	0	I	I	0	0	I	I	0	0	I	I
I	I	0	I	0	I	0	I	0	I	0	I	0	I	0	I	0	I

Boolean algebra is a foundation of digital computing, which on some level justifies inclusion of the table, even though there is no need for computer programmers to comprehend the table, except for logical AND and OR, which programmers, like all people, benefit from understanding. (More on this in the next section.)

In JavaScript, we can manipulate numbers, character strings, and Boolean values. Enter the following expressions into the JavaScript shell (command window) and press Enter or Return after each one. Most cases yield a result, either a number, character string, or a Boolean value. In some instances, though, an error message is generated. As you will discover, an error message could be a statement that reports an invalid function or an error message could be a symbol (e.g., NaN, which is an acronym for Not a Number).

```
4
"4"
6 + 0
6 - 0
6 * 0
6 / 0
a
"a"
6 > 5
5 > 6
6 = 6
6 >= 5
6 >= 6
6 == 6
6 != 6
6 >= 6
6 < 7
6 < 8
6 < 88
6 < 8888888888888888888
```

```
6 < 8888888888888888888888888888888888888888888
Math.round(4.5);
Math.floor(4.5);
Math.sqrt(81);
Math.sqtt(81);
Math.sqrt(-81);
Math.sqr(8);
Math.pow(10, 2);
Math.pow(2, 10);
true
tru
"tru" + "e"
"tru' + "e"
"tru' + "e
false
"f" + "alse"
"
" "
"
'
"Hello, there!"
userHeight = 1.75;
userHeight * 2
print (userHeight);
print ("Maria is" + userHeight + "meters tall.");
```

Creating Variable Names

When you create a variable name, use a word that conveys the data stored in the variable. As evident in the examples, you can use upper and lower case letters. By convention, which is useful to follow for two-word or three-word combinations, use lower case letters, except for the first letter of the second and third words (e.g., userName and numberOfQuestions). We could have called the variable for the user's name userName, but beginning the second word with an upper case letter, as in userName, makes it easier to read because it is immediately clear where the first word ends and the second begins. Alternatively, it is permissible to use the underscore character in a variable name so user_name is also a valid variable name in JavaScript, but programmers will comprehend your code faster if you follow conventional practice. Also note that, occasionally, a single letter is used as a variable name. In statistics, for instance, N is used to represent population size. Consequently, a programmer may wish to use N as the variable name to hold the size of a data set. If you can, for the sake of simplicity, try to keep the length of variable names (*identifiers*, more generally) to fewer than 15–20 characters. The actual maximum length of an identifier varies, but it is often so large (255 characters in some implementations) that the practical limits of human perception are reached long before the actual limit.

When unsure how a programming language feature actually works, programmers have three options: (1) Check the documentation (which typically addresses many topics in great detail, as in the SpiderMonkey JavaScript docs at https://developer.mozilla.org/en-US/docs/Mozilla/Projects/SpiderMonkey); (2) Find a functional example program; or (3) Write a program yourself to test the functionality.

3.1.3 Three Types of Statements

In procedural programming, there are three types of statements: (1) Assignment; (2) Conditional; and (3) Iterative.

Assignment Statements

We have already encountered and implemented the following assignment statement.

```
userName = readline();
```

In that assignment statement, the characters entered by the user were assigned to the variable, userName.

An assignment statement in JavaScript evaluates the expression on the right side of the equal sign and assigns that value to the variable on the left side of the equal sign, as in the following two statements.

```
numberOfQuestions = 10;
totalNumberOfQuestions = numberDayStudents + number
NightStudents;
```

An assignment statement is not an expression of equality. In the Pascal programming language, : = is the assignment operator, rather than = precisely to avoid the potential for false interpretations of an assignment statement as an expressions of equality. In JavaScript, as well as many other procedural programming languages, the equal sign is the assignment operator. When encountering assignment statements in JavaScript (and other programming languages), you may say "becomes" when you encounter an equal sign in an assignment statement.

```
numberOfQuestions = numberOfQuestions + 1;
```

The value of the variable `numberOfQuestions` becomes the current value of `numberOfQuestions` plus one. You may prefer this succinct version: `numberOfQuestions` becomes `numberOfQuestions` plus one.

Conditional Statements

A conditional statement tests a Boolean expression and then, based on whether that expression is true or false, branches to a particular set of statements to execute. For ease of reading (and debugging) source code, the true task and false tasks of an `if` statement are indented, as shown below. The true task is the set of statements executed when the Boolean expression is true whereas the false task is the set of statements executed when the Boolean expression is false. In the example below, if the value of `sum` is 14 when program execution encounters the `if` statement "The sum is 14." is displayed. In contrast, if the value of sum is any number other than 14, the false task executes, which displays, "The sum is not 14."

```
if (sum == 14) {    //true task
  print ("The sum is 14.");
}
else {    //false task
  print ("The sum is not 14.");
}
```

In JavaScript, the comparison operator for equality is ==. This bears repeating! Always recall that in JavaScript, the equal sign (=) is the assignment operator; == is the equality comparison operator. If the programmer mistakenly wrote the following, consider the ramifications below.

```
if (sum = 14) {
  //true task
}
else {
  //false task
}
```

The true task would always be executed because the value of `sum` would be set to 14 (that's what the assignment statement `sum = 14` does). To compare for equality in JavaScript, use the == operator. In JavaScript, there is actually an === operator, as well, which tests for equality of value and data type. For now, remember to use == to compare the values of variables; use = to assign a value to a variable.

Note that the syntax of an `if` statement includes braces {}, which some may call curly brackets. The significance of the braces is that any number of statements can be included within the braces. As such, the braces constitute a *block* of code. In the example above, one statement appears within each pair of braces, which in the example constitute the true task and the false task. As shown below, we could include multiple statements within the braces if we wish to do so.

```
if(sum == 14){    // true task
  print("The sum is 14.");
  print("Well done.");

}

else{    // false task
  print("The sum is not 14.");
  print("6 objects plus 8 objects is 14 objects.");
  print("Try again.");

}
```

Also note that in JavaScript, the programmer can include a comment on one line by inserting // into the code, followed by the comment. Interpreters, which convert high level source code (like JavaScript) to machine code, ignore comments. Comments can also be inserted on more than one line. Such multiline comments begin /* and end */ in JavaScript.

Open a new document in your text editor and enter the following code.

```
/*

  This program provides an example of an if statement.
  The program displays a prompt to elicit a user response.
  Once the user's height is entered, the program
  calculates twice the user's height. The program
  also comments on whether anyone would be twice
  the user's height.

*/

print("Enter your height in meters: ");
userHeight = readline();
doubleHeight = userHeight * 2;
print ("Someone twice as tall as you would be " +
doubleHeight + " meters.");
if(doubleHeight > 3.0){
  print ("Probably nobody is twice as tall as you.");
}
```

Save the file as *sampleIfStatement.js*. Run. Debug as necessary.

In your *practiceAdding.js* program, add the `if` statement below in order to determine whether the user entered the correct answer.

```
print("What is 6 + 8?");
userResponse = readline();
if(userResponse == 14){
  print("You are correct");}
else{
  print("Incorrect. 6 + 8 = 14");
}
```

Now, let's enhance the *practiceAdding.js* program so that the learner encounters different questions. Once 6 + 8 has been learned, it's time to move on. To present different questions, we will generate two random numbers between 1 and 10 and then prompt the learner to add the numbers.

In JavaScript, a random number is generated using the `Math.random` command, which is technically a function, so we use `Math.random()` to generate a random number between 0 and 0.9999999. Multiplying the random number by 10 will yield a number from 0 to 9.9999999 to which we will add 1 for a number in the range 1 to 10.9999999. Then we need only truncate the result using `Math.floor()` to obtain a random number between 1 and 10.

The two random numbers will be assigned to the variables, num1 and num2. (As the programmer, it is your prerogative to create the variable names so if you prefer to substitute augend for num1 and addend for num2, go for it.) Here is the sample *practiceAdding.js* program, which could conceivably be used, provided the learner is willing to restart the program repeatedly. (We will eliminate that requirement in the next section.)

```
num1 = Math.floor(Math.random() * 10 + 1);
num2 = Math.floor(Math.random() * 10 + 1);

print("What is " + num1 + " + " + num2 + "?");
learnerResponse = readline();

if(learnerResponse == num1 + num2){
  print("Correct");}
else{
  print("No, " + num1 + " + " + num2 + " = " + (num1 +
    num2));
}
```

Save and run. Debug as necessary.

In the sample program above, it is a little tricky to distinguish between the plus signs for string concatenation and the plus sign displayed in the prompt and the feedback for an incorrect response. However, consider each pair of quotation marks in order to identify each component. Also note that in the Boolean expression, the addition operation is performed before the comparison, but if you want to be more explicit about this, you can use the following line of code.

```
if (learnerResponse == (num1 + num2)) {
```

As demonstrated in the prior examples, an `if` statement contains a Boolean expression, which evaluates to true or false. A Boolean expression can be a compound expression. For example, if it is sunny and over 25 degrees Celsius, I will go to the beach. Both antecedents (sunny condition and temperature over 25 degrees Celsius) must be true for the consequent (going to the beach) to be true. That's the logical AND operation, which is conjunction. In the case of the logical OR operation, which is disjunction, the consequent is true if either antecedent is true or both antecedents are true. As before, with true represented by 1 and false by 0, Table 3.2 depicts the AND and OR operations for variables x and y. Multiple procedural programming languages also have a `case` statement, which is an alternative form of the `if ... else if ... else` statement. It will suffice to know that you can use an `if` statement structured like the one below when circumstances warrant.

```
if pointsEarned > 89){
  print("Letter grade for " + pointsEarned + "points
    is + "A");
}
else if (pointsEarned > 79){
  print("Letter grade for " + pointsEarned + "points
    is + "B");
}
else if (pointsEarned > 69){
  print("Letter grade for " + pointsEarned + "points
  is + "C");
}
else if (pointsEarned > 59){
  print("Letter grade for " + pointsEarned + "points
    is + "D");
```

Table 3.2 The Truth Tables for AND and OR

x	y	and	or
0	0	0	0
0	1	0	1
1	0	0	1
1	1	1	1

```
}
else {
  print("Letter grade for " + pointsEarned + "points
    is + "F");
}
```

Predict the effect of that if statement for various values of pointsEarned. Then create a new program that allows the user to enter a value for pointsEarned, after which the program will display the corresponding letter grade.

Iterative Statements

An iterative statement creates a loop, which enables the repeated execution of a set of statements. At times, programmers include an iterative statement within an iterative statement (or loop within a loop), which we will do after mastering straightforward loops.

REPETITION A FIXED NUMBER OF TIMES

```
for (i = 1; i <= 7; i++) {// loop body
  print(i);
}
```

The for loop above displays the numbers 1 through 7, each on a separate line. Initially, the loop control variable, i is set to 1. As long as i is less than or equal to 7, the statement or statements in the loop body are executed. Since braces {} surround the loop body, any number of statements can be included in the loop body.

Run the for loop above in the JavaScript shell. Type the first line and hold down the Shift Key before pressing the Enter or Return key. In that way, the first line will not be executed yet. Then type the second line and again hold down the Shift Key before pressing the Enter or Return key. Lastly, enter the final closing brace} and press the Enter or Return key. Alternatively, you could enter the code into your text editor, then save and run.

Once you have that loop working, open a new document in your text editor and enter the following code in order to create a program that calculates the sum of a set of numbers. Save the file as *numberCruncher1.js*.

```
sum = 0;
for (i = 1; i <= 5; i++) {
  print ("Enter a number to include in the sum");
  currentNumber = readline();
  sum = sum + currentNumber;
}

print("The sum is " + sum);
```

Task 3.1 Enhance the *numberCruncher1.js* by also calculating and displaying the mean, which in this case is the sum divided by five (i.e., sum / 5).

Task 3.2 Always calculating the sum of five numbers is a severe limitation. Before the loop begins in *numberCruncher1.js*, prompt the user to enter the population size, N, which is the number of numbers to be summed. The variable you use for population size will replace the 5 in the for loop statement, as well as in the calculation of the mean.

REPETITION AS MANY TIMES AS NECESSARY TO SATISFY A CONDITION

Sometimes we do not know the number of cases to be processed before the task begins. In such cases we may repeat statements until a condition is satisfied. For example, we could accept numbers to be summed until a value such as −99999 is entered.

Open a new document in your text editor and enter the following code. Save the file as *numberCruncher2.js*. Run. Debug as necessary.

```
sum = 0;
N = 0;
print ("Enter a number to include in the sum");
currentNumber = readline();
while (currentNumber != -99999) {
  N = N + 1;
  sum = sum + currentNumber;
  print ("Enter a number to include in the sum");
  currentNumber = readline();
}

print("The sum is " + sum);
print("The mean is " + (sum/N));
```

In JavaScript, like many procedural programming languages, there is an alternative form of the while loop, which tests the condition at the end of the loop body. We could write the program above as shown below. Open a new document in your text editor and enter the following code. Save the file as *numberCruncher3.js*. Run. Debug as necessary.

```
sum = 0;
N = 0;
do {
  print ("Enter a number to include in the sum");
  currentNumber = readline();
  if (currentNumber != -99999) {
    N = N + 1;
    sum = sum + currentNumber;
```

```
    }
} while (currentNumber != -99999);

print("The sum is " + sum);
print("The mean is " + (sum/N));
```

At this point we can rectify the program restart requirement in *practiceAdding.js* in one of two ways: (1) Add a `for` loop that requires the learner to complete a fixed number of practice items; or (2) Add a `while` loop and require the learner to practice until a condition is met, such as achieving ten correct answers. The first option will be left as an exercise. The sample code for the second option follows. The following code is an instructional app!

```
numCorrect = 0;

while (numCorrect < 10) {
  num1 = Math.floor(Math.random() * 10 + 1);
  num2 = Math.floor(Math.random() * 10 + 1);

  print("What is " + num1 + " + " + num2 + "?");
  learnerResponse = readline();

  if (learnerResponse == num1 + num2) {
    print("Correct");
    numCorrect = numCorrect + 1;
  }
  else {
    print("No, " + num1 + " + " + num2 + " = " +
      (num1 + num2));
  }
}
```

Note that to increment the value of `numCorrect`, the sample code uses

```
numCorrect = numCorrect + 1;
```

An alternative would be

```
numCorrect += 1;
```

The alternative relieves the programmer of including the variable name on the right side of the assignment operator. The `+=` operator performs addition with the current value of the variable before assigning the new value to the variable. The `-=` operator performs subtraction with the current value of the variable before assigning the new value to the variable. In the case when the variable is being incremented or decremented by one, the `++` and `--` operators provide yet another alternative. Hence, in the case of incrementing numCorrect in the sample code above, any one of the three statements below is acceptable.

```
numCorrect = numCorrect + 1;

numCorrect += 1;

numCorrect++;
```

Task 3.3 Add one assignment statement to the false task in the sample code above, which will result in the learner needing to get ten consecutive correct answers in order to exit the program.

Task 3.4 Copy the file *practiceAdding.js* and rename the copied file *practiceAdding2.js*. Replace the while loop with a for loop.

Task 3.5 Write a program enabling a learner to practice multiplying numbers between 1 and 12 inclusive. Decide on a mastery threshold. For example, you could set mastery at 8 consecutive answers. Alternatively, you could set mastery at 85 percent correct after a minimum of 15 questions. Exit the program when the learner has attained mastery and congratulate the learner. This is your first instructional app!

3.1.4 Three Data Structures

With knowledge of three data types and the skill to use three statements, you're already capable of creating an instructional app. Congratulations! You know how to create a computer program to implement an instructional method.

By learning three data structures, the functionality of our upcoming programs will surpass our current offerings. For example, to keep track of the values in a data set or to sort the values in a data set, we need a data structure, not numerous variables capable of storing one value each. It is not practical to design a program to store the scores of students in distinct variables, such as scoreStudent1, scoreStudent2, scoreStudent3, and so on. The programmer would need to guess at the number of students in the class, which could be over 200 in a large course. Further, calculating the mean of the student scores would require several lines of code to calculate the sum: scoreStudent1 + scoreStudent2 + scoreStudent3 through to scoreStudent200. That's not practical, especially since the code would need to be rewritten if more students beyond the 200 entered the class. However, with a for loop containing one assignment statement in the loop body, which accesses a one-dimensional array, calculating the cumulative sum of a series of 200, 2,000, or more numbers is accomplished efficiently and easily. Then the mean would be calculated, as always, by dividing the cumulative total by the number of students, in this case.

One-dimensional Array

A one-dimensional array is like a table with one row, as in Table 3.3. The value in each location of a one-dimensional array is accessed through its index. In JavaScript, the index of the first location in the array is 0 and the index is incremented by one for each subsequent location. In Table 3.3, the array (which can also be called a vector because it has magnitude and direction) has 12 locations, numbered from 0 to 11. Arrays store values of one particular data type. In the case of student scores, each location would hold one student's score. The code below calculates the sum of scores in the array called `studentScores`.

```
studentScores = [9, 6, 7, 4, 5, 6, 7, 3, 5, 6, 8,
4, 9, 5, 7, 8, 5, 10, 7, 9];

sum = 0;
for (i = 0; i < studentScores.length; i++) {
sum += studentScores[i];
}

print("The sum is " + sum);
print("The mean is " + (sum/studentScores.length));
```

Conveniently, JavaScript provides the size (or magnitude) of an array through the `length` property. The `for` loop proceeds through each array index, which in this case is 0, 1, 2, through 19 because the `studentScores` array contains 20 values. As the loop control variable `i` increases from 0 through 19, the value at each location in the `studentScores` array is added to the variable `sum`. Open a new document in your text editor, enter the code above, and save the file as *array1.js*. Run. Debug as necessary. Once the program is working for you, change the values in the `studentScores` array and verify that the `sum` and `mean` are calculated correctly.

Sorting an array is common and JavaScript provides a sort function. The `studentScores` array could be sorted in JavaScript with the following statement.

```
studentScores.sort();
```

Table 3.3 A One-dimensional Array

0	1	2	3	4	5	6	7	8	9	10	11

Ultimately, you might include that statement in a JavaScript program, but for practice with iterative statements and one-dimensional arrays, we will write a program to implement a *bubble sort*.

In a bubble sort the values in each consecutive pair of array locations are compared. For a sort in ascending order, if the value in the first location of the pair is greater than the value in the second location, the values are swapped. Passes through the array continue until a pass yields no swapped values. Figure 3.2(a) contains an unsorted array. The array indices, 0, 1, 2, 3, and 4, are also displayed. During the first pass through the consecutive pairs of values, the first comparison would swap the 8 and 12 because the value in array location 0 (12) is greater than the value in location 1 (8). Figure 3.2(b) depicts the unsorted array after that first swap. Then the 12 and 10 would be swapped because the value in array location 1 (12) is greater than the value in location 2 (10). Figure 3.2(c) depicts the unsorted array after the second swap. The comparison of the values in array locations 2 and 3 would not result in a swap because 12 is less than 20. The final comparison of the first pass would swap 20 and 6 because the value in array location 3 (20) is greater than the value in location 4 (6). Figure 3.2(d) depicts the unsorted array after the first pass through the array. The second pass would move the 10 to array location 1 and would then swap the 12 and 6, moving the 6 to

(a) Unsorted array

0	1	2	3	4
12	8	10	20	6

(b) Unsorted array after first swap

0	1	2	3	4
8	12	10	20	6

(c) Unsorted array after second swap

0	1	2	3	4
8	10	12	20	6

(d) Unsorted array after first pass

0	1	2	3	4
8	12	10	6	20

Figure 3.2 States of Array During Bubble Sort.

array location 2 and the 12 to its final position (array location 3). After two more passes through the array, the array would be sorted.

Open a new document in your text editor and enter the code below. Save the file as *ascendingBubbleSort.js*.

```
studentScores = [9, 6, 7, 4, 5];
print("Unsorted Array");
for (i = 0; i < studentScores.length; i++) {
  print(studentScores[i]);
}

numberOfSwaps = -1;
while (numberOfSwaps != 0) {
  numberOfSwaps = 0;
  for (i = 0; i < studentScores.length - 1; i++) {
    if (studentScores[i] > studentScores[i + 1]) {
      sum += studentScores[i];
      tempValue = studentScores[i];
      studentScores[i] = studentScores[i + 1];
      studentScores[i + 1] = temp;
      numberOfSwaps++;
    }
  }
}

print("Sorted Array");
for (i = 0; i < studentScores.length; i++) {
  print(studentScores[i]);
}
```

Run. Debug as necessary.

Task 3.6 Copy the *ascendingBubbleSort.js* file and rename the copied file *descendingBubbleSort.js*. Edit one character in the script in order to create a sort from the largest to the smallest number.

Task 3.7 Replace the numbers in the studentScores array with letters. Determine whether the sorting algorithm still works.

Matrix

A matrix or two-dimensional array is a typical table, which contains rows and columns, such as Table 3.4, which has seven rows and ten columns. To access the values in the locations of a two-dimensional array, use both the row index and column index.

Commonly, programmers process data in a two-dimensional array in *row major* order. That is, for each row from top to bottom, the value in each

Table 3.4 A Two-dimensional Array

	0	1	2	3	4	5	6	7	8	9
0										
1										
2										
3										
4										
5										
6										

column from left to right is processed. Such an approach is consistent with reading left to right and down the lines of a page. To accomplish this in a programming language, a for loop is used to index each row in the two-dimensional array and within its loop body, another for loop is used to index each column. Open a new document in your text editor and enter the following code.

```
gradeBook = [[6, 4, 10, 27, 7], [8, 4, 6, 17, 0],
[6, 0, 8, 29, 10]];
for (studentNum = 0; studentNum < 3; studentNum++) {
  for (assignmentNum = 0; assignmentNum < 5;
assignmentNum++) {
    print (gradeBook[studentNum][assignmentNum]);
  }
}
```

Save the file as *gradeBook.js*. Run. Debug as necessary.

Task 3.8 Edit the array declaration in *gradeBook.js* to increase the number of students in the gradeBook to seven. Edit the outer for loop in order to display the assignment scores for all seven students.

Task 3.9 Edit the array declaration in *gradeBook.js* again to depict that eight assignments have been completed. Edit the inner for loop in order to display all of the assignment scores.

The following example for processing a two-dimensional array imagines a course with three quizzes for which 20 items are randomly drawn from a test bank.

The test bank contains 100 items on the same topic. Open a new document in your text editor. Enter the code below. Notice that the first line declares an empty two-dimensional array. In the examples with one-dimensional arrays, we initialized the array to particular values for studentScores. To declare an empty array of student scores, we would use studentScores = []. In the example below, since quizzes is a two-dimensional array (which can be conceived as a one-dimensional array, each location of which contains a one-dimensional array), the two-dimensional array declaration includes nested brackets, [[ ]] .

```
quizzes = [[]];
for (testNum = 0; testNum < 3; testNum++) {
  for (itemNum = 0; itemNum < 20; itemNum++) {
    quizzes[testNum][itemNum] = Math.floor(Math.random()
* 100 + 1);
    print("For Test " + (testNum + 1) + " Item Number
"+ (itemNum + 1) + ", Use Test Bank question "
+ quizzes[testNum][itemNum]);
  }
}
```

Save the file as *quizItemGenerator.js*. Run. Debug as necessary.

Files

Files are used for data storage and retrieval. Permitting an unknown program to write data to a computer's hard drive poses a large security risk. In general, programmers are trusted to create files on their own computer's hard drive. However, JavaScript is exceptional in this case because JavaScript programs typically run on the web. If a program deployed on the web had permission to write data to the hard drive of the user's computer, that program would have the potential to do serious harm. Therefore, typical JavaScript implementations do not permit file storage. Even reading data from a file in Java-Script is not permissible in general. However, the version of SpiderMonkey JavaScript that we are using enables programmers to read files. In fact, we can do this with one line of code, as follows.

```
fileContents = read("myTextFile.txt");
```

That assignment statement reads the entire contents of a file into the variable, fileContents, which is a character string. Adding the line of code below enables the display of the contents of myTextFile.txt.

```
print(fileContents);
```

Open a new document in your text editor and enter some letters, digits, and punctuation marks. Make sure you have some hard returns in the file so there is more than one line, as in the sample text below. Save the file as *myTextFile.txt*.

This is a sample file of text.
This is Line 2.
Here are some random symbols on Line 3: &^%$#@!)(*{}[]\|'"'<>?/?\\~'
This is Line 4, the final line.

Once again, open a new document in your text editor. This time, enter the code below.

```
fileContents = read("myTextFile.txt");
print(fileContents);
```

Save the file as *readMyFile1.js*. Run. Debug as necessary.

Also try the code below, which splits the file input such that each line in the file is placed into the one-dimensional array, linesInFile.

```
fileContents = read("myTextFile.txt");
linesInFile = fileContents.split("\n");
for (i = 0; i < linesInFile.length; i++) {
  print(linesInFile[i]);
}
```

Save the file as *readMyFile2.js*. Run. Debug as necessary.

The following code will write data to a file, provided you use a non-standard version of SpiderMonkey JavaScript with file writing permission enabled. We will actually write data to a file in Python in Section 3.1.7.

```
var file = new File("myFile.txt");
file.open("write,create", "text");
file.writeln("When to the sessions of sweet silent
thought, I summon up remembrance of things past.");
file.close();
```

At this point, you have succeeded marvelously (or at least made it through to this point, which is great). You can accomplish much with a computer using the statements and data structures you have learned to this point. In 1975, Niklaus Wirth, inventor of the Pascal Programming language, wrote a book called *Algorithms Plus Data Structures = Programs*. You just learned of three data structures and you can write algorithms using assignment, conditional, and iterative statements. Hence, consistent with Niklaus Wirth's perspective, you can write nontrivial apps because you can write computer programs with algorithms and data structures. To increase the confidence you have in your programming ability, opportunities for additional practice are available in Section 3.1.5. First, you have one technique to learn, which increases efficiency and makes coding large programs possible.

3.1.5 One Technique

To complete a complex task, we often divide it into subtasks. Once the subtasks are complete, the entire complex task is done. We may refer to this decomposition technique as the "divide and conquer" strategy. The goal of structured programming is "to subdivide the program into natural parts" in order to correctly code subtasks, which collectively accomplish the main task (Papert, 1980, p. 102). We could probably debate what is meant by a "natural part," but we might agree that a reusable task could be a natural part. In any case, we should not write redundant code; we should program tasks once and reuse them. We do that by coding tasks in *subroutines*, which may also be called *functions* or *methods*.

In the *ascendingSort.js* program above, the following for loop appears twice: First to display the unsorted contents of the studentScores array and then again to display the sorted array.

```
for (i = 0; i < studentScores.length; i++) {
  print(studentScores[i]);
}
```

We eliminate that redundant code by putting that for loop into a subroutine and reusing it to display the contents of the array as desired. The *ascendingSort.js* program below eliminates the code redundancy evident in the original version by including the function, displayArray, which displays the contents of the array. The displayArray function is first called before the sorting algorithm in order to display the unsorted array. The displayArray function is also called after each pass through the array within the sorting algorithm. Lastly, the displayArray function is called after the sorting algorithm in order to display the sorted array. The function is called using the following statement.

```
displayArray();
```

The empty parentheses indicate that no data are passed to the function. (We return to the topic of parameter passing below.) Calling a function transfers execution to the function. When the function finishes executing, control returns to the statement immediately after the function call.

```
function displayArray() {
  for (i = 0; i < studentScores.length; i++) {
    print(studentScores[i]);
  }
}

studentScores = [9, 6, 7, 4, 5];

print("Unsorted Array");
displayArray(); // first call to the function

numberOfSwaps = -1;
while (numberOfSwaps != 0) {
    numberOfSwaps = 0;
    for (i = 0; i < studentScores.length - 1; i++) {
        if (studentScores[i] > studentScores[i + 1]) {
            sum += studentScores[i];
```

```
        tempValue = studentScores[i];
        studentsScores[i] = studentScores[i+1];
        studentScores[i + 1] = temp;
        numberOfSwaps++;
    }
  }
  displayArray(); // second call to the function
}

print("Sorted Array");    //third call to the function
displayArray();
```

Task 3.10 Insert displayArray(); as the last statement in the true task
of the if statement in order to display the contents of the array after each
swap of values in the array.

One advantage of functions is to avoid redundant code. Another key
advantage of functions is to avoid the need to replicate variables. Commonly,
functions have a fixed number of parameters. For example, suppose we want
to calculate the perimeter and area of 100 rectangles. We would not write
200 assignment statements, as depicted below.

```
area1 = width1 * length1;
perimeter1 = 2 * width1 + 2 * length1;
area2 = width2 * length2;
perimeter = 2 * width2 + 2 * length2;
area3 = width3 * length3;
perimeter3 = 2 * width3 + 2 * length3;
.

.

.
area100 = width100 * length100;
perimeter100 = 2 * width100 + 2 * length100;
```

Instead, we would implement the algorithm with a function with two
parameters. Open a new document in your text editor and enter the following code.

```
rectangleLengths = [10, 25, 504, 16, 44, 6, 37, 82,
44, 65536];
rectangleWidths = [9, 4, 4, 6, 24, 6, 7, 8, 40,
1024];

function calculateAreaAndPerimeter (length, width) {
  area = length * width;
```

```
   perimeter = 2 * length + 2 * width;
   print(area, perimeter);
}

for (i = 0; i < rectangleLengths.length; i++) {
   calculateAreaAndPerimeter(rectangleLengths[i],
   rectangleWidths[i]);
}
```

Save the file as *calcAreaPerimeter.js*. Run. Debug as necessary.

Task 3.11 Replace the `rectangleLengths` and `rectangleWidths` arrays with one two-dimensional array called dimensions, which has ten rows and two columns. The first column stores the length and the second column stores the width. Using the same data in the example above, the array declaration would begin `rectangleDimensions[[10,9],` `[25,4], [504,4]];` Ensure that the results for area and perimeter are the same as the previous version.

It is *extremely important* to recognize the effectiveness and efficiency of decomposition (use of functions) and data structures (an array in this case). With functions and arrays, the code is extensible. For example, if we wanted to enhance the program to yield the mean area, we would add one line of code (`sumArea += area`) to the function after the statement that calculates the area (i.e., `area = length * width`). Then after the `for` loop, `sumArea` would be divided by the number of values in the array (`rectangleLengths.length`). Also, if each array is changed to contain 10,000 values, no change is made to the algorithm.

In contrast, even though it is theoretically possible, it would not be practical to write a program that assigns 10,000 values to the 10,000 variables for rectangle lengths and 10,000 values to the 10,000 variables for rectangle widths, as well as coding 30,000 statements to calculate area and perimeter, plus display the results. Further, to accommodate the request to calculate the mean area, the programmer would need to write code to sum 10,000 variables (`area1 + area2 + area3 + ... + area10000`), whereas only `sumArea += area` was needed in the array implementation. Indeed, Niklaus Wirth was well justified in writing: `Algorithms Plus Data Structures = Programs`.

Lastly, in this section, sometimes a function calls itself, which is known as *recursion*. Here is a JavaScript program with a recursive function that calculates 5-factorial (i.e., 5 * 4 * 3 * 2 * 1 = 120).

```
function calculateFactorial (n) {
  if n > 1 {
     return(n * calculateFactorial(n - 1));
  }
  else {
   return(1);
```

```
  }
}
print(calculateFactorial(5));
```

Since we considered iteration previously, you may prefer the following algorithm for calculating 5-factorial.

```
factorial = 1;
n = 5;
for (i = n; i > 1; i-) {
  factorial *= i;
}
```

You may encounter recursion again some time. At some future date, you might write a program with a recursive function to solve the Tower of Hanoi program or you might write a recursive function to create Sudoku puzzles. Given the example above, you will have some awareness of recursion. For now, continue to learn more about the fundamentals of the procedural programming paradigm. Use numeric, character, and Boolean variables, along with assignment, conditional, and iterative statements, as well as the data structures considered previously, arrays and files. Also practice writing and using functions. Programming languages like JavaScript contain libraries of functions to assist with numerical calculations and to facilitate the parsing and searching of strings. To guide your practice, the next section provides multiple opportunities to practice procedural programming.

3.1.6 Practice in Problem Solving through Programming

Enjoy the following practice items. Overcoming the challenges posed by the following problems will increase your programming ability and confidence.

Task 3.12 Write a program that converts temperatures in Celsius to Fahrenheit. The conversion formula is F = 9/5 * C + 32. Display the results as a table from 50C to −50C. For each row of the table, decrement the temperature by 5 degrees.

Tips: Use a `for` loop with the initial value of the loop control variable set to 50. Decrement the loop control variable by 5 each time through the loop. Here are the results for the first five rows of the table.

```
C   F
50  122
45  113
40  104
35  95
30  86
```

Task 3.13 Enhance the previous program for displaying equivalent Celsius and Fahrenheit temperatures by adding a function that pads each Fahrenheit result with leading spaces, if necessary, in order to ensure that the place values of the output values are aligned. Notice in the sample output below that the digits in the ones place, tens place, and hundreds place are properly aligned.

```
C    F
50   122
45   113
40   104
35   95
30   86
```

Tips: Use the built-in function toString() to convert each Fahrenheit temperature to a string. For example, the following statement converts the numeric variable fahrenheitTemperature to its string representation.

```
fahrenheitString = fahrenheitTemperaure.toString();
```

Once converted to a string, the length property (e.g., fahrenheitString. length) reveals the number of characters the string contains and that value can be used to determine the number of spaces to pad on the left of the string. For instance, the function could make all strings 5 characters in length. Then the difference between 5 and fahrenheitString.length is the number of spaces to pad on the left. You could use a loop to insert the necessary spaces, but consider using a substring of a string of spaces. For example, "   ".substr(1,5 − fahrenheitString.length) would extract a string with the correct number of spaces to which fahrenheitString could be appended.

Task 3.14 Write a program with a function that calculates the circumference and area of a circle given the radius.

Tips: Make use of the built-in property, Math.PI. For example, the area of a circle with radius r is Math.PI * r * r and the Circumference is Math.PI * 2 * r.

Task 3.15 Write a program with a function that displays the results of the following math functions: Math.round, Math.floor, Math.ceil (opposite of Math.floor), Math.abs (absolute value), Math.exp (e^x), Math.log (natural logarithm), Math.cos, Math.sin, Math. tan, Math.acos, Math.asin, and Math.atan.

Tips: Define the function to include one parameter (n). Include three or four print statements in the function block. The first print statement appears below. Put Math.abs(n), Math.exp(n), and Math.log(n) in the second print statement. Write one or two more print statements in the function body in order to display the results of the trigonometric functions.

```
print(Math.round(n), Math.ceil(n), Math.floor(n));
```

Task 3.16 Write a program that prompts the user to enter a number. Ensure that the user enters a number. Make use of the built-in function isNaN(). NaN is an acronym for Not a Number.

The function isNaN() returns true when the argument (or actual parameter) passed to the function is not a number and false when the argument is a number. Since isNaN() returns a Boolean value, isNaN() can be used, for instance, in a do ... while statement, as in do {...} while(isNaN()). Learn more about the isNaN() function by entering the following expressions in the JavaScript Console.

```
isNaN("abc");
isNaN(34);
isNan(-3.45);
isNaN("-0.444");
isNaN("!");
isNaN(!);
```

Task 3.17 Write a program that prompts the user to enter an integer. Ensure that the user enters a valid number. Make use of the built-in function, Number.isInteger().

Learn more about the Number.isInteger() method by entering the following expressions in the JavaScript Console.

```
Number.isInteger(34);
Number.isInteger(-42);
Number.isInteger(043);
Number.isInteger(-00044);
Number.isInteger("34");
Number.isInteger("-34");
Number.isInteger($);
Number.isInteger(!);
```

Task 3.18 Enhance the previous program to ensure that the user enters an integer greater than 10.

In JavaScript, a compound conditional statement includes conjunction and/or disjunction of multiple conditions. For instance, the loop in the following code will repeat until the user enters a number between 1 and 5.

```
do {
```

```
    print("Enter a number between 1 and 5");
    userResponse = readline();
} while ((userResponse < 1) && (userResponse > 5));
                               ||
```

As a second example, the loop in the following code will repeat until the user enters an integer less than 5.

```
do {
  print("Enter a whole number less than 5");
  userResponse = readline();
} while(!(Number.isInteger(userResponse))||(userResponse >= 5));
```

Notice the exclamation mark (!) prior to Number.isInteger (userResponse). The exclamation mark negates the result, which in this case ensures that the loop is repeated when the user enters a non-integer.

Task 3.19 Enhance the previous program to ensure that the user enters an integer between 1 and 10 inclusive.

Task 3.20 Write a program that prompts the user to enter two numbers between 1 and 3. Ensure that the user enters two valid numbers.

Tips: Make use of the built-in string function, split().

The split() function divides a string into substrings based on the character argument. Each substring is assigned to an array location. Consider the following example.

```
myString = "This is a sample sentence.";
myValues = myString.split(" ");
for (i = 0; i < myValues.length; i++) {
  print(myValues[i]);
}
```

The output of that code is
 This
 is
 a
 sample
 sentence.

To learn more about the split() function, enter the example code above into a text editor. Save the file as *stringParsing.js*. Run. Debug as necessary. Then vary the input string and the character argument.

Task 3.21 Write a program with a loop that displays the following four lines of characters three times. When the loop terminates, display one line of hyphens. Save this file as *displayGrid.js*.

```
 |  |  |  |
 |  |  |  |
 |  |  |  |
```

When your program has terminated, it will have produced the following grid, which you will use as a tic-tac-toe game board.

```
 |  |  |  |
 |  |  |  |
 |  |  |  |
─────────────
 |  |  |  |
 |  |  |  |
 |  |  |  |
─────────────
 |  |  |  |
 |  |  |  |
 |  |  |  |
─────────────
```

Task 3.22 Copy *displayGrid.js* and rename the copied file, *ticTacToe.js*. Then modify the program by moving the code for displaying the grid to a function. Also modify the middle row of cells to display actual game board data.

Tips: Create a two-dimensional array with four rows and columns to use as the game board. Even though only three rows and columns are necessary for a Tic Tac Toe game board, Row 0 and Column 0 can be ignored. In so doing, references to row and column indices do not need to be decremented by one to access game board locations. Initialize the game board by inserting a ? in the four columns of Row 0 and the four rows of Column 0. While initializing the game board, also insert the letters A, B, C, D, E, F, G, H, and I into the nine game board locations in row major order. (In the next Task, the game board will be initialized to the space character (" "), but it is helpful at this point to be assured that game board data are being displayed so use a visible character for now.)

To display game board data, modify the `print` statement displaying the middle row of cells so that it displays the letter in the gameBoard at Columns 1, 2, and 3 for each row. Depending on your implementation, the following code fragment could be useful.

```
"| " + gameBoard[i][1] + " | " + gameBoard[i][2] + " | "
+ gameBoard[i][3] + " |"
```

When your program has terminated, it will have produced the following grid.

```
  |   |   |   |
  | A | B | C |
  |   |   |   |

  |   |   |   |
  | D | E | F |
  |   |   |   |

  |   |   |   |
  | G | H | I |
  |   |   |   |
```

Task 3.23 Insert another function into *tictactoe.js* that enables the user to enter two integers between 1 and 3 in order to specify which game board location the user wishes to place the user's marker (e.g., let the user's marker be X). If the user selects a valid game board space, put the user's marker in that space.

Tips: Use with the code you developed for Task 3.20 and add one more condition to ensure that the user selects an open space. Once you change the game board initialization from A, B, C, D, E, F, G, H, and I to the space character (" "), an empty space is evident when the game board location is a space.

Task 3.24 Insert another function into *tictactoe.js* to enable the computer's move. Also, ensure that the user and computer take turns for up to nine moves.

Tips: Select random numbers between 1 and 3 for the row and column for the computer's move. Once again, be sure that the computer places its marker (O) in an open space.

Task 3.25 Insert another function into *tictactoe.js* to determine when there is a winner and when the game has ended in a draw.

Tips: Test for a win along the three rows, the three columns, or the two diagonals. If there is no winner after nine moves, the game ends in a draw.

Task 3.26 Write a program to identify all of the bigrams in a text file.

Tips: Split the string containing the contents of the text file using the period (.) character. That would put each sentence of the text file into a separate array location. Then split the text in each array location using the space character (" "). That would put each word into a separate array location. Every two consecutive array locations yields a bigram.

Task 3.27 Write a program that calculates descriptive statistics for values in a data set of 1,000 random numbers between 0 and 99. The descriptive statistics should include the population size, the minimum value, the maximum value, the mean, and the standard deviation.

Task 3.28 Write a program that enables the learner to play a game to guess a word. The learner is given the number of letters in the word and then offers a series of letters that may be in the word. The program indicates where in the word the letter appears, if it appears at all. The learner has seven opportunities to offer a letter or state the word. The learner should be able to play through five words at least.

Task 3.29 A pedagogically sound solution to the previous task would present developmentally appropriate words. Create a file containing at least 50 words for learners at a particular reading level. Enhance your program by adding a function that reads the file and populates an array of words, which will be presented one at a time during game play.

Task 3.30 By completing the practice tasks in this section, you have practiced problem solving through programming, including in the previous practice task, writing a program that implements an instructional app for learners seeking to improve their vocabulary and spelling. Now that you have acquired considerable skill in procedural programming, you can engage in creative expression through programming. Design an instructional app based on your own specifications and write a program that implements it.

3.1.7 Comparing Programming Languages

To make instructional apps ubiquitous across multiple devices, we need to create apps using a wide variety of development platforms. Developers create apps for diverse devices using a variety of computer programming languages, such as Perl, Lua, Swift, C, C++, Java, and Python. Accordingly, knowledge transfer is critical. Soon you will become aware that you are actually capable of programming in multiple imperative programming languages. This section presents a JavaScript program for Task 3.29 and compares it with equivalent programs in Perl, Lua, C, Swift, Java, and Python. As you will discover, the similarities in some languages are striking, which makes for rapid knowledge transfer with a little practice.

To following solution meets the specifications of Task 3.29.

1. The program reads the data file and initializes the array of words.
2. The outermost `while` loop continues game play as long as words remain to be played and the learner has not entered *exit*.

3. The innermost while loop continues the learner's pursuit of a word as long as attempts remain; the learner has not yet determined the word; and the learner has not entered *exit*. Within this loop, there are two main if statements.

    i.   The first if statement updates the learner's progress if the learner entered a single letter; otherwise the learner entered more than one letter, in which case the program checks to determine whether the learner entered the correct word.
    ii. The second if statement executes only when the learner has not yet determined the correct word, in which case the next letter is sought from the learner if attempts remain, otherwise the program reveals the word.

The following programs implement that solution in JavaScript, Perl, Lua, C, Swift, Java, and Python.

JavaScript

```javascript
// Guess the Word
function initialize(fileName) {
  fileContents = read(fileName);
  words = fileContents.split("\n");
}

function getLearnerInput() {
  print(gameString + " attempts remaining: " +
attemptsRemaining);
  print("Enter letter: ");
  learnerResponse = readline();
}

function congratulateLearner() {
  print("Well done! You determined that the word is " +
crntWord + ".\n\n");
  wordNotFound = false;
}
const emptyGameString = "_____";

initialize("wordsReadingLevel9.txt");

wordIndex = 0;
learnerResponse = "";
while ((wordIndex < words.length) && (learnerResponse !=
"exit")) {
```

```
        attemptsRemaining = 7;
        crntWord = words[wordIndex++];
        wordNotFound = true;
        gameString = emptyGameString.substr(1, crntWord.length);

        getLearnerInput();
        while ((attemptsRemaining > 0) && (wordNotFound)
        && (learnerResponse != "exit")) {
            if ((learnerResponse.length == 1) && (crntWord.
match(learnerResponse))) {
                for (i = 0; i < crntWord.length; i++) {
                    if (crntWord.substr(i,1) == learnerResponse){
                        gameString=gameString.substr(0,i)
+ learnerResponse + gameString.substr(i + 1);
                        if (gameString == crntWord) {
                            congratulateLearner();
                        }
                    }
                }
            }
            else if (learnerResponse == crntWord) {
                    congratulateLearner();
            }

            if (wordNotFound) {
                attemptsRemaining—;

                if (attemptsRemaining > 0) {
                    getLearnerInput();
                }
                else {
                    print("The word was " + crntWord + ".\n\n");
                }
            }
        }
    }
}
```

Perl

```
use strict;
use warnings;
```

```perl
# Guess the Word

my $inFile;
my @words;
my $learnerResponse;
my $wordNotFound;
my $wordIndex;
my $attemptsRemaining;
my $crntWord;
my $gameString;
my $i;
my $outFile;

my $EMPTY_GAME_STRING = "_____";

sub initialize {
  open($inFile, "<", $_[0]) or die "Can't open input
  file: $!";
  @words = <$inFile>;
  close($inFile);
}
sub getLearnerInput {
  print($gameString . " attempts remaining: " .
$attemptsRemaining . "\n");
  print("Enter letter: ");
  $learnerResponse = <STDIN>;
  chomp($learnerResponse);
}

sub congratulateLearner() {
  print("Well done! You determined that the word is " .
  $crntWord . ".\n\n");
  $wordNotFound = 0;
}

initialize("wordsReadingLevel9.txt");

$wordIndex = 0;
$learnerResponse = "";
while (($wordIndex < @words) && ($learnerResponse ne "exit")){
  $attemptsRemaining = 7;
  $crntWord = $words[$wordIndex++];
  chomp($crntWord);
  $wordNotFound = 1;
```

```perl
  $gameString   =   substr($EMPTY_GAME_STRING,   1,
length($crntWord));

  getLearnerInput();
  while (($attemptsRemaining > 0) &&
($wordNotFound) && ($learnerResponse ne "exit")) {
    if ((length($learnerResponse) == 1 ) &&
(index($crntWord, $learnerResponse) != -1)) {
      for ($i = 0; $i < length($crntWord); $i++) {
        if (substr($crntWord, $i, 1) eq
$learnerResponse) {
          $gameString = substr($gameString,0, $i).
$learnerResponse.substr($gameString, $i + 1);
          if ($gameString eq $crntWord){
            congratulateLearner();
          }
        }
      }
    }
    elsif ($learnerResponse eq $crntWord) {
      congratulateLearner();
    }

    if ($wordNotFound) {
      $attemptsRemaining--;

      if ($attemptsRemaining > 0) {
        getLearnerInput();
      }
      else {
        print("The word was " . $crntWord . ".\n\n");
      }
    }
  }
}
open($outFile, ">", "learnerProgress.txt");
print $outFile ($wordIndex);
close($outFile) or die "Failed to close learnerProgress.
txt file";
```

The structure of JavaScript and Perl programs is similar. The first two lines in the
Perl program are optional, but often useful. Since the Perl program above was
compiled using strict mode, all variables are declared before use. The names of
scalar variables in Perl begin with a dollar sign ($) and entire array variables begin
with @. A scalar variable is a simple unstructured variable that stores one value

of one particular data type. By convention in Perl, $EMPTY_GAME_STRING appears in all upper-case letters because it is treated as a constant.

With respect to functions, rather than use the JavaScript keyword function, Perl uses sub. In the declaration of a subroutine in Perl, it is not necessary to specify parameters. Any actual parameters passed to a Perl subroutine are automatically stored in a special array, beginning at index 0. Only one actual parameter (the name of the file to be opened, wordsReadingLevel9.txt) is passed to the initialize subroutine, which is accessed through the special array variable $_[0].

There are no true and false keywords in Perl so in the Perl program above, the number 0 is used for false and the number 1 for true. The while loops and if statements in the Perl and JavaScript programs are nearly identical. Rather that the JavaScript else if, Perl uses elsif. The comparison operators for numbers (==, !=, >, <, <=, >=) are identical in JavaScript and Perl. However, comparison operators for strings are different. JavaScript uses the same comparison operators for numbers and strings whereas Perl uses two-letter abbreviations for the string comparison operators (eq for equals, ne for not equal, lt for less than, gt for greater than, le for less than or equal, and ge for greater than or equal).

Since Perl permits writing data to a file, the final three lines of code store the number of the last word encountered, which we might regard as the learner's progress or, at least, one measure of the learner's progress. An enhanced version of this program would tally the number of correct and incorrect responses in order to assess the learner's progress. Those tallies would be saved in an output file along with the number of the last word encountered. Then, as part of the program's initialization process, the program would read the file containing the learner's progress in order to resume the game at the last word encountered. Alternatively, in light of the learner's progress (perhaps the ratio of correct to incorrect responses after 50 words), the program might present words from a different file if the learner progressed sufficiently.

Lua

```
-- Guess the Word
function initialize(fileName)
  words = {}
  for crntLine in io.lines(fileName) do
    words[#words + 1] = crntLine
  end
end

function getLearnerInput()
  print(gameString .. "  attempts  remaining:
  " .. attemptsRemaining);
```

```
    print("Enter letter: ");
    learnerResponse = io.read();
end

function congratulateLearner()
    print("Well done! You determined that the word is
      " .. crntWord .. ".\n\n");
    wordNotFound = false;
end

EMPTY_GAME_STRING = "_____"
initialize("wordsReadingLevel9.txt")

wordIndex = 1
learnerResponse = ""
while (wordIndex <= #words) and (learnerResponse ~= "exit") do
    attemptsRemaining = 7
    crntWord = words[wordIndex]
    wordIndex = wordIndex + 1
    wordNotFound = true
    gameString = string.sub(EMPTY_GAME_STRING, 1,
    string.len(crntWord));

    getLearnerInput()
    while ((attemptsRemaining > 0) and (wordNotFound)
    and (learnerResponse ~= "exit"))do
        if ((string.len(learnerResponse)==1) and
(string.find(crntWord,learnerResponse))) then
            for i = 1, string.len(crntWord) do
                if(string.sub(crntWord,i,i)==learner
Response) then gameString = string.sub(gameString,
1, i-1) .. learner Response .. string.sub(gameString,
i+1);
                if (gameString == crntWord) then
                congratulateLearner()
                end
            end
        end
    elseif (learnerResponse == crntWord) then
        congratulateLearner()
    end

    if (wordNotFound) then
        attemptsRemaining = attemptsRemaining - 1
```

```
         if (attemptsRemaining > 0) then
           getLearnerInput()
         else
           print("The word was " .. crntWord .. ".\n\n")
             end
         end
     end
end

outFileHandle = io.open("learnerProgress2.txt", "w")
outFileHandle:write(wordIndex)
outFileHandle:close()
```

Lua is somewhat similar to JavaScript, particularly with respect to the syntax of functions. Parameter passing and the function definition are very similar. Like JavaScript, Lua also use the standard set of control statements, if, for, and while. Unlike JavaScript, compound conditional expressions in Lua use the words and, or, and not. Blocks of code are also different. Whereas JavaScript uses { }, Lua uses do . . . end. Also unlike JavaScript, arrays and strings in Lua begin at index 1.

File input and output (IO) is straightforward in Lua. This example demonstrates how each line of a file is read and assigned to consecutive array locations. Since files are often large, reading data one line at a time is quite practical. In the case of this program, the file is sufficiently small that all words in the input file can easily be read into an array before processing. Like Perl, Lua permits the writing of data to a file. The final three lines of code store the number of the last word the user encountered.

C

```c
#include <stdio.h>
#include <string.h>

/* Guess the Word */

int initialize(char *strings[], char *fileName) {

  FILE *fileHandle;
  char fileContents[1024];
  int index;
  char crntLines[1000][255];

  index = 0;
  fileHandle = fopen(fileName, "r");
  if(fileHandle) {
```

```
        while (fscanf(fileHandle, "%s", fileContents) != EOF) {
            strcpy(crntLines[index],fileContents);
            strings[index] = &crntLines[index];
            index++;
/*          strcpy(strings[index++], fileContents); */
        }
        fclose(fileHandle);
    }
    return index;
}

char * getLearnerInput(char *gameString, int attempts
Remaining) {
    char aRstring[100];
    char learnerResponse[255];
    char *learnerResponsePtr;
    int strLength;

    sprintf(aRstring, "%d", attemptsRemaining);
    printf("%s%s%s\n", gameString, " attempts remaining: ",
    aRstring);
    printf("Enter letter: ");

    scanf("%s", learnerResponse);
    learnerResponsePtr = &learnerResponse;
    strLength = strlen(learnerResponsePtr);

    return learnerResponsePtr;
}

int congratulateLearner(char *crntWord) {
    printf("%s%s%s", "Well done! You determined that the
    word is ", crntWord, ".\n\n");

    return 0; /* to make wordNotFound = false */
}

int main() {

    const char * EMPTY_GAME_STRING = "_____";

    char *words[1000];
    int wordIndex;
    char *learnerResponse;
    char *crntWord;
    int i;
    int attemptsRemaining;
    char *gameString;
```

```
int wordNotFound;
int numWords;
int strCompareResult1;
char mySubstring[255];
FILE *fileHandle;

for (i = 0; i < 1000; i++) {
   words[i] = "";
}

numWords = initialize(words, "wordsReadingLevel9.txt");

for (i = 0; i < numWords; i++) {
   crntWord = words[i];
}

attemptsRemaining = 7;

wordIndex = 0;
learnerResponse = "";
strCompareResult1 = strcmp(learnerResponse,"exit")!=0;
while((wordIndex < numWords) && (strCompareResult1)) {
   attemptsRemaining = 7;
   crntWord = words[wordIndex++];
   wordNotFound = 1;

   i = 0;

   while (i < strlen(crntWord)) {
       mySubstring[i] = EMPTY_GAME_STRING[i];
       i++;
   }
   mySubstring[i] = '\0';
   gameString = &mySubstring;

   learnerReponse = getLearnerInput(gameString,
attemptsRemaining);
   strCompareRe sult1 = strcmp(learnerResponse,
exit") != 0;
   while ((attemptsRemaining > 0) && (wordNotFound)
&& (strCompareResult1)) {
       if (strlen(learnerResponse) == 1) {/* && (strstr
(crntWord,learnerResponse) != NULL) */
           for (i = 0; i < strlen(crntWord); i++) {
              if (crntWord[i] == learnerResponse[0]) {
                 gameString[i] = learnerResponse[0];
                 if (strcmp(gameString, crntWord) == 0) {
                     wordNotFound = congratulateLearner
(crntWord);
```

```
                }
              }
            }
          }
        else if (strcmp(learnerResponse, crntWord) == 0) {
            wordNotFound = congratulateLearner
(crntWord);
          }
        if (wordNotFound) {
          attemptsRemaining--;

          if (attemptsRemaining > 0) {
            learnerResponse=getLearnerInput
(gameString, attemptsRemaining);
            strCompareResult1=strcmp(learnerResponse,
"exit") != 0;
          }
          else {
            printf("%s%s%s", "The word was", crntWord,
".\n\n");
          }
        }
      }
    }

  fileHandle = fopen("learnerProgress3.txt", "w");
  fprintf(fileHandle, "%d", wordIndex);
  fclose(fileHandle);
}
```

C is a strongly typed language, which makes it much different from JavaScript. Parameter passing to functions is also different, as is the manner in which strings are implemented. In C, strings can be represented as a one-dimensional array of characters or as a pointer to a memory location, which points to a null-terminated string. Like JavaScript, C uses the standard set of control statements, if, for, and while and logical operators, as well as braces { } for code blocks.

Like Perl and Lua, C permits the writing of data to a file. Once again, the final three lines of code store the number of the last word the user encountered.

Many compilers are written in C, perhaps owing to its "old" age compared with other "high level" computer programming languages. Use of pointers in C suggests that C is somewhat lower in level among "high level" programming languages, though C is certainly not an assembly language. Compared with C, newer computer programming languages have made programming easier, with respect to consistent string implementation, for instance. Progress in compiler writing continues.

Swift

```
// Guess the Word

import Foundation
var fileContents: String = ""
var learnerResponse: String?
var words: [String]
var crntWord: String
var wordIndex: Int
var wordNotFound: Bool
var gameString: String
var attemptsRemaining: Int
var i: Int
let EMPTY_GAME_STRING = "_____"

func initialize(fileName: String) {

  if let dir = FileManager.default.urls(for:
.documentDirectory, in: .userDomainMask).first {
    let path = dir.appendingPathComponent(fileName)
    do {
      fileContents = try String(contentsOf: path,
encoding: String.Encoding.utf8) //read contents of
file into string
    }
    catch {
      print("Error reading file: " + fileName)
    }
  }
}

func getLearnerInput(gameString: String,
attemptsRemaining: Int) {
  print(gameString + " attempts remaining: " +
  String(attemptsRemaining));
  print("Enter letter")
  learnerResponse = readLine(strippingNewline: true)
}
func congratulateLearner(crntWord: String) -> Bool {
```

```
  print("Well done! You determined that the word is
" + crntWord + ".\n\n");

  return(false) // to set wordNotFound to false
}
func finalize(wordIndex: Int) {
  var wordIndexString: String

  wordIndexString = String(wordIndex)
  if   let   dir   =   FileManager.default.urls(for:
.documentDirectory, in: .userDomainMask).first {

    let path = dir.appendingPathComponent
("learnerProgress5.txt")

    do{
      try wordIndexString.write(to: path, atomically:
false, encoding: String.Encoding.utf8)
    }
    catch {
      print("Error writing file: learnerProgress5.txt")
    }
  }
}

initialize(fileName: "wordsReadingLevel9.txt")

words = fileContents.components(separatedBy: "\n")
for i in 0..<words.count {
  print(words[i])
}

wordIndex = 0;
learnerResponse = "";
while((wordIndex<words.count) && (learnerResponse !
= "exit")) {
  attemptsRemaining = 7
  crntWord = words[wordIndex]
  wordIndex += 1
  wordNotFound = true;

  gameString   =   EMPTY_GAME_STRING.substring(to:
EMPTY_GAME_STRING.index(EMPTY_GAME_STRING.
startIndex, offsetBy: crntWord.characters.count))
  getLearnerInput(gameString: gameString, attemptsRemaining:
attemptsRemaining)

    while ((attemptsRemaining > 0) && (wordNotFound)
    && (learnerResponse != "exit")){
```

```
        if ((learnerResponse!.characters.count == 1) &&
(crntWord.range(of: learnerResponse!) != nil)) {
            for i in 0..<crntWord.characters.count {
                if (String(crntWord[crntWord.
index(crntWord.startIndex, offsetBy:i)]) ==
learnerResponse) {
                    gameString = (gameString.
substring(to: EMPTY_GAME_STRING.index(EMPTY_
GAME_STRING.startIndex,offsetBy: i + 0))) +
learnerResponse! + (gameString.substring(from:
EMPTY_GAME_STRING.index(EMPTY_GAME_STRING.
startIndex, offsetBy: i + 1)))
                    if (gameString == crntWord) {
                        wordNotFound =
                        congratulateLearner
                        (crntWord: crntWord)
                    }
                }
            }
        }
    else if (learnerResponse == crntWord) {
        wordNotFound = congratulateLearner(crntWord:
crntWord)
    }

    if (wordNotFound) {
        attemptsRemaining -= 1

        if (attemptsRemaining > 0) {
            getLearnerInput(gameString: gameString,
attempts Remaining: attemptsRemaining)
        }
        else {
            print("The word was " + crntWord + ".\n\n")
        }
    }
}
}

finalize(wordIndex: wordIndex)
```

Swift, like JavaScript and all procedural programming languages, uses the control statements, if, for, and while. The syntax of the for loop changed with Swift 3 and the C-style for loop (e.g., for (i = 0; i < 10;

`i++) {...})` is no longer permitted in Swift. The symbols for the comparison operators (`== != < <= > >=`) are the same ones used in JavaScript and other languages. Arrays in Swift and JavaScript are similar, as is evident in the example above.

Strings are implemented differently in Swift 3. In Swift 2, strings were implemented as arrays of characters, which was similar to JavaScript and enabled access to substrings using an integer for the index. In Swift 3, strings were implemented as *collections* and the programmer needs to provide an open or closed range to index a string. In the example above, you may have noticed the rather long expressions involving substrings. Swift is a relatively new language and open-source project with seemingly monthly builds (https://swift.org/download/).

Functions in Swift use named parameters, which is unlike JavaScript and the other languages in this section. Functions permit access to global variables, though programmers can choose to pass parameters to functions, as well as return values. In the example code above, the `congratulateLearner` function returns the Boolean result `false`, which is assigned to the `wordNotFound` variable. While on the topic of variables, Swift departs somewhat from other languages at times. Variables may include a question mark after the name to denote an *optional*, which makes explicit that a variable may not have a value. One implication of an *optional* is that the compiler will at times force the optional to be resolved, which puts an exclamation mark after the variable name. This adds some programming complexity (and flexibility) at times.

Borrowing in part from Objective-C, Swift is object oriented, though flexible for particular implementations. For example, the code above is a command line app, consistent with the other examples in this section. In the case of command line apps, one places Swift code in a main file, which does not force a class definition. When creating an iOS app, which runs on the iPhone, iPad, and iPod Touch, the Xcode interface to Swift projects automatically creates a ViewController class. Just as computer programming languages are improving, so too are the tools for app development. Apple's Xcode development environment detects compile time errors in real time, much as a word processor detects spelling errors and offers recommendations for correcting errors.

Java

```
import java.io.*;
// Guess the Word
public class guessTheWord2 {
    public static String initialize(String fileName)
    {
        String fileContents = "";
        String prefix = "";
```

```
        try {
            BufferedReader in = new
BufferedReader(new FileReader(fileName));
            String str;
            while ((str = in.readLine()) != null) {
                fileContents += prefix + str;
                prefix = "\n";
            }
        } catch (IOException e) {
        }
        return (fileContents);
    }

    public static String getLearnerInput(String
gameString, int attemptsRemaining) {
        Console crntConsole;
        String learnerResponse = "";
        System.out.println(gameString + " attempts
remaining: " + attemptsRemaining);
        try {
            crntConsole = System.console();

            if (crntConsole != null) {
                learnerResponse = crntConsole.
                readLine("Enter letter: ");
            }
        } catch(Exception ex) {
        }
        return(learnerResponse);
    }

public static boolean congratulateLearner(String
crntWord) {
    System.out.println("Well done! You determined
that the word is " + crntWord + ".\n\n");
    return (false); // to set wordNotFound to false;
}

    public static void finalize(String fileName, int wordIndex) {
        try {
            BufferedWriter out = new BufferedWriter
            (new FileWriter(fileName));
            out.write(wordIndex + "");
            out.close();
        }
```

```
                catch (IOException e) {
                }
        }
public static void main(String args[]) {
    int wordIndex;
    String fileContents;
    String[] words;
    int i;
    String learnerResponse;
    boolean wordNotFound;
    String crntWord = "";
    int attemptsRemaining;
    String gameString;
    String exitStr = "exit";

    String EMPTY_GAME_STRING="                    ";

    String str = "Hello World";
    String anotherString = "hello world";

    fileContents = initialize("wordsReadingLevel9.txt");

    words = fileContents.split("\n");

    wordIndex = 0;
    learnerResponse = "";
      while ((wordIndex < words.length) && (! learnerResponse.
equals(exitStr))) {
            attemptsRemaining = 7;
            crntWord = words[wordIndex++];
            wordNotFound = true;

            gameString = EMPTY_GAME_STRING.substring(1,
            crntWord.length() + 1);

            learnerResponse = getLearnerInput(gameString,
attemptsRemaining);
            while ((attemptsRemaining > 0) && (wordNotFound)
&& (! learnerResponse.equals(exitStr))) {
                    if ((learnerResponse.length() == 1) &&
(crntWord.indexOf(learnerResponse) >= 0)) {
                        for (i = 0; i < crntWord.length(); i++) {
                            if (learnerResponse.equals(crntWord.
                            substring(i,i+1))) {
                                gameString = gameString.
substring (0, i) + learnerResponse + gameString.substring
(i + 1);
```

```
                              if (gameString.equals(crntWord)) {
                                  wordNotFound = congratulate
                                  Learner(crntWord);
                              }
                          }
                      }
                  }
              else if (learnerResponse.equals(crntWord)) {
                  wordNotFound = congratulateLearner(crntWord);
              }

              if (wordNotFound) {
                  attemptsRemaining--;

                  if (attemptsRemaining > 0) {
                      learnerResponse = getLearnerInput
                      (gameString, attemptsRemaining);
                  }
                  else {
                      System.out.println("The word was " +
crntWord + ".\n\n");
                  }
              }
          }
      }
      finalize("learnerProgress4.txt", wordIndex);
  }
}
```

Like JavaScript, Java includes the common control statements, `if`, `for`, and `while`, as well as braces `{}` for code blocks. The symbols in Java for the comparison operators (`== != < <= > >=`) are also the same as JavaScript. In addition, strings in Java are implemented in a manner similar to JavaScript. Arrays in Java and JavaScript are similar too.

In contrast, the program structure is much different. Other than any imported library routines (the io library in this case), Java programs begin with the program's class definition, which reveals that Java is object oriented. The file name of the source code must be *classname.java*, with a suitable substitution for the actual class name. The source code file name for this example is *guessTheWord2.java*.

Some languages, like Java, have a `try {} catch {}` statement, which enables error reporting and (more graceful) program termination for particular errors, such as file not found. In the example above, file reading and writing include the `try {} catch {}` statement. Like Perl, Lua, C, and Swift, Java permits the writing of data to a file. The final line of code in the main function calls the `finalize` function, which stores the number of the last word the user encountered.

Python

```
# Guess the Word
words = []
learnerResponse = ""
wordNotFound = True
def initialize(fileName):
    global words

    inFile = open(fileName, "r")
    fileContents = inFile.read()
    inFile.close()
    words = fileContents.split("\n")

    for i in range(0, len(words)):
        print(i, words[i])
def getLearnerInput():
    global learnerResponse

    print(gameString + " attempts remaining: " +
    str(attemptsRemaining))
    learnerResponse = input("Enter letter: ")

def congratulateLearner():
    global wordNotFound

    print("Well done! You determined that the word
is " + crntWord + ".\n\n")
    wordNotFound = False

EMPTY_GAME_STRING = "_____";

initialize("wordsReadingLevel9.txt")

wordIndex = 0
learnerResponse = ""
while ((wordIndex < len(words)) and (learnerResponse
!= "exit")):
    attemptsRemaining = 7
    crntWord = words[wordIndex]
    wordIndex += 1
    wordNotFound = True
    gameString = EMPTY_GAME_STRING[1:len(crntWord)+1]
    print("game string is'" + gameString + "'")
```

```
      getLearnerInput()
      while ((attemptsRemaining > 0) and (wordNotFound)
and (learnerResponse != "exit")):
            if ((len(learnerResponse) == 1) and (crntWord.
            find(learnerResponse) >= 0)):
                  for i in range(0, len(crntWord)):
                        if (crntWord[i] == learnerResponse):
                              gameString = gameString[0:i] +
learnerResponse + gameString[i + 1:len(gameString)]
                              if (gameString == crntWord):
                                    congratulateLearner();
            elif (learnerResponse == crntWord):
                  congratulateLearner();
      if (wordNotFound):
            attemptsRemaining -= 1

      if (attemptsRemaining > 0):
            getLearnerInput()
      else:
            print("The word was " + crntWord +
            ".\n\n");

outFile = open("learnerProgress.txt", "w")
outFile.write(str(wordIndex))
outFile.close()
```

Python uses the standard set of control statements, if, for, and while, but code blocks in Python are different from those in JavaScript and many other languages. Python uses indentation to mark blocks of code, rather than braces { } or keywords, such as do ... end. Like Lua, Python uses logical operators, and, or, and not in compound conditional expressions.

Like Perl, Lua, C, Swift, and Java, Python permits the writing of data to a file. Once again, the final three lines of code store the number of the last word the user encountered.

With respect to functions, Python uses def to begin a function definition and requires explicit references to any global variables. String processing in Python includes functions such as string length (len) and split. The built-in len function can also be used to determine the size of an array. Unlike JavaScript, Python uses *slicing*, which requires the provision of array indices to access substrings. File IO is straightforward in Python.

In summary, Table 3.5 identifies similarities and differences between JavaScript, Perl, Lua, C/C++, Swift, Java, and Python.

3.2 App Development Environments

Just as there are different types of apps (e.g., desktop apps, tablet apps, smartphone apps, web apps, social robot apps), there are multiple development tools

Table 3.5 Comparing Features of Procedural Programming Languages

	JavaScript	Perl	Lua	C/C++	Swift	Java	Python
Variable names	Weakly typed	D	NI	SD	SD	SD	NI
Strings	Implicit string type	S	S	D	D	S	SD
Assignment statement	=	NI	S	S	S	S	S
Conditional statement	if {} else if {} else {}	NI	S	S	S	S	S
Comparison operators	== != < <= > >=	SD	NI	S	S	S	NI
Fixed iteration	for	NI	SD	S	SD	S	SD
Conditional Iteration	while	NI	S	S	S	S	S
1-dimensional array		NI	S	S	S	S	NI
2-dimensional array		NI	S	S	S	S	NI
Files	In general, read only	SD	SD	D	SD	D	SD
Code Block	{...}	I	D	I	I	I	D
Function Scope/ Parameter Passing	Free to access global variables	D	S	D	SD	D	SD
Program Structure		S	S	D	SD	D	SD

I: Identical; NI: Nearly Identical; S: Similar; SD: Somewhat Different; D: Different

or environments for creating the apps. Compilers and interpreters are app development tools because they translate high-level source code into machine executable code. Section 3.2.1 discusses acquisition of compilers and interpreters. Section 3.2.2 describes use of Software Development Kits (SDKs) for app development. SDKs, such as Unity and Unreal Engine, provide visual interfaces for working with visible objects and multimedia assets in addition to code translation features for building executable code for multiple platforms. Those SDKs also include debugging tools. Another app development option, which is mentioned in Section 3.2.3, involves use of somewhat non-standard hardware, such as the Raspberry Pi, though there are many low-cost single board computers that offer more speed and functionality.

3.2.1. Compilers and Interpreters

Computer manufacturers sometimes bundle compilers and interpreters with the operating system. Compilers and interpreters translate source code, which we write, to machine code, which the Central Processing Unit (CPU) executes. When not included with the operating system, a compiler or interpreter is often available free of cost. Even if bundled, one may choose to acquire and install the latest version of a compiler or interpreter. As experienced with SpiderMonkey JavaScript, developers typically use a command line interface in a Terminal or Command Window to run a compiler or interpreter.

Perl

Perl compilers are often distributed with Unix operating systems. Since Mac computers provide a graphical interface over Unix, Perl comes with a Mac. In a Mac Terminal Window, one can type `which perl` to locate the directory of the Perl compiler. Typing `perl -v` in a Mac Terminal Window will display the Perl version number.

Developers on Windows and Mac computes can download and install a recent version of Perl from www.perl.org. Alternatively, a community (free of cost) version of Perl could be obtained from Active State, which according to their slogan is *The Open Source Languages Company* (www.activestate. com/activeperl/downloads).

Lua

Lua Binaries for Mac OS X are available from Rudix (http://rudix.org/packages/lua.html), which according to their slogan is *The Hassle-free way to get Unix programs on OS X*. It is also possible to install the Lua shell and compiler on a Mac using one command in the Mac Terminal Window. On a Mac with Homebrew installed, the following command will install Lua:

```
brew install lua
```

To obtain Lua Binaries for Windows, see https://sourceforge.net/projects/luabinaries/files/5.3.3/

C/C++

Since many Unix installations include a C/C++ compiler, Mac OS X comes bundled with clang, which is a C/C++/Objective C compiler. The compiler produces object code (an `a.out` file), which is run from the command line by entering `./a.out`

Developers using computers running Microsoft Windows can access a C compiler using Visual Studio Express.

Swift

On a Mac, Swift is available through Apple's Xcode development tool, which is a free download from the Apple Mac Store. There is also a Swift build for

Ubuntu (which is built on Linux). A Swift build for Windows is available, with work still in progress (http://swiftforwindows.codeplex.com/).

Java

Since many Unix installations include a Java compiler, Mac OS X comes bundled with javac, which is a Java compiler. Within the Mac Terminal Window, entering `which java` will display the location of the Java Complier. Further, entering `java -version` will display version and build numbers. The compiler produces an executable class file, which is run from the command line by entering `java classname.java`, with a suitable substitution for the actual class name.

Java developers on either Mac or Windows can download and install the latest Java Development Kit (JDK) from Oracle. The JDK is used to compile java source code. www.oracle.com/technetwork/java/javase/downloads/index-jsp-138363.html#javasejdk

Python

The Python Software Foundation provides an Integrated Development Environment (IDLE) for Microsoft Windows and Mac OS X (www.python.org/downloads/), which is free of monetary cost. Active State also offers a Community Edition of Python (www.activestate.com/activepython/downloads). Like the SpiderMonkey JavaScript environment, the IDLE development environment has two modes. Developers can execute individual Python statements in the shell or drop down the File Menu and create a new Python source file (extension .py) or open an existing file.

3.2.2 Software Development Kits

When not using a compiler or interpreter to create apps, a developer may use a Software Development Kit (SDK), which is a special purpose programming environment. Such environments often include debugging tools in addition to a compiler. SDKs may enable developers to use a visual drag-and-drop interface or a symbolic interface to create apps. Luterbach and Hubbell (2015) compared a variety of SDKs. App development environments continue to improve in a manner commensurate with advances to target devices.

Android Studio (https://developer.android.com/studio/index.html) for Apple Mac and Microsoft Windows enables development of apps for Android devices (mobile, TV, auto, wearables, Internet of Things). Developers use the Java programming language to create apps in Android Studio, which offers a hybrid (visual and symbolic) interface for developing apps.

The Corona SDK (https://coronalabs.com/) for Apple Mac and Microsoft Windows enables development of 2D games and other apps for a variety of target devices (mobile, desktop, TV) using the Lua programming language. The Corona SDK provides a symbolic interface for app development with rapid run-time testing.

As mentioned in the previous section for running Swift code, developers use Apple's Xcode to create iOS, Mac, wearable (watch), and TV apps. Xcode runs only on a Mac and offers a hybrid visual and symbolic interface.

Unity 3D for Apple Mac and Microsoft Windows enables cross-platform app development. That is, one can develop apps for iOS and Android devices in Unity, as well as HTML apps, and apps for desktop (PC, Mac, and Linux), Xbox One, PlayStation 4, Tizen OS (mobile, wearable, TV) and Microsoft Windows. We will use Unity 3D, which provides visual and symbolic interfaces, to develop the apps in Chapter 5. You may deploy those apps on iOS and Android devices (or other devices of your choosing). Unity can also be used to develop VR apps.

The Unreal Engine by Epic games for Apple Mac and Microsoft Windows is a cross platform development environment used to create iOS and Anroid apps, as well as HTML, Linux, and VR (Gear, Oculus, Steam, Daydream) apps.

Microsoft Visual Studio for Microsoft Windows computers offers an integrated development environment for creating mobile apps and Windows apps using C# (C Sharp), C++, Visual Basic, TypeScript, F#, or a third party language such as JavaScript.

3.2.3 Create Your Own Device

The point of this section is to draw attention to the possibility of using a Single Board Computer (SBC), such as the Asus Tinker Board ($60), Raspberry Pi ($35), Banana Pi ($46), Orange Pi ($49), PineA64+ ($15–$29), NanoPi M3 ($35), C.H.I.P. ($9), NanoPi NEO Air (40mm by 40mm, $20), HummingBoard Gate ($70), Beagleboard ($57), or similar such computer (Beebom Media, 2017; Slant Community), to create your own device. A keyword search on the web for the name of the board followed by the word *projects* (e.g., NanoPi projects) will reveal numerous possibilities. Consider creating a unique wearable device or a new device for distributing instructional apps, whether wearable or not.

Note

1   If necessary, install the Google Chrome browser after acquiring it from www.google.com/chrome/browser or install Firefox after acquiring it from www.mozilla.org/firefox

References

Beebom Media (2017). https://beebom.com/best-raspberry-pi-3-alternatives/

Kedar, S. (2011). *Principles of programming languages.* Shaniwar Peth, Pune, Maharashtra, India: Technical Publications.

Luterbach, K. & Hubbell, K. (2015). Capitalizing on App Development Tools and Technologies. *TechTrends, 59*(4), 62–70.

Papert, S. (1980). *Mindstorms: Children, computers, and powerful ideas.* Hemel Hempstead, UK: Harvester Press.

Slant Community (2017). www.slant.co/topics/6106/~raspberry-pi-alternatives

Thompson, S. (2011). *Haskell: The craft of functional programming.* Edinburgh Gate, Harlow, UK: Pearson Education.

Part 2

Creating Instructional Apps

Chapter 4

Instructional Apps for Building Knowledge Foundations

In this chapter, we review behavioral instruction briefly and consider the diversity of instructional apps that build knowledge foundations through behavioral instruction. Then we use JavaScript to create two instructional apps. The first app presents a web interface for practicing multiplication, which leverages code written in the previous chapter. The second web app enables one to learn words in English, French, and Spanish for colors.

4.1 Implementing the Instructional Method

Behavioral instruction presents an instructional stimulus; elicits a response; and provides feedback. Such a teaching method may be called *direct instruction* or *didactic instruction*, which some regard as *drill-and-practice*. Over time, engagement in only one instructional method would likely make learners crave an alternative approach to learning. Some critics of behavioral instruction suggest that learners are passive when engaged in the instruction. That's absurd. Behaviorists studied observable behaviors only so learners engaged in behavioral instruction are active. If not responding to stimuli, learners are not engaged in behavioral instruction. Perhaps those critics favor another form of instruction, but that would limit their versatility. Rather than pick a favorite instructional method, many instructional designers favor an eclectic approach, which enables selection of an instructional method appropriate for the instructional objectives and learners.

4.2 Diversity of the Apps

There are many options for presenting content, eliciting a response, and providing feedback through text, images, sound, and video. In addition to use of multiple media, learners can provide responses through multiple means (e.g., mouse; keyboard; stylus; finger tap, swipe, and drag; multi-touch; and voice). Further, the instructional method can be implemented variably, which may involve game play, rather than electronic flash cards or multiple-choice items, for instance.

I highly recommend that you go to the following websites and consider the examples of web apps that implement behavioral instruction. You will gain a sense for the variability of these instructional apps. Additionally, you may identify features that you would like to implement in instructional apps that you create.

Kerntype: A Kerning Game
Mark MacKay for Method of Action
http://type.method.ac/

Geography Game
Techslides
http://techslides.com/demos/d3/dragdrop-geo-game.html

Converting Volumes
George Wiger
http://science.widener.edu/svb/tutorial/convertvolcsn7.html

Additional drill-and-practice items on numerous topics are available at
http://science.widener.edu/svb/tutorial/index.html
George Wiger and Scott Van Bramer

4.3 Learning Times Tables

In Chapter 3, Task #5 required development of a command-line app for learners to practice multiplication (times tables). Regarding distribution of that app, each learner would need to download the executable file (which might have been sent as an email attachment, for instance) and then run the app in a command-line window. Some computer users do not know how to open such a window because that has not been necessary for them previously. Further, some computer users may not know which folder contains downloaded files. To eliminate the need for distributing the instructional app and the instructions necessary to guide the learner through installation and execution of the app, we will create a web app. To run a web app, the learner need only enter the URL of the app into a web browser's address field or simply click on a link in an email message, for instance.

To create a web app, rudimentary knowledge of the Hypertext Markup Language (HTML) is required. Consequently, we will first create a couple of web pages in HTML. Then we will add the few lines of JavaScript necessary to implement the app.

HTML is not a programming language; it contains no iterative statements or conditional statements. Tim Berners-Lee (2000) designed web technologies to provide a standard method for sharing content, which prior to 1990 was challenging because mainframe computers, minicomputers, and microcomputers emerged with multiple operating systems, as well as a variety of external storage devices and software for displaying text and images.

Creating Web Pages in HTML

To create a web page in HTML, open *Notepad* on Windows or *TextEdit* on a Mac. Enter the text below and save the file as *webPage1.html*.

```
<html>
    <head>
    <title>Basic Web Page</title>
    </head>

    <body>
    This is a very simple web page.
    </body>
</html>
```

The first example illustrates fundamental structural elements of a web page. In particular, web pages contain tags, such as `<html>` `</html>`, `<head>` `</head>`, `<title>` `</title>`, and `<body>` `</body>`. Tags almost always come in pairs and are arranged hierarchically. Within the opening `<html>` and closing `</html>` tag, a typical web page contains two parts, the head and the body. The head is not absolutely necessary, but it is helpful to provide a title, which appears in the tab of a web browser. The tags and text in the body are rendered by the web browser to display the content of the web page.

After entering the HTML above and saving the file as *webPage1.html*, double-click the file icon, which will open the web page in a web browser. Notice that *Basic Web Page* appears in the browser's tab because `<title>` `</title>` surrounds *Basic Web Page*. Also notice that *This is a very simple web page* appears in the content space of the web browser because that text appears in the body of the web page (within `<body>` `</body>`).

Copy *webPage1.html* to *webPage2.html*. Open *webPage2.html* in your text editor. Edit the body section, as shown below, in order to display two levels of headings and multiple paragraphs, as well as text that appears bold, underlined, and in italics.

```
<html>
<head>
<title>Literature</title>
</head>

<body>
<h1>Genres of Literature</h1>
<p>There are two main categories or genres of literature,
<i>fiction</i> and <i>nonfiction</i>.</p>

<h2>Genres of Fiction</h2>
<p>Fiction derives from the author's imagination. Genres
of fiction include drama, mystery, humor, poetry, science
fiction, fables, and fairy tales, for instance.</p>
```

```
<p>Enjoy reading <i><u>fiction</u></i>.</p>
<h2>Genres of Nonfiction</h2>
<p>Nonfiction works are <u>factual</u>.</p>
```

```
<p>Enjoy reading <i><u>nonfiction</u></i>, such as
<i>Design and Development of Robust Instructional
Apps</i>. Genres of nonfiction include essays, speeches,
biographies, autobiographies, and textbooks, for
instance.</p>
</body>
</html>
```

After entering the HTML above and saving the file as *webPage2.html*, double-click the file icon. Notice the size difference in headings for Level 1 (h1) and Level 2 (h2) headings. Web page developers also use heading levels 3–6 (h3, h4, h5, h6). For the heading levels, the closing part of the tag is very important. If forgotten, the remaining text of the document will appear in the size of the opening tag (unless there is another opening heading tag). For instance, in your text editor, delete </h1>; save the file; and reload the page in the web browser (Ctrl-R on a Windows PC; Command-R on a Mac). Notice that all text until the Level 2 heading (<h2>), Genres of Fiction, is the size of Level 1 headings. Then re-insert </h1> in its proper place. Also try some different heading levels. For instance, replace <h2> and </h2> with <h5> and </h5>. Always save and reload the page to view the effects of the changes. Rarely would one use italics and underline, as in <i><u>fiction</u></i> for one word or phrase. This is done in the example only to demonstrate how tags are nested. Add the bold tag <b></b>, as in <b><i><u>fiction</u></i></b>, and view the effect.

Copy *webPage2.html* to *webPage3.html*. Open *webPage3.html* in your text editor. Edit the body section, as shown below, in order to display the genres of fiction and nonfiction as unordered lists. In addition, the sample web page below introduces hyperlinking.

```
<html>
<head>
<title>Literature</title>
</head>
```

```
<body>
<h1>Genres of Literature</h1>
<p>There are two main categories or genres of literature,
<i>fiction</i> and <i>nonfiction</i>.</p>
```

```
<h2>Genres of Fiction</h2>
<p>Fiction derives from the author's imagination.
Consider the following genres of fiction.
```

```
<ul>
```

```
<li>Drama</li>
<li>Mystery</li>
<li>Humor</li>
<li>Poetry</li>
<li>Science fiction</li>
<li>Fables</li>
<li>Fairy tales</li>
</ul>
</p>

<p>Enjoy reading fiction.</p>

<h2>Genres of Nonfiction</h2>
<p>Nonfiction works are <u>factual</u>.</p>

<p>Enjoy reading nonfiction, such as <i>Design and
Development of Robust Instructional Apps</i>. Consider
the following genres of nonfiction.

<ul>
<li>Essays</li>
<li>Speeches</li>
<li>Biographies</li>
<li>Autobiographies</li>
<li>Textbooks</li>
</ul>
</p>

<p>When you are ready for a change, view the <a
href="webPage1.html">first web page you created</
a> and the <a href="www.routledge.com">Routledge</
a> website.
</body>
</html>
```

After entering the HTML above and saving the file as *webPage3.html*, double-click the file icon. Notice that effect of <ul> </ul> tag in combination with the <li> </li> tag, which produces a list of bullet points. Then replace <ul> and </ul> with <ol> and </ol>; save the file; and reload the page to view the ordered list, which inserts consecutive numbers for the bullet points.

Also test the hyperlinks. Notice that clicking a hyperlink replaces the current web page with another web page. You may return to the original web page by clicking the web browser's back arrow icon or pressing the previous page key (Ctrl-Left arrow on a Windows PC or Command-Left arrow on a Mac). Hyperlinks are created using anchor tags <a> . . . </a> and can be implemented to open a new tab for the new web page, which prevents replacement of the current web page. This is achieved by setting the target attribute to blank, as shown below.

```
<a href="webPage1.html" target="blank">first web
page</a>
```

Make that change in your text editor in both anchor tags. Save, reload the page, and notice the effect. Now take note of the `href` attribute, which determines the web page to be displayed when the hyperlink is clicked. In the anchor tag above, the first web page created in this chapter, *webPage1.html*, is displayed. In the anchor tag below, the `href` attribute provides an explicit reference to a web server (i.e., www.routledge.com). An explicit reference to a particular web server always begins http:// and is followed by the web server name, which may also be called the *domain name*. Such a reference is called an *absolute* hyperlink. In contrast, there is no http:// and no web server name in the `href` attribute above, which makes the reference to the target web page a *relative* hyperlink. Use relative hyperlinks to reference web pages you create and absolute hyperlinks to reference web pages at other websites.

```
<a href="www.routledge.com">Routledge</a>
```

Task 4.1 In *webPage1.html*, insert one anchor tag in order to link to *web-Page2.html* and a second anchor tag in order to link to *webPage3.html*. Also copy the anchor tag in *webPage3.html* that links to *webPage1.html* and paste that anchor tag into *webPage2.html*. Save all three web pages and test the hyperlinks to ensure that all of them function properly. Then insert anchor tags into *webPage2.html* and *webPage3.html* to link those web pages directly. Save those two web pages and test the links to ensure that they function properly. Lastly, in *webPage1.html*, insert anchor tags with absolute references to three or four websites of interest to you. Save the web page and ensure that all links function properly.

Task 4.2 In the folder containing *webPage1.html* and the other web pages you developed above, create a subfolder called `images`. In the `images` folder, put a file named `myPhoto.png`, `myPhoto.jpg`, or use any image file with a png, gif, jpg, or jpeg file name extension. I will use `myPhoto.png` in the example below and you can substitute the filename you are using if it differs from `myPhoto.png`. Insert either image tag below into *webPage1.html* in order to display the image.

```
<img src="images/myPhoto.png" alt="Ken's Photo">
```
or
```
<img src="images/myPhoto.png" alt="Ken's Photo"
height="300" width="200">
```

Save *webpage1.html*, reload the page, and view the image. The `height` and `width` attributes are optional. The `alt` attribute provides alternative text in case the image cannot be viewed, whether due to a slow Internet connection, an error in the `src` attribute, or the user may be accessing the web page with a screen reader.

Task 4.3 You may wish to reinforce what you have learned about HTML and learn more HTML tags by proceeding through a free tutorial, such as the one provided by w3schools, which is available at www. w3schools.com/html/default.asp.

Adding JavaScript Code to Web Pages to Interact with Learners

In your text editor, open a new document and enter the text below in order to display an input field and a button on a web page. An input field enables the user to enter a response to a prompt. The button in the web page enables submission of the response to the prompt. Save the file as *webPage4. html*.

```
<html>
<head>
<title>Get Learner Input</title>
</head>

<body>
<p>Let us create a field that enables a learner to
type a response and then click a button to submit
the response.</p>
Enter your first name: <input id="learnerResponse"
type="text" size="30"></input>

<button  id="submitButton"  type="button"  onclick
="getResponse()">Submit Name</input>
</body>
</html>
```

After entering the HTML above and saving the file as *webPage4.html*, double-click the file icon. Notice that after the preliminary line of text, there is the prompt to enter your name, a field for name entry, and a button to submit the name. Enter your name into the text field and click the submit button. Since we have yet to write the getResponse() function in JavaScript and include it in the script, the submit button fails. However, the text field enables user interactivity and the browser has detected why the button failed. Reload the web page by pressing Ctrl-R on a Windows PC or Command-R on a Mac. Then open the web browser's JavaScript Console in the Google Chrome web browser (Control-Shift-I on a Windows PC; Option-Command-J on a Mac). Once again, enter your name and click the submit button. Notice in the JavaScript Console that a Reference Error has been detected because getResponse is absent from the script.

To make the script functional, the getResponse() function need only contain one or two lines of JavaScript. As shown below, JavaScript code is included in the web page using the HTML script tag <script> </script>.

```
<html>
<head>
<title>Get Learner Input</title>
</head>

<body>
<p>Let us create a field that enables a learner to
type a response and then click a button to submit
the response.</p>
Enter your first name: <input id="learnerResponse"
type="text" size="30"></input>
<button id="submitButton type="button" onclick="get
Response()">Submit Name</input>
<script>
  function getResponse() {
    alert("Name submitted");
  }
</script>
</body>
</html>
```

After adding the getResponse() function within <script> and
</script>, save the file; reload the page; enter your name; and click the
submit button. We now have a functional interactive app, but we should
ensure ourselves that we have access to the name entered by the user. Add
the following line of text to the getResponse() function and edit the
alert statement, as shown below.

```
userName = document.getElementById("learnerResponse").
value;
alert("Name submitted: " + userName);
```

Save the file; reload the page; enter your name; and click the submit button.

Web app developers can retrieve values entered using the getElementById
method, provided the HTML element includes the id attribute, which does appear
in the input tag: <input id="learnerResponse" type="text"
size="30"></input>.

Using an alert to popup a dialog box is useful at times, but at other times the
popup is annoying. Consider replacing alert("Name submitted: "
+ userName) with console.log("Name submitted: " +
userName). Alternatively, during debugging, you can use both the alert
and console for output if you wish.

Even better, display the name entered by the user in the web page, as
shown below in the final version of *webPage4.html*.

```
<html>
<head>
<title>Get Learner Input</title>
</head>

<body>
<div id="inputSpace">
<p>Let us create a field that enables a learner to
type a response and then click a button to submit
the response.</p>

Enter your first name: <input id="learnerResponse"
type="text" size="30"></input>

<button    id="submitButton    type="button"    onclick=
"getResponse()">Submit name</input>
</div>

<div id="outputSpace"> </div>

<script>
function getResponse() {
  userName = document.getElementById("learnerResponse").
value;
  alert("Name submitted: " + userName);
  console.log("Name submitted: " + userName);
  document.getElementById("outputSpace").
innerHTML = userName;
}
</script>
</body>
</html>
```

The final version of *webPage4.html* demonstrates a technique for dynamically modifying the content of a web page by altering a section of the web page marked by the <div> </div> tag. In this case the user's name is displayed in the div tag with id="outputSpace".

Once you have tested *webPage4.html* to ensure proper functionality, make one final change. Replace <div id="outputSpace"> </div> with the following HTML.

```
<div id="outputSpace">text to be replaced</div>
<p>This text follows the section of the web page
changed dynamically.</p>
```

Save and reload. Notice that clicking the submit button changes the outputSpace section of the web page only.

At this point, we have covered sufficient HTML and JavaScript to create interactive instructional web apps.

Web App 1: Practicing Multiplication

TARGET LEARNERS: People capable of entering digits on a keyboard or numeric keypad who have mastered addition.
INSTRUCTIONAL OBJECTIVE: The learner will be able to answer one-digit multiplication questions correctly at least 80 percent of the time.

DESIGN

This web app will repeatedly display a one-digit multiplication question (the instructional stimulus) and provide a field that enables the learner to enter the answer (elicit a response). The learner's response will be compared with the correct answer and appropriate feedback provided. Figure 4.1(a) displays an initial question; Figure 4.1(b) displays the response with feedback and the second question; and Figure 4.1(c) displays the state of the app at the fourth question.

DEVELOPMENT

Open a new document in your text editor and enter the following HTML. Save the file as *webApp1pa.html*.

4 * 3 = [   ]

Figure 4.1 (a). Initial question displayed in web browser.

4 * 3 = 12 Correct
5 * 8 = [   ]

Figure 4.1 (b). Response to initial question, the feedback, and second question.

4 * 3 = 12 Correct
5 * 8 = 45 No, 5 * 8 = 40
2 * 3 = 6 Correct
9 * 10 = [   ]

Figure 4.1 (c). State of the web browser window at fourth question.

Figure 4.1 States of App through Four Questions.

```
<html>
<head>
    <title>Practice Adding</title>
</head>
<body>

<div id="workSpace" style="display:inline">4 * 3 =
</div><input type="text" size="4" id="learnerResponse"
onKeyPress="processKeyPress(event)">

</body>
</html>
```

After entering the HTML above and saving *webApp1pa.html,* double-click the file icon to open the web page in a web browser. Notice that the content displayed in the web browser is the same as Figure 4.1 (a).

At this point, we already have the basic web page in place with a section identified as the workSpace (`<div id="workSpace"` ... `</div>`) and a field for the learner's response to the question. Although random numbers from 1–10 will be drawn, the initial question appears as 4 * 3 = in order to display the question in Figure 4.1 (a). The `<div>` tag also includes the style attribute `style="display:inline"` to ensure that the input field appears on the same line as the question.

As per Chapter 3, this example will create an app for practicing addition, which will enable you to make changes necessary for learners to practice multiplication. Recall the following code from *practiceAdding.js* in Chapter 3 (Section 3.1.3).

```
num1 = Math.floor(Math.random() * 10 + 1);
num2 = Math.floor(Math.random() * 10 + 1);
print("What is " + num1 + " + " + num2 + "?");
learnerResponse = readline();
if (learnerResponse == num1 + num2) {
  print("Correct");}
else {
  print("No, " + num1 + " + " + num2 + " = " + (num1
  + num2));
}
```

We will use the first two assignment statements without modification in order to generate two random numbers to form the question presented to the learner, rather than always starting with 4 * 3. In the next version of this app, we will add a function to select two random numbers and present the learner the opportunity to enter the sum of those two numbers. In your text editor, modify *webApp1pa.html* as shown below.

```
<html>
<head>
    <title>Practice Adding</title>
</head>
<body onload="init()">
<div id="workSpace" style="display:inline"> </div> <input
onKeyPress="processKeyPress(event)" id="learnerResponse"
style="font-size: 11pt" type="text" size="4">
<script type="text/javascript">
    function init() {
        num1 = Math.floor(Math.random() * 10 + 1);
        num2 = Math.floor(Math.random() * 10 + 1);

        document.getElementById("workSpace").
innerHTML = num1 + " + " + num2 + " =";
        document.getElementById("learnerResponse").
focus();
    }
</script>

</body>
</html>
```

After making the changes above and saving *webApp1pa.html*, reload the web page. At this point, the app runs an initialization function to draw two random numbers for the opening question. The following statement is used to display the opening question.

```
document.getElementById("workSpace").innerHTML = num1
+ " + " + num2 + " = ";
```

As before, the `getElementById` method enables access to a component of the web page. In this case, we need access to the section of the web page called the `workSpace`, which is created with the `<div>` ... `</div>` tag. Setting the `innerHTML` attribute of the `workSpace` to the question will display the question in the web browser's content space. The following statement ensures that the cursor will appear in the `learnerResponse` field so the learner will not need to click in the field or press the Tab key in order to enter a response into the field.

```
document.getElementById("learnerResponse").
focus();
```

Since two random numbers must be drawn for all questions, not just the opening question, we will move the two assignment statements producing the random numbers to a function named `getQuestion`, and call that function both during initialization and after providing the learner with feedback. In your text editor, modify *webApp1pa.html* as shown below.

```
<html>
<head>
  <title>Practice Adding</title>
</head>

<body style="font-family: Courier"; onload="init()">

<div id="workSpace" style="display:inline"> </div> <input
onKeyPress="processKeyPress(event)" id="learnerResponse"
style="font-size: 11pt" type="text" size="4">
<script type="text/javascript">
  var crntQuestion;
  var resultString;
  var num1, num2;

  function getQuestion() {
      num1 = Math.floor(Math.random() * 10 + 1);
      num2 = Math.floor(Math.random() * 10 + 1);
      return (num1 + " + " + num2 + " = ");
  } // "getQuestion"

  function init() {
      document.getElementById("workSpace").
innerHTML = getQuestion();
      document.getElementById("learnerResponse").
focus();
  }
</script>

</body>
</html>
```

The getQuestion function generates two random numbers between 1 and 10 and uses the numbers to form the question. The question is returned to the init() function as a string of characters (e.g., 3 + 4 =) . Now we need to get the learner's response; provide feedback; and present the next question. In your text editor, modify *webApp1pa.html* as shown below. In particular, add the processKeyPress function.

```
<html>
<head>
  <title>Practice Adding</title>
</head>
```

```html
<body style="font-family: Courier"; onload="init()">

<div id="workSpace" style="display:inline"> </div> <input
onKeyPress="processKeyPress(event)" id="learnerResponse"
style="font-size: 11pt" type="text" size="4">
<script type="text/javascript">
  var crntQuestion;
  var resultString;
  var num1, num2;

  function getQuestion() {
     num1 = Math.floor(Math.random() * 10 + 1);
     num2 = Math.floor(Math.random() * 10 + 1);
     return (num1 + " + " + num2 + " = ");
  } // "getQuestion"

  function init() {
     document.getElementById("workSpace").
innerHTML = getQuestion();
     document.getElementById("learnerResponse").
focus();
  }

  function processKeyPress(e) {
     if (e.keyCode == 13) {
        learnerResponse = document.getElementById
("learnerResponse").value;
        if (learnerResponse == num1 + num2) {
           resultString = learnerResponse + " Correct";
        }
        else {
          resultString = learnerResponse + " No, " +
num1 + " + " + num2 + " = " + (num1 + num2); // " No,
correct answer is "
        }

     document.getElementById("learnerResponse").
value = "";
     document.getElementById("workSpace").
innerHTML = document.getElementById("workSpace").
innerHTML + " " + resultString + "<br />" +
getQuestion();
     }
  }
</script>

</body>
</html>
```

Rather than require the learner to press a button in order to submit the response, the `processKeyPress` function detects when the learner has pressed the Enter/Return key. Every user interaction, such as a key press, a mouse click, or mouse movement, triggers an event or events. A mouse click, for instance, triggers *mouse down* and *mouse up* events. JavaScript provides an `onKeyPress` event to detect when a key press is complete (a key that was once pressed down is now back up). The input tag for the `learnerResponse` field directs the computer to call the `processKeyPress` function (`onKeyPress="processKeyPress(event)"`) after each key press. Given the first statement in the `processKeyPress` function, all key presses except the Enter/Return key are ignored. Some keyboards have a Return key while other keyboards have an Enter key. Although the label is different, the Enter and Return key produce the same key code, which is decimal value 13. When that key is detected, the following statement retrieves the user response and assigns it to the `learnerResponse` variable.

```
learnerResponse    =    document.getElementById
("learnerResponse").value;
```

Then, using the subsequent `if` statement, the learner's response is compared with the correct answer and the appropriate feedback string is produced. Lastly, the feedback and the next question are displayed by the following statement.

```
document.getElementById("workSpace").innerHTML    =
document.getElementById("workSpace").innerHTML+" "+
resultString + "<br />" + getQuestion();
```

Task 4.4 Copy *webApp1pa.html* to *webApp1pm.html*. Then, as in Chapter 3, replace the addition operator (+) with the multiplication operator (*) to enable the learner to practice multiplication. Also change each statement producing a random number to yield a random number between 1 and 12. Further, replace the word *adding* with the word *multiplying* in the `<title> </title>` tag.

Task 4.5 In *webApp1pm.html*, vary the maximum random number generated in accordance with the learner's performance. For example, after obtaining five consecutive correct answers (or achieving 80 percent correct answers on at least five attempts) with random numbers from 1 to 4, increase the maximum random number to 6. Then, after obtaining five consecutive correct answers (or achieving 80 percent correct answers on at least five attempts) with random numbers from 1 to 6, increase the maximum random number to 8. Continue the pattern until the maximum random number is 12.

Task 4.6 Write an app that enables learners to practice subtraction. Ensure that the difference is always a positive number or zero.

Task 4.7 Consider designing and writing an app that enables learners to practice division. Would such an app be helpful? What would be some of the benefits and limitations of the app?

4.4 Learning Words in Multiple Languages

Instruction often involves use of multiple media, which enables learners to consider information in multiple forms. Educational research has revealed that consideration of information in multiple forms to facilitate dual coding is beneficial for learning (Mayer, 2009; Paivio, 1971, 1986). To help learners recognize spoken words for colors, this web app uses sound and colored rectangles.

Web App 2: Learning Words for Colors in Multiple Languages

TARGET LEARNERS: People capable of selecting a rectangle upon hearing a sound.
INSTRUCTIONAL OBJECTIVE: The learner will be able to correctly recognize spoken words for colors in English, French, and Spanish at least 80 percent of the time.

Design

This app presents color swatches (rectangles). For color image, see Figure 4.2 in the eResources. Though unknown to the learner, this app also loads audio files

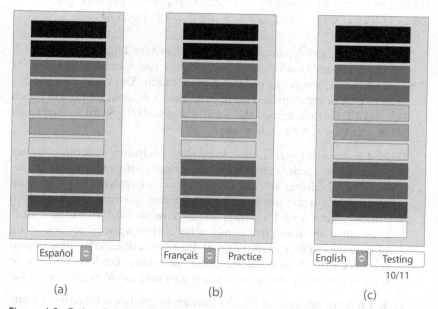

(a)   (b)   (c)

Figure 4.2 Color Swatches with Language Selection Menu and Mode Button.

of the spoken words of the colors in English, Spanish, and French. When the learner clicks a swatch, the app plays the file that speaks the color of the swatch. The learner can select to learn the color words in English, Spanish, or French, as per Figure 4.2(a). The learner can also toggle between Practice and Test modes (see Practice/Test toggle button in Figure 4.2(b)). In Test mode, the app plays the file that speaks a color in the selected language and the learner responds by clicking the appropriate rectangle. The app keeps a tally of correct answers and displays a tally of correct replies to total items, as per Figure 4.2(c).

Development

This web app could be implemented with a series of colored buttons, but in order to introduce graphics programming on a two-dimensional grid, this app use the HTML *canvas* element. The first stage of development will display the colored rectangles on the canvas, load the sound files (which are included in the eResources), detect each mouse click on the canvas, and play the spoken word in Spanish for the color clicked.

The second stage will add the drop-down menu enabling the learner to select either English, Spanish (*Español*), or French (*Français*). In this second stage of development we will make the program more robust by changing the data structures from one-dimensional arrays to two-dimensional arrays. The sound files for English and French will be loaded in order for words to be spoken in those languages, in addition to Spanish.

The third and final stage of development for this web app will add the button to toggle between Practice and Test modes. Code for the test mode will be added to select a color at random, speak the world for the color, and determine whether the learner selected the swatch matching the color spoken.

FIRST STAGE OF DEVELOPMENT

Open a new document in your text editor and enter the following text. Save the file as *webApp2swr.html*. (The acronym swr is used for Spoken Word Recognition.)

```
<html>
<head>
<title>Practice   Colors   in   Multiple   Languages
</title>
</head>
<body onload="init()" style="margin: 0px">
<canvas id="theCanvas" width="150" height="300">
</canvas>
<script>
  var canvas;
```

```
  var canvasContext;

  var colorStringEnglish =
"black:brown:gray:red:pink:orange:yellow:green:
blue:purple:white";
  var colorStringSpanish = "negro:marron:gris:rojo
:rosa:naranja:amarillo:verde:azul:violeta:blanco";
  var colorWordsEnglish = [];
  var colorWordsSpanish = [];
  var colorRefs = [];

  function init() {
    colorWordsEnglish = colorStringEnglish.split(":");
    colorWordsSpanish = colorStringSpanish.split(":");

    canvas = document.getElementById("theCanvas");
    canvasContext = canvas.getContext("2d");
    canvasContext.fillStyle = "#E0E0E0"; // light gray color
    canvasContext.fillRect(0,0,150,300); // to see the canvas

    for (var i = 0; i <= 10; i++) {
      canvasContext.fillStyle = colorWordsEnglish[i];
      canvasContext.fillRect(30, 15 + i * 25, 90, 20);
    }
  } // "init"
</script>
</body>
</html>
```

The opening <body> tag, which appears below, contains two attributes, namely onload and style. As in the previous web app, the onload attribute is used to execute the initialization code in the init function when the web page loads. Setting the margin to 0 in the style attribute eliminates the default white space at the top of the web browser's content space.

```
<body onload="init()" style="margin: 0px">
```

The canvas element is added using the line of HTML below. The width and height attributes specify the canvas size in pixels. As before, the id attribute enables subsequent access to the component.

```
<canvas id="theCanvas" width="150" height="300">
</canvas>
```

The javascript code within the <script> ... </script> tag begins with seven variable declarations and ends with the code for the initialization function. The need for the variables will become clear in light of the statements in the initialization function, `init`.

The first line of JavaScript in function `init()` appears below.

```
colorWordsEnglish = colorStringEnglish.split(":");
```

That line initializes each value of the `colorWordsEnglish` array to one color. The variable, `colorStringEnglish` contains 11 colors separated by the : character. Following are the values in `colorWordsEnglish` array due to the `split` command.

```
colorWordsEnglish[0]  is "black"
colorWordsEnglish[1]  is "brown"
colorWordsEnglish[2]  is "gray"
colorWordsEnglish[3]  is "red"
colorWordsEnglish[4]  is "pink"
colorWordsEnglish[5]  is "orange"
colorWordsEnglish[6]  is "yellow"
colorWordsEnglish[7]  is "green"
colorWordsEnglish[8]  is "blue"
colorWordsEnglish[9]  is "purple"
colorWordsEnglish[10] is "white"
```

With the following line of JavaScript, the `colorWordsSpanish` array is initialized to equivalent color words in Spanish.

```
colorWordsSpanish = colorStringSpanish.split(":");
```

```
colorWordsSpanish[0]  is "negro"
colorWordsSpanish[1]  is "marron"
.
.
.
colorWordsSpanish[10] is "blanco"
```

The next two lines set the `canvas` and `canvasContext` variables. The `canvas` variable enables access to the canvas context and `canvasContext` enables drawing on the canvas.

```
canvas = document.getElementById("theCanvas");
canvasContext = canvas.getContext("2d");
```

The following two lines are optional, but useful. Without them, the canvas would not be visible in the web browser (assuming a default white background color for the web page). The canvas is made visible by drawing a rectangle in light gray over the entire canvas. To accomplish this, the fill color, technically the `fillStyle`, of the canvas context is set to a hexadecimal (base 16) number representing a mix of red, green, and blue. These primary colors are mixed in equal parts (decimal value 224, which is E0 in hexadecimal) to produce the light gray. [You do not need to know how to convert between decimal and hexadecimal to program this app. Just know that in the following line of code, the # character indicates that a hexadecimal number follows.] With the `fillStyle` set to light gray, the `fillRect` method fills the rectangle from the upper left of the canvas, which has coordinates (0,0), to the bottom right corner, which has coordinates (150,300) and is the precise width and height of the canvas.

```
canvasContext.fillStyle = "#E0E0E0"; // light gray color
canvasContext.fillRect(0,0,150,300); // to see the canvas
```

The following loop sets the `fillStyle` to each of the colors in the `colorWordsEnglish` array and displays a rectangle 90 pixels wide and 20 pixels high in each of the 11 colors in the `colorWordsEnglish` array. The upper-left corner of each rectangle begins in Column 30. The row of the upper-left corner of each rectangle varies according to the expression, $15 + i * 25$ where i is the color number, which goes from 0 to 10. The first rectangle has index (i) equal to 0, which puts the upper-left corner at (30,15). The second rectangle has i equal to 1, which puts the upper-left corner at (30,40). The remaining rectangles, with i going from 2 to 10, have upper-left corners at (30,65), (30,90), (30,115), (30,140), (30,165), (30,190), (30,215), (30,240), and (30,265).

```
for (var i = 0; i <= 10; i++) {
    canvasContext.fillStyle = colorWordsEnglish[i];
    canvasContext.fillRect(30, 15 + i * 25, 90, 20);
}
```

[Note: The default brown color may be unsatisfying. We adjust the brown color below.]

At this point we have colored rectangles on a light gray background. That alone may not be too thrilling for users, but you should be delighted because attaining this state of the app requires mastery of HTML and JavaScript. Well done. Next we enable interactivity by adding mouse click detection and responding to each mouse click by playing the sound file that speaks the appropriate color word.

In the folder containing the *webApp2swr.html* file, create a folder called audio, and place the ten Spanish audio files in the audio folder (or put all 30 audio files in the eResources into the audio folder because all 30 audio files will be needed soon). The following code will be inserted into the `init()` function to ensure that the audio files are loaded when the web page is rendered in the web browser, which will make the sounds available when needed.

```
for (var i = 0; i <= 10; i++) {
   colorRefs[i] = new Audio("audio/" + colorWordsSpanish
[i] + ".mp3");
   }
```

At times it may help to insert some alerts in the code to assist with debugging (in case you do not write perfect code). For example, it may be helpful to insert the following alert statement to display the path used to access each audio file.

```
for (var i = 0; i <= 10; i++) {
   alert("audio/" + colorWordsSpanish[i] + ".mp3");
   colorRefs[i] = new Audio("audio/" + colorWordsSpanish
[i] + ".mp3");
   }
```

You may prefer displaying output for debugging purposes to the console. If so, just substitute `console.log` for `alert`. During debugging, we will also insert a few other statements to assure ourselves that we are making progress. For example, we will insert the following statement in a strategic place in the `init()` function in order to verify that the last sound file loaded properly because the code below will play the file to speak the word in Spanish for white, which is *blanco*.

```
colorRefs[10].play();
```

In order to detect mouse clicks on a canvas object in a web page, we need to add an *event listener* to the canvas. (Similarly, event listeners are added to various objects in other app development environments in order to enable user interactivity.) Adding the event listener is accomplished with the following line of code.

```
canvas.addEventListener("mouseup",    mouseUpDetected,
false);
```

In JavaScript, an event listener is added to a web page canvas using the `addEventListener` function, which has three parameters: (1) The event to be detected; (2) The name of the function to call when the event is detected; and (3) A Boolean variable for the capture phase. In this case, we are looking for a `mouseup` event, which occurs when the user releases the mouse button. When a `mouseup` event has been detected, the code will call the `mouseUpDetected` function (which appears below). Without getting into too much technical detail about phases of mouse clicks, we set the third parameter to false because the capture phase (mouse button down) has ended prior to the `mouseup` event. Recall that we set the canvas variable using the following statement:

```
canvas = document.getElementById("theCanvas");
```

We will add the event listener to the canvas immediately after that statement. When the program runs, the mouseUpDetected function must exist because it is identified in the addEventListener method.

```
function mouseUpDetected() {
    console.log("mouse click detected");
} // "mouseUpDetected"
```

In your text editor, insert the loop above to load the sound files. Also insert the statement to add the event listener and include the mouseUpDetected function above. Lastly, include the statement to play the last sound file, which enables us to verify that the software for playing audio and the hardware (the computer's speaker) is functional. The code below implements those changes. Save the changes, run, and debug as necessary.

```
<html>
<head>
<title>Practice    Colors    in    Multiple    Languages
</title>
</head>
<body onload="init()" style="margin: 0px">
<canvas id="theCanvas" width="150" height="300">
</canvas>
<script>
  var canvas;
  var canvasContext;

  var colorStringEnglish = "black:brown:gray:red:
pink:orange:yellow:green:blue:purple:white";
  var    colorStringSpanish    =    "negro:marron:gris:
rojo:rosa:naranja:amarillo:verde:azul:violeta:
blanco";
  var colorWordsEnglish = [];
  var colorWordsSpanish = [];
  var colorRefs = [];

  function init() {
    colorWordsEnglish = colorStringEnglish.split(":");
    colorWordsSpanish = colorStringSpanish.split(":");
    for (var i = 0; i <= 10; i++) {
      alert("audio/" + colorWordsSpanish[i] + ".mp3");
```

```
      colorRefs[i] = new Audio("audio/" +
colorWordsSpanish[i] + ".mp3");
    }
    colorRefs[10].play();

    canvas = document.getElementById("theCanvas");
    canvas.addEventListener("mouseup",
    mouseUpDetected, false);
    canvasContext = canvas.getContext("2d");
    canvasContext.fillStyle = "#E0E0E0"; // light gray
color
    canvasContext.fillRect(0,0,150,300); // to see the
canvas

    for (var i = 0; i <= 10; i++) {
      canvasContext.fillStyle = colorWordsEnglish[i];
      canvasContext.fillRect(30, 15 + i * 25, 90, 20);
    }
  } // "init"

  function mouseUpDetected() {
    console.log("mouse click detected");
  } // "mouseUpDetected"
</script>
</body>
</html>
```

Currently, this web app detects mouse clicks on the canvas and you have verified that the last sound file loaded is working. To complete this first stage of development, we need only play the appropriate color word for each mouse click over a colored rectangle. A "mouse up" event provides the position of the tip of the mouse cursor when the mouse button is released. (A computer mouse may have more than one button. In those cases, programmers can determine which button was clicked in addition to the mouse cursor position.) The position of the tip of the mouse is a point, which is available through its x and y coordinates.

In the updated mouseUpDetected function below, notice the event parameter in the function definition. The event parameter is an object containing information about the mouseup event, which is used to determine the point at which the user clicked the canvas. The first two statements of the mouseUpDetected function below set the variables x and y to the position of the tip of the mouse cursor at the time of the "mouse up" event (i.e., when the mouse button is released). The third statement in the function calculates the index into the colorRefs array in order to play the correct color word. The first rectangle, which is the black rectangle, has its upper-left corner at (30,15). Since the width of each rectangle is 90 pixels and the height is 20 pixels, the lower right corner is at (120,35). Every click on a rectangle will be between columns 30 and 120. The row (or y coordinate) determines which rectangle is clicked. If the y coordinate is between 15 and 35, the first (black) rectangle was clicked. The second (brown) rectangle is between 40 and 60; the third is between 65 and 85. The pattern continues through the last (white) rectangle, which is on rows 265 to 285. If you subtract 15 from the y-coordinate (which is the offset from the top of the canvas to the first rectangle), divide that difference by 25, and truncate the result (which eliminates the decimal part), you get the correct index to the color array. Hence, the following statement is used to set the index variable.

```
index = Math.trunc((y - 15) / 25);
```

There is a 4-pixel gap between each rectangle. Technically, no color word should be spoken when the user clicks between rectangles. Ensuring that does not happen is left as an exercise (Task 4.8).

In your text editor, replace the mouseUpDetected() function with the following.

```
function mouseUpDetected(event) {
    var x = event.pageX;
    var y = event.pageY;
    var index = Math.trunc((y - 15) / 25);
    if (x > 29 && x < 121 && y > 14 && y < 286) {
        colorRefs[index].play();
    }
    alert(x + " " + y + " " + index);
} // "mouseUpDetected"
```

Save, run, and debug as necessary. Remove alerts after the program is functioning well. You can "comment out" an alert statement by inserting two forward slash characters before the statement or by deleting the alert statement.

If you want to see the codes for the left, middle, and right mouse buttons, insert console.log(event.button) in the mouseUpDetected function. Even if your mouse has only one button, you could verify that the mouse button code for a one-button mouse is 0. You could also try Shift-mouse click, Alt-mouse click, and Ctrl-mouse click to determine the results.

At this point, the app is playing the sound of the color clicked, but that occurs even when gray space between the colored rectangles is clicked. Implement the following remedy.

Task 4.8 Ensure that the app does not play a sound file when the learner clicks in the gray space between the colored rectangles.

Tips: The gray space between the first two rectangles occurs at rows 36, 37, 38, and 39. Since each rectangle and the gray space below it comprise 25 pixels, the gray space between the second and third rectangles occurs at rows 61 (36 + 25), 62 (37 + 25), 63 (38 + 25), and 64 (39 + 25). Adding 25 to 61, 62, 63, and 64 yields 86, 87, 88, and 89, which are the rows in the canvas of the gray space between the third and fourth rectangles. The pattern continues. What do 36, 61, and 86 have in common? They are the first row of gray space between two colored rectangles and the remainder after dividing each of those numbers by 25 is 11. Given a number and a divisor, the arithmetic operator called the *modulus* will calculate the remainder of the number after division by the divisor. In JavaScript, the percent symbol (%) is the modulus operator. [You are probably already very familiar with searching the web for such a detail. Indeed, a Google search for *javascript modulus operator* yields hyperlinks to multiple web pages listing the arithmetic operators in JavaScript. For instance, try the Google search or see www.w3schools.com/js/js_arithmetic.asp. In addition to finding the modulus operator at w3schools, the web search also provided a particular link to a web page containing the answer at the Mozilla Developer Network (http://developer.mozilla.org).] In the `mouseUpDetected` function, setting a variable to `y % 25` is useful for determining when the learner has clicked between rectangles. In addition to 11, determine the other three values of `y % 25` for clicks in the gray space between rectangles. Then modify the `if` statement in the `mouseUpDetected` function accordingly to prevent a color word from playing when the learner clicks the gray space between the colored rectangles. After all, the learner has not clicked on a colored rectangle so no color name should be heard.

SECOND STAGE OF DEVELOPMENT

In this developmental stage we will insert a drop-down menu, which will enable the learner to select one of three languages. (You may wish to add more languages, which is encouraged, per Task 4.9.) In the first developmental stage we used one-dimensional arrays for specific languages (e.g., `colorWordsSpanish`, `colorStringSpanish`, `colorWordsEnglish`, and `colorStringEnglish`), which works, but an approach that favors extensibility is preferred. Rather than use one-dimensional arrays for each language, we will use two-dimensional arrays (one two-dimensional array for the file name of each color in each language and one two-dimensional array for the contents of each audio file in each language). The first index in the two-dimensional arrays will be the language code (0 for English; 1 for Spanish; and 2 for French). The second index will be the color index (0 for black; 1 for brown; 2 for gray; 3 for red; 4 for pink; 5 for orange; 6 for yellow; 7 for green; 8 for blue; 9 for purple; and 10 for white).

In HTML, a drop-down menu is created with the select tag, as shown below.

```
<select id="languageCode" onChange="getLanguageCode()">
  <option value="0">English</option>
  <option value="1">Español</option>
  <option value="2">Français</option>
</select>
```

Two attributes appear in the `select` tag. The `id` attribute provides a reference to the drop-down menu. The `onChange` attribute identifies the function called when a new item is selected from the menu. Each option tag identifies a unique menu item. The value attribute in each option tag is the language code. When the learner changes the language by selecting a new menu item, the `getLanguageCode` function uses the following line of code to set the `crntLanguageCode` variable to the value of the menu item selected.

```
crntLanguageCode       =       document.getElementById
('languageCode').value;
```

With respect to the JavaScript, which in HTML always appears within the `<script> </script>` tag, some variable declarations have changed from the previous version. In particular, `colorStringEnglish` and `colorStringSpanish` were replaced with `colorStrings`, which is now a one-dimensional array initialized to the three strings of the words in English, Spanish, and French for the 11 colors we are using. In each string, the words are separated by the colon (`:`) character. Note that in the list of French words for colors, *marron, gris*, and *orange* appear as `marronF`, `grisF`, and `orangeF` because *marron, gris*, and *orange* appear previously in either the English or Spanish words for colors. Each name in `colorStrings` must be unique in order to read the audio file for the color.

Also in the variable declarations, `colorWordsEnglish = []` and `colorWordsSpanish = []` have been replaced with `colorWords = []`, which will be a two-dimensional array. If the version of JavaScript used in web browsers was the same as Spider Monkey JavaScript, `colorWords = []` would have been declared as `colorWords = [[]]` (an array of arrays, as per the declaration in Chapter 3). However, the version of JavaScript in web browsers requires the syntax for a one-dimensional array and then, in the JavaScript code, a one-dimensional array is inserted into a one-dimensional array, thereby making a two-dimensional array. We will return to this after one more comment about a variable declaration.

In the variable declarations, the statement `crntLanguageCode = 0;` is used to set English as the default language. However, that default value is arbitrary, as is the order of the strings in the `colorStrings` variable. Replacing the 0 with 1 would make Spanish the default language;

replacing the 0 with 2 would make French the default language. Alternatively, the default language could be changed by reordering the strings in the `colorStrings` variable. Crucially, the programmer must be consistent. Since we established the language codes earlier (0 for English; 1 for Spanish; and 2 for French), we will retain the current order of the strings in the `colorStrings` variable.

Having completed the discussion of the variable declarations, we proceed with the changes to the `init()` function, which brings us back to the method for initializing the two-dimensional arrays, namely `colorWords` and `colorRefs`. The following code initializes those two arrays.

```
for (i = 0; i < colorStrings.length; i++) {
    crntColorWords = colorStrings[i].split(":");
    colorWords.push(crntColorWords);

    for (var j = 0; j < crntColorWords.length; j++) {
        crntColorRefs[j]    =    new    Audio("audio/"    +
colorWords[i][j] + ".mp3");
    }

    colorRefs.push(crntColorRefs);
}
```

The first time in the outer loop, `i = 0`. Hence, in the first statement of the loop body, the one dimensional array `crntColorWords` becomes the color words in English (i.e., `crntColorWords[0]` is black, `crntColorWords[1]` is brown, `crntColorWords[2]` is gray, ..., `crntColorWords[10]` is white). The second statement in the loop body (i.e., `colorWords.push(crntColorWords);`) sets the first entry of the two-dimensional `colorWords` array to the `crntColorWords` array, which appears as the first row of data in Table 4.1. The inner loop (which varies the loop control variable `j` from 0 to 10 because there are 11 color words), stores the audio object for each of the color words in English in the array, `crntColorRefs`. The last statement in the body of the outer loop (i.e., `colorRefs.push(crntColorRefs);`) sets the first entry of the two-dimensional `colorRefs` array to the `crntColorRefs` array. The second and third iterations of the outer and inner loops above set the second and third rows of the `colorWords` and `colorRefs` arrays.

Structurally, the two-dimensional arrays are identical, as per Table 4.1, but `colorWords` is filled with strings (one for each color word) whereas each element in the `colorRefs` array is an audio object. The row index is the language code (0, 1, or 2) and the column index is the color code (0, 1, 2, ... 10). Given this method for initializing the arrays, access to the Spanish word "*rojo*," for instance, would be through `colorWords[1][3]` and access to the audio object for "*rojo*" (the spoken word "*rojo*") would

Table 4.1 Values in the colorWords array after initialization

	0	1	2	3	4	5	6	7	8	9	10
0	black	brown	gray	red	pink	orange	yellow	green	blue	purple	white
1	negro	marron	gris	rojo	rosa	naranja	amarillo	verde	azul	violeta	blanco
2	noir	marronF	grisF	rouge	rose	orangeF	jaune	vert	bleu	violet	blanc

be through `colorRefs[1][3]`. In the code below, notice the explicit reference to `colorWords[0][1]`, which is the English word "brown" (per Table 4.1). Web browsers seem to render that "brown" like a red (even after adjusting the angle of eyes relative to the computer monitor) so in the code below, `colorWords[0][1]` = `"#8B4513";` replaces the word "brown" with a hexadecimal value for a mix of red, green, and blue, which appears more like brown. To avoid any possible side effect of this "hack," `colorWords[0][1]` is set back to "brown" a couple of lines of code later. Both of those assignments statements are optional. If satisfied with the default "brown" color displayed in your web browser, you are free to delete the following two statements from the code below.

```
colorWords[0][1] = "#8B4513";
colorWords[0][1] = "brown";
```

The key changes between the first and second developmental stages of this app are the introduction of a drop-down menu to enable language selection and implementation of the two-dimensional arrays, which together make this app extensible. For example, adding another language requires inserting one more option to the `languageCode` drop-down menu, plus adding one more string of color words to `colorStrings` and adding 11 more audio files with unique file names.

The magnitude of the changes is of such significance that you might wish to retain the code for the first version of this app. Indeed, it is often helpful to apply version control during the development process in order to retain prior versions of computer programs. (Computer programmers sometimes revert to prior versions.) Accordingly, rename *webapp2swr.html* to *webapp2swr001.html*. Then copy *webapp2swr001.html* to *webapp2swr002.html*. In your text editor, edit *webapp2swr002.html* to contain the code below. (Some alerts are "commented out," but if you wish, you can enable those alerts by deleting the two slash characters in front of the alert.) Save the file. Ensure that all 30 audio files are in the audio folder. Double-click the *webapp2swr002.html* icon in order to run the program. Debug as necessary; smile when the code is functional.

```
<html>
<head>
<title>Practice    Colors    in    Multiple    Languages
</title>
```

```
</head>

<body onload="init()" style ="margin: 0px">
<canvas    id="theCanvas"    width="150"    height="300">
</canvas>
<p></p>
<div style="padding-left: 35px">
<select id="languageCode" onChange="getLanguageCode()">
  <option value="0">English</option>
  <option value="1">Español</option>
  <option value="2">Français</option>
</select>
</div>

<script>
    var canvas;
    var canvasContext;

    var colorStrings = ["black:brown:gray:red:pink
:orange:yellow:green:blue:purple:white",
"negro:marron:gris:rojo:rosa:naranja:amarillo:verde:a
zul:violeta:blanco",
"noir:marronF:grisF:rouge:rose:orangeF:jaune:vert:ble
u:violet:blanc"];

    var crntColorWords = [];
    var crntColorRefs = [];
    var colorWords = [];
    var colorRefs = [];
    var crntLanguageCode = 0;

    function init() {
        for (i = 0; i < colorStrings.length; i++) {
            crntColorWords = colorStrings[i].split(":");
            colorWords.push(crntColorWords);

            for (var j = 0; j < crntColorWords.length; j++) {
                crntColorRefs[j] = new Audio("audio/"
+ colorWords[i][j] + ".mp3");
            }
            colorRefs.push(crntColorRefs);
        }
//colorRefs[crntLanguageCode][10].play();

        canvas = document.getElementById("theCanvas");
        canvas.addEventListener("mouseup", mouseUpDetected,
false);
```

```
        canvasContext = canvas.getContext("2d");
        canvasContext.fillStyle = "#E0E0E0";
        canvasContext.fillRect(0,0,150,300);

        colorWords[0][1] = "#8B4513";
        for (var i = 0; i <= 10; i++) {
            canvasContext.fillStyle = colorWords[0][i];
            canvasContext.fillRect(30, 15 + i * 25, 90, 20);
        }
        colorWords[0][1] = "brown";
    } // "init"

    function mouseUpDetected(event) {
        var x = event.pageX;
        var y = event.pageY;
        var crntColorIndex = Math.trunc((y - 15) / 25);
        var yMod25 = y % 25;

        if (x > 29 && x < 121 && y > 14 && y < 286 &&
(yMod25 < 10 || yMod25 > 14)) {
            colorRefs[crntLanguageCode][crntColorIndex].
            play();
        }
    //alert(x + " " + y + " color index: " + crntColorIndex +
" language code: " + crntLanguageCode);
    //console.log("event button code: " + event.button);
    } // "mouseUpDetected"

    function getLanguageCode() {
        crntLanguageCode = document.getElementById
('languageCode').value;
//alert(crntLanguageCode);
    } // "getLanguageCode"
</script>
</body>
</html>
```

Task 4.9 Implement another language or languages.

Tips: Insert the string for the 11 new color words, separated by the : character, into the `colorStrings` variable. (You may find translate.google. com helpful for determining color words in numerous languages.) Those words will be the filenames to the sound files, which you will need to record. (The Google translation tool at translate.google.com will also speak the words if you wish to hear them before recording each word.)

Also, as noted previously, add one item to the drop-down menu for each new language you implement. For example, you could insert the following HTML <option> ... </option> tags if implementing Portuguese and German.

```
<option value="3">Português</option>
<option value="4">Deutsche</option>
```

THIRD STAGE OF DEVELOPMENT

In this stage of development, we add a button enabling the learner to switch (toggle) between Practice and Test mode. Practice mode is precisely the functionality achieved at the end of the second stage of development. In Test Mode, the app selects a color word at random and presents the sound of the word. The learner responds by clicking a colored rectangle, which should be the color of the word spoken. To provide feedback, the app will tally and display the number of correct answers and the number of items presented. Such feedback may be regarded as rather subtle and learners might conceive of such feedback favorably or unfavorably. (You will have the opportunity to alter the feedback in Task 4.12.)

The following HTML tag adds the button enabling the user to toggle between Practice and Test mode.

```
<button id="toggleMode" type="button" style="width:
70px" onclick="processButtonClick()">Practice</button>
```

The button has three attributes. The id attribute provides a reference to the button. The `onclick` attribute identifies the function called when the learner clicks the button. The style attribute sets the width of the button to 70 pixels. In Practice mode, the button label is *Practice*. In Test mode, the button label is *Testing*. Since the button labels, *Practice* and *Testing*, render in different sizes, specifying a fixed button width (70 pixels in this case) is necessary to avoid the dynamic resizing of the button, which many users would find annoying.

The following HTML tag allocates space for the feedback.

```
<div id="feedback" style="margin-top: 3px; margin-left:
90px"></div>
```

The `id` attribute provides a reference to the feedback space, which is where the tallies of correct answers and total items will be displayed. Rather than display the feedback at the left edge of the browser window, the style attribute positions the output underneath the toggle button (as per Figure 4.2c).

Regarding new code, we will add the four variable declarations below. The first variable declaration below makes Practice mode the default mode. This is not arbitrary: In this case, learners will have the opportunity to practice before testing. (An alternative scenario could implement a pretest. A pretesting scenario would prevent the learner from entering Practice mode at will.)

```
var crntMode = "Practice";
var randomNum;
var numItems = 0;
var numCorrect = 0;
```

The code for this development stage includes two new functions. The processButtonClick function processes each click on the toggle button. The getTestItem() function generates a test item.

The code for the processButtonClick function appears below.

```
function processButtonClick() {
    crntMode = (crntMode == "Practice") ? "Testing" :
"Practice";

    document.getElementById('toggleMode').
innerHTML = crntMode;
    if(crntMode == "Testing") {
        numItems = 0;
        numCorrect = 0;
        getTestItem();
    }
    document.getElementById('feedback').innerHTML = "";
} // "processButtonClick"
```

The first line of code in the processButtonClick function toggles the value of the crntMode variable. The first line of code is equivalent to the following.

```
if (crntMode == "Practice") {
    crntMode = "Testing"
}
else {
    crntMode = "Practice";
}
```

The second line of code in the processButtonClick function changes the button label to either *Practice* or *Testing*.

Within the if statement, which is executed in Test Mode, the tallies of total test items and total number of correct answers for the current test administration are set to zero. Also, the getTestItem function is called to get the next test item.

As per the code below, the getTestItem function selects a random number between 0 and 11, retrieves the sound object for the color word randomly selected, and plays the sound object.

```
function getTestItem() {
    var crntSound;

    randomNum = Math.floor(Math.random() * 11);
    crntSound = colorRefs[crntLanguageCode][randomNum];
    crntSound.play();
```

```
} // "getTestItem"
```

Lastly, for this stage of the web app, one `if` statement is added to the `mouseUpDetected` function in order maintain the correct answer tally during Test mode and to play the color word sound during Practice mode.

Copy *webapp2swr002.html* to *webapp2swr003.html*. In your text editor, edit *webapp2swr003.html* to make the changes discussed above for the third developmental stage (which will result in the code below). Save the file. Then double-click the *webapp2swr003.html* icon in order to run the program. Debug as necessary; smile when the code is functional.

```html
<html>
<head>
<title>Practice    Colors    in    Multiple    Languages
</title>
</head>

<body onload="init()" style ="margin: 0px">

<canvas  id="theCanvas"  width="150"  height="300">
</canvas>
<p></p>

<select   id="languageCode"   onChange="getLanguage
Code()">
  <option value="0">English</option>
  <option value="1">Español</option>
  <option value="2">Français</option>
</select>

<button  id="toggleMode"  type="button"  style="width:
70px" onclick="processButtonClick()">Practice</button>
<div id="feedback" style="margin-top: 3px; margin-left:
90px"></div>

<script>
  var canvas;
  var canvasContext;

  var  colorStrings  =  ["black:brown:gray:red:pink:
orange:yellow:green:blue:purple:white",
"negro:marron:gris:rojo:rosa:naranja:amarillo:
verde:azul:violeta:blanco",    "noir:marronF:grisF:
rouge:rose:orangeF:jaune:vert:bleu:violet:blanc"];

  var crntColorWords = [];
  var crntColorRefs = [];
  var colorWords = [];
  var colorRefs = [];
```

```
var crntLanguageCode = 0;
var crntMode = "Practice";
var randomNum;
var numItems = 0;
var numCorrect = 0;
function init() {
   for (i = 0; i < colorStrings.length; i++) {
      crntColorWords = colorStrings[i].split(":");
      colorWords.push(crntColorWords);

      for (var j = 0; j < crntColorWords.length; j++) {
      crntColorRefs[j]  =  new  Audio("audio/"  +
      colorWords[i][j] + ".mp3");
      }
      colorRefs.push(crntColorRefs);
   }
//colorRefs[crntLanguageCode][10].play();

   canvas = document.getElementById("theCanvas");
   canvas.addEventListener("mouseup", mouseUpDetected,
false);

   canvasContext = canvas.getContext("2d");
   canvasContext.fillStyle = "#E0E0E0";
   canvasContext.fillRect(0,0,150,300);

   colorWords[0][1] = "#8B4513";
   for (var i = 0; i <= 10; i++) {
      canvasContext.fillStyle = colorWords[0][i];
      canvasContext.fillRect(30, 15 + i * 25, 90, 20);
   }
   colorWords[0][1] = "brown";
} // "init"

function mouseUpDetected(event) {
   var x = event.pageX;
   var y = event.pageY;
   var crntColorIndex = Math.trunc((y - 15) / 25);
   var yMod25 = y % 25;

   if (x > 29 && x < 121 && y > 14 && y < 286 &&
(yMod25 < 10 || yMod25 > 14)) {
      if (crntMode == "Testing") {
         numItems++;
         if (crntColorIndex == randomNum) {
           numCorrect++;
         }
         document.getElementById('feedback').
innerHTML = numCorrect + "/" + numItems;
```

```
              getTestItem();
              }
              else {
                colorRefs[crntLanguageCode][crntColor
Index].play();
              }
          }
//alert(x + " " + y + " color index: " + crntColorIndex
+ " language code: " + crntLanguageCode);
//console.log("event  button  code:  "  +  event.
button);
  } // "mouseUpDetected"

  function getLanguageCode() {
    crntLanguageCode  =  document.getElementById
('languageCode').value;
//alert(crntLanguageCode);
  } // "getLanguageCode"

  function getTestItem() {
    var crntSound;

    randomNum = Math.floor(Math.random() * 11);
    crntSound = colorRefs[crntLanguageCode][randomNum];
    crntSound.play();
  } // "getTestItem"

  function processButtonClick() {
    crntMode = (crntMode == "Practice") ? "Testing" :
"Practice";
document.getElementById('toggleMode').
innerHTML = crntMode;
    if (crntMode == "Testing") {
        numItems = 0;
        numCorrect = 0;
        getTestItem();
    }
    document.getElementById('feedback').
innerHTML = "";
  } // "processButtonClick"
</script>

</body>
</html>
```

Task 4.10 Modify the design of the interface to display the word for each
color. Implement the design modification.

Figure 4.3 Text Position Determined by Upper-left Corner of Bounding Box.

Tips: To display text on a web page canvas, a developer may use the fillText method, as shown below. The example below displays "Hello, World!" Though not visible on the actual canvas, there is actually a bounding box surrounding "Hello, World!" and the upper-left corner of the bounding box is at (100,30), which is 100 pixels from the left edge of the canvas and 30 pixels down from the top row of the canvas, as per Figure 4.3.

```
canvasContext.fillText("Hello, World!",250,90);
```

If you want to set the font size and type before displaying text on a canvas, use the font method, as shown below.

```
canvasContext.font = "30px Arial";
canvasContext.fillText("Hello, World!",100,30);
```

If you prefer to outline the text, rather than fill the text, use strokeText, as shown below.

```
canvasContext.font = "30px Arial";
canvasContext.strokeText("Hello, World!",100,30);
```

For additional information about fillText and strokeText, see this web page: www.w3schools.com/graphics/canvas_text.asp

For information about common fonts in HTML, you may wish to see this web page: www.yourhtmlsource.com/text/font.html

Task 4.11 Consider design options for enabling the learner to determine whether the color words (implemented in Task 4.10) are visible or hidden. Reflect on how adding features to an existing app or to a new app complicates both the design and development of the app. Also reflect on the uncertainties of design choices. Perhaps many users will favor your design decisions, but some users may not: Then what should you do? Implement a design option that enables the learner to display or hide the color words.

Task 4.12 Incrementing a tally is a rather subtle form of feedback. Consider design options, which may involve text and/or sound, for making the feedback obvious. Implement at least one design option for providing obvious feedback.

Task 4.13 Display an image on a canvas element. The `drawImage` method is similar to the `fillText` method. In fact, the second and third parameters of both methods are identical. The difference is in the first parameter. The first parameter of `fillText` is the string of text to be displayed, whereas the first parameter of `drawImage` is the image object to be displayed. Notice the `myImage.onload = function()` `{...}` code below. An image cannot be displayed until loaded. The `onload` method is used to trigger a function when an image has loaded. Hence, in the code below, when `myImage` has been loaded, `myImage.onload` triggers execution of the function assigned to `myImage.onload`, which in the code below results in the display of the image. Consider the effect of both the presence and absence of the `myImage.onload` trigger function. After you have the sample code below working, comment out the `myImage.onload` code, leaving only the `drawImage` method, as shown below.

```
//myImage.onload = function() {
  canvasContext.drawImage(myImage,30,30);
//}
```

Notice that the image is not displayed when the `onload` trigger function is not executed. Without the trigger function, the `drawImage` statement is executed before the image has been retrieved so it is not possible to display the image. Once you have learned about the importance of the `onload` function, restore its functionality by removing the comment symbols (`//`).

Additional information about the `drawImage` method is readily available on the web if you wish to consider the function in greater detail.

SAMPLE CODE

```html
<html>

<head>
<title>Display Image on Canvas</title>
</head>

<body>

<canvas id="theCanvas" width="350" height="450">
</canvas>

<img id="sourceImage" src=" circle1nb.png" style="display:
none">
<script>
  var myImage = document.getElementById("sourceImage");
  var canvas = document.getElementById("theCanvas");
  var canvasContext = canvas.getContext("2d");
//    document.getElementById("sourceImage").style.
display = "block";

  canvasContext.fillStyle = "#E0E0E0";
  canvasContext.fillRect(0,0,350,450);

  myImage.onload = function() {
    canvasContext.drawImage(myImage,30,30);
  }
</script>

</body>
</html>
```

Task 4.14 Animate an image on a canvas element.

The sample code below loads an image and then moves it along a descending line. The code for loading the image is different from the sample code in Task 4.13. Rather than use a hidden <img> tag, the sample code below creates an Image object and assigns the path to the image file to the Image object.

Once you have the code below running, you can modify it to move an object up, down, left, or right simply by changing how x and y are incremented or decremented. You may also add sound effects, such as a *boing* when the image contacts an edge, for instance. You could also add an eventListener to the canvas and make a sound effect (and/or other effects) when the user clicks the image.

The code below implements animation by repeatedly (every 1/10 of a second) clearing the entire canvas and drawing the image in a location close to its previous position. [A more subtle and refined approach to animation is to redraw, in the canvas background color, only the object being moved (thus eliminating it from view) and then, as before, drawing the object in a location close to its previous position.] The setInterval method identifies a function to be called every finite period of time. In the sample code below, setInterval(animate, 100) ensures that the animate function is called every 100 milliseconds (i.e., every 1/10 of a second). Using clearTimeout(timerInterval), the animation is stopped when the object nears the right edge of the canvas. Conceivably, the animation could be stopped by a button click, which might be a suitable technique to use when implementing an instructional game, for instance.

Additional information about the setInterval and clearTimeout methods is readily available on the web.

SAMPLE CODE

```
<html>
<head>
<title>Animate Image</title>
</head>
<body>

<canvas id="theCanvas" width="350" height="450">
</canvas>
<script>
  var myImage = new Image();
  var canvas = document.getElementById("theCanvas");
  var canvasContext = canvas.getContext("2d");

  var timerInterval;
  var x = 0;
  var y = 0;

  myImage.src = 'Images/circle2nb.png';
  myImage.onload = function() {
    timerInterval = setInterval(animate, 100);
  }
  function animate() {
    canvasContext.clearRect(0,0,canvas.width,
canvas.height);
    canvasContext.drawImage(myImage,x,y);
    x += 1;
    y += 1;
```

```
    if (x > 300) {
        clearTimeout(timerInterval);
    }
}
</script>
</body>
</html>
```

Task 4.15 Design at least one instructional app and implement it on a web page using HTML and JavaScript. You may involve target learners during the design, development, and testing stages.

References

Berners-Lee, T. (2000). *Weaving the web: The original design and ultimate destiny of the World Wide Web*. New York, NY: HarperCollins.

Mayer, R. E. (2009). *Multimedia learning* (2nd ed.). New York, NY: Cambridge University Press.

Paivio, A. (1971). *Imagery and verbal processes*. New York, NY: Holt, Rinehart & Winston.

Paivio, A. (1986). *Mental representations*. New York, NY: Oxford University Press.

## Chapter 5

Instructional Apps for Problem Solving

In this chapter, we review cognitivist instruction briefly and consider the variability of instructional apps that implement cognitivist instruction to help learners increase their problem solving capabilities. Then we transfer knowledge of JavaScript to C# (C Sharp) in order to create two instructional apps, which you can deploy on your iOS or Android smartphone, for instance. The first app provides an interface to help learners solve the Farmer, Wolf, Goat, and Cabbage problem. The second app provides a drag-and-drop interface to help learners solve a coin problem.

We will create these two apps in the Unity development environment. For non-commercial purposes, Unity Technologies makes available a *Personal* version of Unity, which is free of cost and runs on both Apple Mac and Microsoft Windows computers (http://unity3d.com). This chapter discusses all of the code necessary for the two apps. The eResources for the book include videos demonstrating how to create the app.

5.1 Implementing the Instructional Method

As discussed in Chapter 1, the development of mental models is critical to cognitive conceptions of learning. Multiple instructional methods help learners *assimilate* new information into their mental models. Further, when new information seems to contradict existing mental models, learners are said to *accommodate* or alter their mental models (Piaget, 1936). For example, children may first conceive of mammals as land animals, but upon discovering that dolphins are mammals, not fish, children refine their conceptions of mammals and fish. Also as discussed in Chapter 1, *advance organizers* (Ausubel, 1960), *concept mapping* (Novak & Gowin, 1984), and *dual coding* (Mayer, 2009; Paivio, 1971, 1986) facilitate formation and refinement of mental models. In addition to concept development, educators and cognitive psychologists also attend to development and refinement of tactical models, which include models for problem solving (Cognition and Technology Group at Vanderbilt, 1990, 1993). The two instructional apps we design and develop in this chapter seek to help learners refine their problem solving capabilities.

5.2 Diversity of the Apps

As noted in the previous chapter, instructional apps may use a combination of text, images, sound, and video to present content or problems, for instance. Learners may interact with the app using a mouse, keyboard, or stylus, or use a finger to tap, swipe, and drag objects. Alternatively, learners may interact with an instructional app using a multi-touch interface or use their voice for input. Another option is to implement an interface enabling collaboration between multiple learners. Beyond the media and learner interaction techniques, a variety of instructional methods can be implemented to help learners refine mental models of concepts and solutions, which may include advance organizers, concept mapping, or dual coding. Importantly, the learners need to be challenged in order to extend their extant mental models. For the two apps in this chapter, the learner will seek to solve two puzzles or problems. Engagement in puzzle solving may seem like game play. There is a specific goal and particular rules of engagement. Learners may not succeed initially, but the apps provide opportunities to practice. Through practice gained using the instructional app, learners may refine their problem solving strategies and solve the puzzles. Conceivably, the instructional apps could be extended to track performance, which could be used to offer tips and, if permission granted, could also be used for research purposes.

Consider the following examples of cognitivist instruction, which are helpful for developing mental models.

Newton's Cradle
Erik Neumann
www.myphysicslab.com/engine2D/newtons-cradle-en.html
Similar types of physics simulations, which enable modification of variables to refine knowledge of concepts and principles, are available at the following URL. www.myphysicslab.com/

Virtual Piano
https://virtualpiano.net/

Lemonade Stand
Bob Jamison, 1973; Charlie Kellner, 1979
Function Historical Reference at https://archive.org/details/Lemonade_Stand_1979_Apple

Contemporary Versions available at no cost from:

- App Store for iPhones: https://itunes.apple.com/us/app/classic-lemonade-stand/id1077016153?mt=8
- Microsoft Windows Store: www.microsoft.com/en-us/store/p/lemonade-stand/9wzdncrfj4wg

The historical version enabled entry of three values: (1) Cups of lemonade to make at the start of the day; selling price per cup; and number of advertising signs. The app calculated profit or loss (revenue minus expenses) and the learner could adapt values entered based on lessons learned from sales in prior days. This enabled learners to gain a personal sense for business profit and loss. A more sophisticated game could enter into the realm of constructivist instruction, but this version limited learners to gaining a sense for profit and loss based on three decisions and random events.

5.3 Farmer, Wolf, Goat, and Cabbage Problem

A farmer seeks to transport a wolf, goat, and cabbage across a river one at a time without either the goat or cabbage being eaten. The farmer can cross the river in a boat with one of the wolf, goat, or cabbage. If ever the wolf is alone with the goat, the goat perishes. If ever the goat is alone with the cabbage, the cabbage is consumed. How can the farmer get the wolf, goat, and cabbage across the river safely?

Download and install the *Personal* version of Unity by clicking the *Get Unity* link at https://unity3d.com. Then click the checkbox to confirm eligibility to download the Personal version because you are using the software for personal study rather than commercially. Lastly, click the button to download the installer and proceed with installation.

The code below is entered into the Unity development environment. For tips on using the editing features in Unity to create the visual interface, view the video demonstrations in the eResources.

TARGET LEARNERS: People capable of selecting a button in a computer interface who are developing problem solving capability.
INSTRUCTIONAL OBJECTIVE: The learner will solve the Farmer, Wolf, Goat, and Cabbage problem.

Design

The visual design of this app appears in Figure 5.1. When the boat is docked, clicking one of the four buttons in the footer will toggle the position of the farmer, wolf, goat, or cabbage. For example, if the goat is on the bank and the learner clicks the Goat button, the goat will be moved to the boat. Conversely, if the goat is on the boat and the learner clicks the *Goat* button, the goat will be moved to the bank. When the learner has loaded the boat and clicks the Sail button, the app moves the boat to the opposite bank. The learner then unloads the boat by clicking the appropriate button or buttons in the footer before clicking the *Sail* button to go to the opposite bank. At any time during game play, if the goat is left with the cabbage or the wolf with the goat, the game ends. The learner is informed that the game did not end well and is invited to click a button to play again. When the learner succeeds, the game terminates with a message of success. Again, the learner may restart the game.

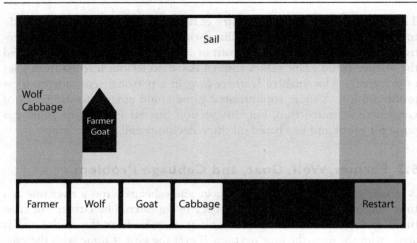

Figure 5.1 Visual Design of Instructional App for Solving the Farmer, Wolf, Goat, and Cabbage Problem.

Development

Create a new 2D Unity project. In the Unity project window, create a new folder called *Scripts*. Within the *Scripts* folder, create a new C# script called *Controller*. Double-click the icon for the *Controller* script. Unity will open the script using a text editor called *MonoDevelop*, which also enables you to enter C# code and compile the script to check for syntax errors. The *MonoDevelop* editor also has a look-ahead feature that anticipates what you may be typing. When the editor is correct in anticipating what you want to type, press the Tab key or the Space bar to add the actual text to be entered. Pressing the ESCape key removes the window displaying predicted text.

C# is object oriented, which extends procedural programming by introducing objects. Regarding the code below, each of the first five lines, which begin with `using`, simply imports a library routine. The object-oriented code begins with the declaration of `public class Controller`, which is of type `MonoBehavior`, the base class for all programs in Unity. Just as you have a mental model for several concept classes (animal, vegetable, fruit, mineral, water, metal, plastic, wood, chair, etc.), an object-oriented program creates concept classes. In this case, since we named the script *Controller*, we are defining the `Controller` class and making it available publicly (though we have just this one script so other objects will not be interacting with it). In object-oriented programming, objects contain data and functions. In object-oriented programming, *functions* are often called *methods*.

The `Controller` class begins with ten lines of variable declarations followed by three dictionary declarations. A dictionary in C# acts like an associative array. Rather than use a number to index an array, a character string (called a *key*) is used to access a value in an associative array. We use the dictionaries to keep track of the location of the puzzle items, namely the farmer, wolf, goat, and cabbage. The first dictionary declaration below defines the variable `onBank1`. If we were to `print(onBank1["Farmer"])`, the result would be true because the `Farmer` entry in `onBank1` is set to `true`. In looking at Figure 5.1, Bank1 is the left bank, which is where the farmer, wolf, goat, and cabbage appear initially. Since those four puzzle entities are on Bank 1 (the left bank), the `onBank1` array entry for all four of those entities is initially set to `true`. The dictionary definition entries for `onBank2` are all set to `false`, as are the initial entries of `onBoat` because there are no puzzle items on the right bank nor on the boat at the start of the game. Figure 5.1 depicts a state of the puzzle after the goat and farmer have been moved to the boat (by clicking the *Goat* and *Farmer* buttons in the footer).

After the declarations, the `Controller` class defines *methods*. There are three public methods, namely `EntityButtonClicked`, `TraverseRiver`, and `RestartGame`. Public methods and variables are available outside the script, which in Unity makes public methods and variables accessible to other scripts and accessible within the app development environment. Consequently, developers can set public variables in the visual editing environment and can connect buttons in the visual editor to functions in the script. For instance, the *Sail* button is linked to the `TraverseRiver` method; the *Reset* button to the `RestartGame` method; and the *Farmer, Wolf, Goat,* and *Cabbage* buttons to the `EntityButtonClicked` method. (See the eResources for dynamic depictions of this linking.) Consequently, the `EntityButtonClicked` method executes every time any one of the *Farmer, Wolf, Goat,* and *Cabbage* buttons is clicked. The `TraverseRiver` method executes when the *Sail* button is clicked and the `RestartGame` method runs when the *Restart* button is clicked. The *Restart* button becomes active when the puzzle ends, whether in failure or success. In either case, the learner may restart the puzzle game. In the comments below, each method is described, after discussion of the `Start` method, which is where program execution begins.

The `Start` method `inactivates` the *Reset* button and sets eight objects to variables, namely the *Sail, Boat, Farmer, Wolf, Goat,* and *Cabbage* buttons, as well as the two panels (rectangles) *Bank1* and *Bank2*. The two panels and the boat image each have a child text field for displaying the items on the river banks and the boat.

The `EntityButtonClicked` method retrieves the name of the entity button clicked (either *Farmer, Wolf, Goat,* or *Cabbage*). Then `EntityButtonClicked` calls `ToggleResource` to move an entity from a river bank (either Bank1 or Bank2) to the boat or from the boat to a river bank. The Boolean variable `boatOnBank1` is used to pass the appropriate river bank list to the `ToggleResource` function (which is private because the key word public does not appear in the function declaration). The `ToggleResource` function uses an `if` statement to ensure that the learner is making a valid move (which could move the *Farmer, Wolf, Goat,* or *Cabbage* from a river bank to the boat or vice versa) before updating the boat and river bank lists to visually depict the move. The learner can move the *Farmer, Wolf, Goat,* or *Cabbage* to or from the bank at which the boat is docked. Given a valid move, once the appropriate river bank list and the boat list have been updated, `ToggleResource` calls the `UpdateDisplayStrings` method. In `UpdateDisplayStrings`, the `for` loop puts the list of occupants into the `crntOccupants` string, which is then assigned to the child text field of the bank or boat object. Lastly in the `EntityButtonClicked` method, the state of the game is checked to determine whether the learner has succeeded or failed to solve the puzzle, or whether the outcome has not yet been determined. In the case of success or failure, the `GameDone` method is called to activate the *Restart* button, which provides feedback to the learner by reporting the outcome (success or failure) and an opportunity to play again. In addition, text displayed on the feedback panel provides encouragement to try again in the case of failure or the opportunity to go again in the case of success. The `GameDone` method also disables the *Farmer, Wolf, Goat,* and *Cabbage* buttons to ensure that the game can no longer be played until restarted.

The `TraverseRiver` method toggles the `boatOnBank1` variable, which effectively moves the boat from one river bank to the other. Visually, the learner views the boat instantly move from one river bank to the other, which is accomplished by setting the x and y coordinates of the `boatGameObject.transform.position`. In Unity, every visible object has a *transform*, which determines the object's position, rotation, and scale.

The `RestartGame` method sets variables to the initial game state, hides the feedback panel, `inactivates` the *Restart* button by setting its *interactable* attribute to false, moves the boat to the left bank, displays the words *Farmer, Wolf, Goat,* and *Cabbage* on the left bank, sets the words displayed on the right bank and the boat to the empty string, and enables the *Farmer, Wolf, Goat,* and *Cabbage* buttons by setting the interactable attribute of each button to true.

Enter the following code into the *Controller* script. As you develop this app, you may insert `print()` statements to view the values of variables, such as `print("Number of items on boat: " + numOnBoat);`

As demonstrated on the companion website, attach the Controller script to the six buttons (*Farmer, Wolf, Goat, Cabbage, Sail,* and *Restart*). Debug as necessary.

```
using System.Collections;
using System.Collections.Generic;
using UnityEngine;
using UnityEngine.UI;
using UnityEngine.EventSystems;
public class Controller : MonoBehaviour {
    static bool boatOnBank1 = true;
    static int  numOnBoat = 0;
    GameObject[] occupantsGameObjects = new GameObject[4];
    string[] occupantsKeys = new string[] {"Farmer",
"Wolf", "Goat", "Cabbage"};
```

```
    string crntButtonName;
    public GameObject restartGameObject;
    public GameObject feedbackPanel;
    GameObject sailGameObject;
    GameObject boatGameObject;
    GameObject bank1GameObject, bank2GameObject;

    static Dictionary<string, bool> onBank1 =
new Dictionary<string, bool>()
        {
            {"Farmer", true},
            {"Wolf", true},
            {"Goat", true},
            {"Cabbage", true}
        };
    static Dictionary<string, bool> onBank2 =
new Dictionary<string, bool>()
        {
            {"Farmer", false},
            {"Wolf", false},
            {"Goat", false},
            {"Cabbage", false}
        };
    static Dictionary<string, bool> onBoat =
new Dictionary<string, bool>()
        {
            {"Farmer", false},
            {"Wolf", false},
            {"Goat", false},
            {"Cabbage", false}
        };

    void Start () {
        restartGameObject.SetActive(false);

        sailGameObject = GameObject.Find("Sail");
        boatGameObject = GameObject.Find("Boat");
        bank1GameObject = GameObject.Find("Bank1");
        bank2GameObject = GameObject.Find("Bank2");

        for (var i = 0; i < occupantsKeys.Length; i++) {
            occupantsGameObjects[i] =
GameObject.Find(occupantsKeys[i]);
        }
        //GameObject.Find("Sail").GetComponent<Button>().
interactable = true;
    }// "Start"
```

```
        public void RestartGame() {
            print ("In Restart Game");
            for (var i = 0; i < occupantsKeys.
Length; i++) {
                onBank1[occupantsKeys[i]] = true;
                onBank2[occupantsKeys[i]] = false;
                onBoat[occupantsKeys[i]] = false;
            }

            print (onBank1["Farmer"]+" "+onBank1["Wolf"]
+ " " + onBank1["Goat"] + " " + onBank1["Cabbage"]);

            restartGameObject.SetActive(false);
            numOnBoat = 0;
            boatOnBank1 = true;
            boatGameObject.transform.position =
new Vector2(248,320);
            UpdateDisplayStrings(onBank1,
bank1GameObject);
            bank2GameObject.GetComponentInChildren
<Text>().text = "";
            boatGameObject.GetComponentInChildren
<Text>().text = "";

            for (var i = 0; i < occupantsKeys.Length; i++) {
                occupantsGameObjects[i].GetComponent
<Button>().interactable = true;
            }
        } // "RestartGame"

    void UpdateDisplayStrings(Dictionary<string,
bool> onBank, GameObject crntGameObject) {
            string crntOccupants = "";

            foreach (string key in onBank.Keys) {
                if (onBank[key]) {
                    crntOccupants = crntOccupants
+ key + "\n";
                }
            }

            crntGameObject.GetComponentInChildren
<Text>().text = crntOccupants;
        } // "UpdateDisplayStrings"

    void ToggleResource(Dictionary<string, bool>
onBank, GameObject crntGameObject) {
            if (onBoat[crntButtonName]) {
```

```
                onBoat[crntButtonName] = false;
                numOnBoat--;
                onBank[crntButtonName] = true;
                UpdateDisplayStrings(onBank,
crntGameObject);
                UpdateDisplayStrings(onBoat,
boatGameObject);

                if (crntButtonName == "Farmer") {
                    sailGameObject.GetComponent
<Button>().interactable = false;
                }
            }
            else if (numOnBoat < 2 && onBank[crntButton
Name]) {
                onBoat[crntButtonName] = true;
                numOnBoat++;
                onBank[crntButtonName] = false;
                UpdateDisplayStrings(onBank,
crntGameObject);
                UpdateDisplayStrings(onBoat,
boatGameObject);

                if (crntButtonName == "Farmer") {
                    sailGameObject.GetComponent
<Button>().interactable = true;
                }
            }
    }  // "ToggleResource"

    public void TraverseRiver () {
            print("Traverse River");
            boatOnBank1 = ! boatOnBank1;
            print(boatGameObject.transform.position);
            if (boatOnBank1) {
                boatGameObject.transform.position
= new Vector2(248,320);
            }
            else {
                boatGameObject.transform.position
= new Vector2(888,320);
            }
    }  // "TraverseRiver"

    void GameDone (string feedback) {
```

```
            sailGameObject.GetComponent<Button>().
interactable = false;
            for (var i = 0; i < occupantsKeys.Length; i++) {
                    occupantsGameObjects[i].
GetComponent<Button>().interactable = false;
            }

            restartGameObject.GetComponent
InChildren<Text>().text = feedback;
            restartGameObject.SetActive(true);
        }  // "GameDone"

    public void EntityButtonClicked () {
            crntButtonName = EventSystem.current.
currentSelectedGameObject.name;
            print(crntButtonName);

            if (boatOnBank1) {
                    ToggleResource(onBank1,
bank1GameObject);
            }
            else {
                    ToggleResource(onBank2,
bank2GameObject);
            }
            print("after call to toggle Resource: " +
crntButtonName + " on   Bank 1: " + onBank1[crntButtonName]
+ "        on Bank 2: " + onBank2[crntButtonName] + "        on
Boat: " + onBoat[crntButtonName]);

            // check game state
            if ((((onBank1["Wolf"] && onBank1["Goat"])
|| (onBank1["Cabbage"] && onBank1["Goat"]))
&& !onBank1["Farmer"]) ||
                    (((onBank2["Wolf"] && onBank2["Goat"])
|| (onBank2["Cabbage"] && onBank2["Goat"])) &&
!onBank2["Farmer"]) ||
                    ((onBoat["Wolf"] && onBoat["Goat"])
|| (onBoat["Cabbage"] && onBoat["Goat"])))) {
                    GameDone("Oops\nTry Again");
            }
            else {
                    if (onBank2["Farmer"] && onBank2["Wolf"]
&& onBank2["Goat"] && onBank2["Cabbage"]) {
                            GameDone("You did it!\nGo Again");
                    }
                    else {
```

```
                print("play on");
            }
        }
    }  // "EntityButtonClicked"
}
```

Task 5.1 Determine what each method and statement does. In order to do that you may comment out a statement or group of statements and predict the effect. Then run the program to test your predictions. For example in GameDone, comment out the first assignment statement or the first statement and the for loop. You might (properly) predict that the *Sail* button will not be disabled when the first assignment statement is commented out (which means // appears at the start of the line of code to prevent its execution). What does the for loop after that assignment statement do? Test your prediction. Continue in this manner until you have convinced yourself that you know how the program works.

Task 5.2 What do you regard as strengths and weaknesses of this app?

Task 5.3 Change the feedback to the learner. In particular, alter the if statement that provides general feedback about failure (i.e., "Oops") in order to provide specific feedback. In particular, identify whether the error was leaving the goat and cabbage together or the wolf and goat together. There is also a third case in which all three entities, goat, cabbage, and wolf, are left alone on a river bank. Your program should provide feedback for all three cases. Feedback should be brief. Optionally, you may reposition the feedback to display in the center of the screen.

Tip: Like JavaScript, C# has an if statement structure like the following, which enables testing of multiple conditions.

```
if (condition) {}
else if (condition) {}
else {}
```

Task 5.4 Consider design options for feedback of invalid input. For example, consider use of sound for invalid button clicking, such as when the boat is filled to capacity and a button is clicked in an attempt to get a third entity on the boat. Should buttons be disabled (by setting the interactable property to false) when clicking them would be counter to the rules? The *Sail* button, for instance, is enabled only when the farmer is on the boat.

Task 5.5 Add sound to indicate invalid button clicking. In particular, when any of the *Farmer, Wolf, Goat,* or *Cabbage* buttons are clicked in error, play a brief sound.

Tips: Add an empty `GameObject` to the scene and change its default name to *SoundObject*. Add an Audio Source component to *SoundObject*. Drag an audio file (e.g., one ending .mp3 or .wav) into the Resources folder in the Project window. The audio file might contain a brief (one-quarter or one-tenth second) buzzer sound. Then drag the audio file icon from the Resources folder to the `AudioClip` attribute in the Audio Source.

In the *Controller* script, add the following declaration to the Controller Class.

```
AudioSource audioPlayer;
```

In the `Start` method, include the following line of code, which will enable the sound to be played.

```
audioPlayer = GameObject.Find("SoundObject").
GetComponent<AudioSource>();
```

Lastly, insert the following line of code into the `ToggleResource` method in such a way that the sound plays when the learner clicks any of the *Farmer*, *Wolf*, *Goat*, or *Cabbage* buttons in error.

```
audioPlayer.Play();
```

Task 5.6 Consider design options for imagery. Could you scale images of a farmer, wolf, goat, and cabbage to a size that would fit into a boat on a mobile app? How would the C# code need to change in order to replace the words Farmer, Wolf, Goat, and Cabbage with representative images?

Task 5.7 Words used to describe a game may be open to interpretation, whether written or verbal. For example, the description of the Farmer, Wolf, Goat, and Cabbage problem in the first paragraph of this section does not explicitly state that the wolf and cabbage, for instance, cannot both be on the boat simultaneously, yet the program above does not permit that. Clarity is often helpful to human beings, but it is not always apparent to messengers (clients) when perceivers of their messages (designers and developers) will need additional information. In your view, might particular target learners benefit from disabling the buttons to prevent invalid selections? Could disabling buttons inhibit learning?

Task 5.8 List items on the boat in the order in which the learner selects them.

Tips: Consider adding another dictionary declaration called `onBoatOrder` using the data types `<string, int>` rather than `<string, bool>`. Then the digits 1 and 2 (from the variable `numOnBoat`) can be used to determine the order in which puzzle items are added to the boat. The digit 0 can be used to denote no items on the boat. Retain the `onBoat` dictionary because its use of Boolean values makes for easy comparisons.

Task 5.9 Consider redesigning the app to add avocados, which goats also eat (as well as cardboard and clothing, and they might even try to eat tin cans). Is there a solution under the current rules with the extension that the goat can't be alone with either the avocados or cabbage? Consider changing the rules to allow a third entity on the boat. How would you change the app to include avocados and the rule extension? Could you redesign and reprogram the app to permit the learner to choose which items to include on the river bank and how many items can be transported on the boat? What limitations would you put on the number of items on the river bank and the number of items on the boat? Conceivably, a robust app, which enables learners to select items to transport and number of items permitted on the boat would enable learners to refine their problem solving abilities sufficiently to form rules about when a solution exists. The problem could be made even more complex by permitting combinations of items to be safe from consumption, but consumed when on the river bank individually. Increasing the complexity of the app creates the potential for learners to increase the sophistication of their mental models.

Task 5.10 Build options: You may build your app for deployment on a variety of devices, including mobile devices and desktop computers. Deployment to Apple iOS devices involves one level of indirection beyond Android implementation. Unity will deploy your app directly to an Android device, but Apple requires that apps be distributed through Xcode. Consequently, the output from the Unity build process for iOS apps is input to Xcode for deployment on your iOS device. An Apple developer ID is required for that, which can be obtained free of cost for deployment of apps to your own iOS devices. Deployment methods to various devices continue to be refined. A good start is to follow the directions at Unity Technologies (2017) for loading the app to a device connected to your development computer with a USB cable. A subsequent step for mass deployment would be to distribute the app through Google Play or Apple's App Store. For those instructions, you may consider the latest documentation. The documentation also has instructions for deployment to desktop computers and all other supported devices.

5.4 A Coin Problem

A puzzle has coins arranged in two groups, as depicted in Figure 5.2. You may conceive of the light gray circles as coins of one particular value and the dark gray circles as coins of another value. The goal is to get the coins on the left side to the right side and vice versa. There are two valid moves: (1) A coin can move forward one space, provided the space is empty. Coins originally on the left side move right and coins originally on the right side move left so forward is relative to the original position of a coin. (2) A coin can move forward two spaces if the space two positions ahead is empty and the coin jumped over is in the opposite coin group.

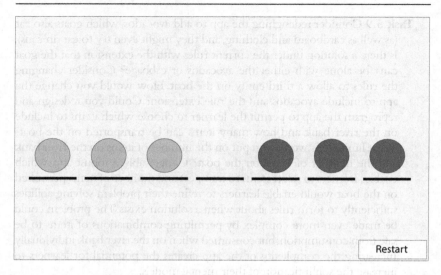

Figure 5.2 Visual Design of Instructional App for Solving the Coin Problem.

TARGET LEARNERS: People capable of dragging an object in a computer interface who are developing problem solving capability.
INSTRUCTIONAL OBJECTIVE: The learner will solve the coin puzzle.

Design

As per Figure 5.2, two sets of coins (circles) are grouped on opposite sides of the game board. The goal is to get the coins on the left side to the right side while getting the coins on the right side to the left side. A coin can be moved forward one space if the space is empty or ahead two spaces if jumping over a coin from the other side to an open space. To create an app enabling learners to solve this puzzle, we will implement a drag-and-drop feature that checks for a valid move. A valid move conforms to one of the two rules for coin movement. Moving coins in accordance with the rules does not guarantee success in solving the puzzle. For example, if each of the three coins from one side is advanced one space, the goal to move the coins to opposite sides of the game board can never be reached. The learner is free to click the restart button at any time. After some trials and errors, learners may refine their problem solving strategy sufficiently to complete the puzzle successfully.

Development

Create a new 2D Unity project. In the project window, create a new folder called *Scripts*. Within the *Scripts* folder, create two new C# scripts, one named *MoveMe* and one named *RestartPuzzle*. Double-click the icon for the *RestartPuzzle* script. Unity will open the script in a text editor called *MonoDevelop*, which also enables you to enter C# code and compile the script to check for syntax errors. As noted previously, the *MonoDevelop* editor also has a look-ahead feature that anticipates what you may want to type. When the editor is correct in anticipating what you want to type, press the Tab key or the Space bar to add the actual text to be entered. Pressing the ESCape key removes the window displaying predicted text.

The *MoveMe* script below begins with five `using` statements to import Unity library routines. Then the *MoveMe* script below includes the class definition for a `Player`. Conceive of the coins as players. Each coin/player has a team color, direction, and a name. Since the indices of a one-dimensional array increase from left to right, the direction is set to positive one for players moving left to right and set to negative one for players moving right to left. The player objects are created in the *Start* method, which is discussed subsequently.

The definition of the `MoveMe` class begins with five lines of variable declarations, followed by a Dictionary definition. The `coinImages` variable is a one-dimensional array that stores the positions of the coins on the screen. Technically, this array stores information of type `RectTransform`, which defines the position, rotation, and scale of the coin images (which are images of red and green circles). The variable `crntTransform` is used to store the position of the current coin. The `myGBcolumn` variable holds the Game Board (GB) column in which the current coin (i.e., the coin dragged and dropped by the learner) currently resides. The `playerNames` variable is a one-dimensional array of names for the coins. The `gameboard` variable is the primary data structure in the app. It is a one-dimensional array with seven positions indexed from 0 to 6; each position contains a `Player` object. The `playerNamesDictionary` acts as an associative array, which specifies the initial game board position (column) of each coin.

The MoveMe class contains five methods. The `Start` method locates and stores the reference to each of the six coins. It also creates one `Player` object for each of the six coins and a *bogus* `Player` object for the open space. Each `Player` object is stored in the `gameboard` array. Though created, the values of the three variables in each `Player` object have not yet been initialized. The player objects are initialized in the `InitGameBoard` method, which occurs next because the last statement in the `Start` method calls the `InitGameBoard` method.

The `InitGameBoard` method assigns the first three coin `Players` in the `gameboard` array to the "red" team, which moves in direction 1 (left to right), and sets the name of each coin player. Then the fourth element in the `gameboard` array, the open space, is assigned the "null" team color, the direction 0, and the name "open." The second set of coin players is assigned to the "green" team and has direction −1. The names of the coin players from left to right on the `gameboard`, in accordance with the `playerNames` array, are `"RedCircle3"`, `"RedCircle2"`, `"RedCircle1"`, `"open"`, `"GreenCircle1"`, `"GreenCircle2"`, `"GreenCircle3"`. The final two statements in `InitGameBoard` set the `myGBcolumn` variable (which is short for my Game Board Column) on the current coin object and positions it on the screen.

Instruction begins with the learner dragging a coin, any coin. The one statement in the OnDrag method moves the coin being dragged by updating the x and y coordinates of the center of the coin.

When the learner drops the coin (by releasing a mouse button if running the app on a desktop computer or laptop, or raising a finger if running the app on a smartphone or a laptop with a trackpad or touchscreen), Unity invokes the OnDrop method.

Each time the learner makes a valid move, the app places the coin in its proper position by setting the x and y coordinates appropriately. The learner need only drop the coin in a valid column and the app will move the coin to its exact location in the new column. When the learner does not drop the coin in a valid column, the app returns the coin to the column from which the drag operation started. You may notice that the OnDrop method is not invoked when a coin is dragged underneath another coin. All coins are subordinate to the Background panel, which makes them siblings of the parent Background panel. Each sibling has an ordinal value called an *index*. When Object A is dragged to Object B, Object A appears on top of Object B if the sibling index of Object A is greater than or equal to that of Object B; otherwise Object A appears underneath Object B. Setting the sibling index of all coin objects to the same value will ensure that the coin being dragged is always on top. You will implement this in Task 5.12 to ensure that the coin being dragged always appears on top of other coins (which also ensures that the onDrop method is triggered every time a coin is dropped).

The only other method in the MoveMe class script, PuzzleSolved, determines whether all coins are in the final goal state. If so, the method returns the Boolean value true, which results in the word *Congratulations* being displayed on the screen.

Enter the following C# code into the MoveMe script. Save and build the script. Debug as necessary. As demonstrated in a video in the eResources, add the MoveMe script to each of the six coin objects created in the Unity visual development environment.

```
using System.Collections;
using System.Collections.Generic;
using UnityEngine;
using UnityEngine.UI;
using UnityEngine.EventSystems;

public class Player {
        public string teamColor;
        public int direction;
        public string name;
}

public class MoveMe : MonoBehaviour, IDragHandler,
IDropHandler {
```

```
        private RectTransform[] coinImages = new
RectTransform[7];
        public RectTransform crntTransform;
        private int myGBcolumn;
        string[] playerNames = new string[] {"RedCircle3",
"RedCircle2", "RedCircle1", "open", "GreenCircle1",
"GreenCircle2", "GreenCircle3"};

        static Player[] gameboard = new Player[7];

        Dictionary<string, int> playerNamesDictionary =
new Dictionary<string, int>()
                    {
                        {"RedCircle3", 0},
                        {"RedCircle2", 1},
                        {"RedCircle1", 2},
                        {"GreenCircle1", 4},
                        {"GreenCircle2", 5},
                        {"GreenCircle3", 6}
                    };
    void Start () {
            for (var i = 0; i < 7; i++) {
                if (i != 3) {
                        coinImages[i] = new Rect
Transform();
                        coinImages[i] = GameObject.
Find(playerNames[i]).GetComponent<RectTransform>();
                }
            }

            for (var i = 0; i < 7; i++) {
                    gameboard[i] = new Player();
            }
            InitGameBoard();
    } // "Start"

    public void InitGameBoard() {
            string crntTeamColor = "Red";
            int    crntDirection = 1;
            for (var i = 0; i < 7; i++) {
              if (i != 3) {
                gameboard[i].teamColor = crntTeamColor;
                gameboard[i].direction = crntDirection;
                gameboard[i].name = playerNames[i];
                coinImages[i].position = new Vector2
(88 + i * 160, 280);
                }
```

```
                else {
                        gameboard[i].teamColor = "null";
                        gameboard[i].direction = 0;
                        gameboard[i].name = layerNames[i];

                        crntTeamColor = "Green";
                        crntDirection = -1;
                }
        }
     myGBcolumn = playerNamesDictionary[crntTransform.
name];
        crntTransform.position = new Vector2(88 +
myGBcolumn * 160, 280);
} // "InitGameBoard"

bool  PuzzleSolved() {
                bool  solved = true;
                string[]    finalOrderNames = new
string[] { "GreenCircle1", "GreenCircle2",
"GreenCircle3", "open", "RedCircle3", "RedCircle2",
"RedCircle1"};
                for (var i = 0; i < 7; i++) {
                        if (gameboard[i].name !=finalOrder
Names[i]) {
                                solved = false;
                        }
                }
                return solved;
        } // "PuzzleSolved"
     public void OnDrag(PointerEventData
eventData) {
     crntTransform.position +=
new Vector3(eventData.delta.x, eventData.delta.y);
        }  // "OnDrag"

     public void OnDrop(PointerEventData eventData) {
                string myName;
                string myTeamColor;
                int myDirection;

                intdroppedInColumn=(int)(crntTransform.
position.x / 160);
                int dropTolerance = (int) crntTransform.
position.x % 160;

                myName = gameboard[myGBcolumn].name;
```

```
        myTeamColor   =   gameboard[myGBcolumn].
teamColor;
        myDirection   =   gameboard[myGBcolumn].
direction;

        if (dropTolerance > 33 && dropTolerance
< 143) {
            int   seeksToMove   =   Mathf.Abs
(myGBcolumn - droppedInColumn);
            int   expectedTargetColumn   =
myGBcolumn + seeksToMove * myDirection;

            if ((droppedInColumn == expected
TargetColumn) && ((seeksToMove == 1 && gameboard
[droppedInColumn].name == "open") ||
                (seeksToMove == 2 && (game
board[myGBcolumn + myDirection].teamColor != myTeam
Color) && gameboard[droppedInColumn].name ==
"open"))) {
                gameboard[droppedInColumn].
teamColor = myTeamColor;
                gameboard[droppedInColumn].
direction = myDirection;
                gameboard[droppedInColumn].
name = myName;

                gameboard[myGBcolumn].
teamColor = "null";
                gameboard[myGBcolumn].
direction = 0;
                gameboard[myGBcolumn].name =
"open";

                myGBcolumn=droppedInColumn;

                crntTransform.position   =
new Vector2(88 + droppedInColumn * 160, 280);

                if (PuzzleSolved()) {
                    GameObject.Find
("Restart").GetComponent<RestartPuzzle>().
DisplaySuccessButton();
                }
            }
            else {
                crntTransform.position =
new Vector2(88 + myGBcolumn * 160, 280);
```

```
                }
           }
           else {
                crntTransform.position = new Vector2
(88 + myGBcolumn * 160, 280);
           }
     }   // "OnDrop"
}
```

There is a second script in this app. All of the code could have been placed in a single script, but apps often include multiple scripts and include a specific script in a particular object. To demonstrate that functionality in this app, the `RestartPuzzle` script is included in the `Restart` button object. The `RestartPuzzle` script contains three initial lines of code to include Unity library routines. Then the script contains the definition of the `RestartPuzzle` class. There is one variable and three methods in the `RestartPuzzle` class. The one variable is the `successButton`, which is a non-interactable button used only to display the word *Congratulations* when the learner solves the puzzle. The `Start` method contains one line of code, which sets `successButton` to inactive in order to hide it before the interface is displayed on the screen. The `DisplaySuccessButton` method is called from the `MoveMe` script when the learner has completed the puzzle successfully. When the user clicks the *Restart* button, the `Restart` method calls the `InitGameBoard` method in the `MoveMe` script and sets `successButton` to inactive in order to hide the word *Congratulations*. The `InitGameBoard` method is called six times, one time for each instantiation of the `MoveMe` script. After all, the `MoveMe` script is attached to each of the six coin objects.

Enter the following C# code into the `RestartPuzzle` script. Save and build the script. Debug as necessary. Then, as demonstrated on the companion website, add the `RestartPuzzle` script to the `Restart` button created in the Unity visual development environment.

```
using System.Collections;
using System.Collections.Generic;
using UnityEngine;

public class RestartPuzzle : MonoBehaviour {
     public        GameObject successButton;

     void Start() {
          successButton.SetActive(false);
          print ("Screen width and height: "  +
Screen.width + " " + Screen.height);
     } // "Start"

     public void DisplaySuccessButton () {
```

```
        successButton.SetActive(true);
    } // "DisplaySuccessButton"

    public void Restart () {
        string[] playerNames = new string[] {"Red
Circle3", "RedCircle2", "RedCircle1", "open", "Green
Circle1", "GreenCircle2", "GreenCircle3"};

        for (var i = 0; i < 7; i++) {
            if (i != 3) {

                GameObject.Find(playerNames[i]).
GetComponent<MoveMe>().InitGameBoard();
            }
        }

        successButton.SetActive(false);
    } // "Restart"
} // "RestartPuzzle"
```

Task 5.11 One of the challenges to developing this app is keeping proper track of the two types of coin objects. Each coin object on the screen has a transform, which in Unity is a RectTransform data type. The variables coinImages and crntTransform are of type RectTransform so those two variables pertain to the coin images displayed on the screen. Also, each coin is a Player object in the gameboard array. The gameboard variable is used to keep track of which column in the 7-column game board each coin is in and which column is the empty space. Determine what each method and statement does. In order to do that you may comment out a statement or group of statements and predict the effect. Then run the program to test your predictions.

Task 5.12 Add the IBeginDragHandler to the MoveMe class definition, as shown below.

```
public class MoveMe : MonoBehaviour, IBeginDragHandler,
IDragHandler, IDropHandler {
```

Then add the method below to set the sibling index of each coin to the same value.

```
public void OnBeginDrag(PointerEventData eventData) {
//    print(crntTransform.GetSiblingIndex());
    crntTransform.SetSiblingIndex(15);
} // "OnBeginDrag"
```

Notice that the dragged coin now always appears on top when dragged over other coins. Further, this code implements the remedy to the problem with the `onDrop` method, which did not trigger when a coin was dropped behind another coin.

Task 5.13 Build the app and deploy it to iOS, Android, Windows, and Mac OS devices. You could also deploy the app to a Linux device if you have access to one.

Task 5.14 Create or locate images of coins. You may, for instance, search a creative commons site enabling free use of images. Creating a coin image is another option. Once you have two distinct coin images, drag each file into the Project Window and then drag the image from the Project Window to the object in the Inspector Window in Unity. Build the app again and deploy to devices.

Task 5.15 Add sound to enhance the experience of success. You may record a sound (a chime, for instance) or obtain a sound file from a creative commons site that produces a pleasing sound, which could be applause, though you may well find other sounds more appealing.

Task 5.16 How do you know when no valid moves remain? How soon can it be known that the game is lost? What code would you insert to determine when no valid moves remain? Should you prompt the learner to press the Restart button when no valid moves remain? Why or why not?

Task 5.17 Insert the following line of code into the `Start` method of `RestartPuzzle` in order to view the size of the screen in pixels. Then insert a print statement to calculate the screen width divided by 9.

```
print("Screen width and height: " + Screen.width +
" " + Screen.height);
```

Task 5.18 The result from Task 5.17 (screen width / 9) indicates the number of pixels available for displaying the game board (including the space between the lines) of a coin puzzle with eight coins. What code needs to be changed to implement the puzzle with eight coins and what changes to the interface must be made? Make a backup copy of the app by copying the entire folder (and its subfolders); then implement the changes necessary to enable learners to solve the puzzle with eight coins.

Task 5.19 With respect to user interactivity, the two apps in this chapter use panels, text fields, and buttons. Many apps require additional user interface components, such as text entry fields, sliders, toggles, and drop down menus.

Whether implementing a text entry field, a slider, a toggle, or a drop down menu, you can follow the same general three-step process you used to implement a button: (1) Insert the user interface object into the scene using the visual editor; (2) Write a function to process the user's input; and (3) Link the user interface object to the function.

Open a new Unity project. Add an *Input Field* to the empty scene. Position the field in the upper left corner with its anchor and pivot also in the upper left corner. Create a C# script called *ProcessUserInput* and enter the following code.

```
using System.Collections;
using System.Collections.Generic;
using UnityEngine;
using UnityEngine.UI;
using UnityEngine.EventSystems;

public class ProcessUserInput : MonoBehaviour {

        public void ProcessEvent() {
                print (EventSystem.current.currentSelected
GameObject.name);
                print(EventSystem.current.currentSelected
GameObject.GetComponent<InputField>().text);
        } // "ProcessEvent"
} // "ProcessUserInput"
```

In the Inspector dialog, add the *ProcessUserInput* script to the object. Then, in the On End Edit section of the Inspector dialog, click the + sign; drag the *Input Field* from the Hierarchy and drop it on the Object field in the Inspector dialog. Lastly, select the `ProcessEvent` function associated with the `ProcessUserInput` class in order to link the *Input Field* to the script. Test and debug as necessary.

Implement at least one other user interface element (e.g., a drop down menu, a slider, or a toggle). Check the documentation when necessary (https://docs.unity3d.com/Manual/comp-UIInteraction.html).

Task 5.20 Design and develop an app for deployment on mobile devices that enables a learner to practice multiplication.

Tips: Use `Random.Range(1,13)` to generate a random number between 1 and 12. Generate two such random numbers and display them in a text string surrounding the multiplication operator, such as 3 * 7. Note that the integer variable num1 can be converted to a string using `num1.ToString()`. Further, the plus sign (+) is the string concatenation operator in C#.

Position an *Input Field* beside the text string displaying the question. Provide feedback to indicate whether the value entered by the learner is correct. You may use sound or another text field, for instance, to provide feedback. You are the one designing the app so you determine how to provide feedback.

The app must provide the learner with an unlimited number of practice items, but need not keep a history of items completed. Consequently, one text field to display the item and one *Input Field* for the learner's response is sufficient.

Behavioral instruction is helpful for particular types of math practice, such as when learning to multiply numbers from 1 to 12. However, once learners have mastered multiplying such numbers, how might you enhance the design of the app to help learners refine their mental models of multiplication?

References

Ausubel, D. P. (1960). The use of advance organizers in the learning and retention of meaningful verbal material. *Journal of Educational Psychology, 51*, 267–272.

Cognition and Technology Group at Vanderbilt (1990). Anchored instruction and its relationship to situated cognition. *Educational Researcher, 19*(6), 2–10.

Cognition and Technology Group at Vanderbilt (1993). Anchored instruction and situated cognition revisited. *Educational Technology, 33*(5), 52–70.

Mayer, R. E. (2009). *Multimedia learning* (2nd ed.). New York, NY: Cambridge University Press.

Novak, J. D. & Gowin, D. B. (1984). *Learning how to learn.* New York, NY: Cambridge University Press.

Paivio, A. (1971). *Imagery and verbal processes.* New York, NY: Holt, Rinehart & Winston.

Paivio, A. (1986). *Mental representations.* New York, NY: Oxford University Press.

Piaget, J. (1936). *Origins of intelligence in the child.* London: Routledge & Kegan Paul.

Unity Technologies (2017). Building your Unity game to an Android device for testing. https://unity3d.com/learn/tutorials/topics/mobile-touch/building-your-unity-game-android-device-testing

Unity Technologies (2017). Building your Unity game to an iOS device for testing. https://unity3d.com/learn/tutorials/topics/mobile-touch/building-your-unity-game-ios-device-testing?playlist=17138

Unity Technologies (2017). Getting started with Android development. https://docs.unity3d.com/Manual/android-GettingStarted.html

Unity Technologies (2017). Getting started with iOS development. https://docs.unity3d.com/Manual/iphone-GettingStarted.html

Chapter 6

Instructional Apps for Experimentation

In this chapter, we review constructivist instruction briefly and consider the variability of instructional apps implementing constructivist instruction for experimentation. Since constructivist instruction situates learners in authentic environments to pursue real-world tasks, we will engage as educational researchers seeking to advance the field by implementing machine learning techniques as tools for experimentation. In the simulated research scenarios, we will use Python to create two instructional apps to produce machine learning tools for experimentation and knowledge discovery.

First, we will create an app that implements a machine learning technique (algorithm) to find patterns in data intended to improve learner satisfaction with instruction. According to Baker and Yacef (2009), improving instruction is one of the goals of Educational Data Mining (EDM). Another goal of EDM is to advance learning analytics through machine learning methods (Hung & Crooks, 2009; Tsai, Ouyang, & Chang, 2015), which may also be referred to as data mining methods. Machine learning and intelligent tutoring also offer methods for improving personalized learning environments (Verdú, Regueras, Gal, de Castro, Verdú, & Kohen-Vacs, 2017). Since we are simulating the work of educational researchers, we will use fictitious data.

Second, we will create an app that implements a machine learning technique to discover a valid and reliable method for identifying effective K-12 teachers. As before, we will use fictional data for this simulation. However, school administrators in actual school districts and some educational researchers in U.S. States, Canadian Provinces, and regions throughout the world have access to real data. In actual educational research, a literature review would inform selection of measurements useful for identifying effective teachers. Measures of teacher effectiveness selected in light of prior research would then be triangulated with (compared with) measures used by school districts and to national models of teacher effectiveness, for instance.

6.1 Implementing the Instructional Method

Engagement in constructivist instruction leads each learner to develop a unique personal view of the subject matter. Learners engage in authentic tasks, seeking to understand and resolve problems that may not have an obvious solution and may have multiple solutions. In constructivist instruction, learners seek to perform like experts, whether mathematicians, writers, researchers, managers, entrepreneurs, architects, engineers, botanists, or golfers, for instance. Consistent with Bednar, Cunningham, Duffy, and Perry (1991), constructivist instruction does not lead instructional designers to decompose authentic tasks into predetermined instructional objectives. There is an instructional goal (accomplish the authentic task) and a knowledge base upon which to draw, but the path to task accomplishment is not entirely clear. Evaluation is based on the extent to which the learner can justify actions taken, results obtained, and conclusions drawn.

6.2 Diversity of the Apps

In the case of constructivist instruction, apps vary in accordance with authentic tasks. Instructional apps for retail management simulate operations in particular types of stores. Apps for novice entrepreneurs facilitate decision making in business. Apps that simulate operating rooms enable surgical practice. Flight simulators facilitate practice for pilots. Such apps enable authentic practice.

With respect to authentic tasks, professionals in data analytics, such as geopolitical risk analysts, seek to persuade clients to accept their analyses. Educational researchers engage in knowledge discovery and theory building. Conditions in actual schools and school districts might initiate a search for a solution to a particular problem and some educational researchers might seek to contribute to such a search, ultimately to advance theory. An early step for educational researchers would be to search scholarly journals for partial solutions evident in prior work, as well as to gain insights into methodologies used in the disciplined inquiries. Hypotheses pertaining to new approaches to a particular problem might emerge from such a literature search. Testing hypotheses leads researchers to deduce answers, which is consistent with the hypothetico–deductive research tradition (Cook & Campbell, 1979). In Section 6.3 we hypothesize that learners are more satisfied with instruction when accurately informed of the approximate completion time. Literature on design heuristics considered in Chapter 2 indicates that users like to feel in control of apps and that displays of system status, such as percentage of lesson completed, might contribute to satisfaction with apps. Certainly, some instructional apps and other instructional materials provide estimates of completion time, but how accurate and satisfying are those general estimates? Can apps be developed to provide predictions of completion time customized to each learner? If so, is it possible to measure the learner's satisfaction with customized predictions of completion time versus general predictions for a large population of learners? In Section 6.3 we consider fictional data that would address one component of that educational research scenario. In particular, we seek to determine how to create a customized prediction of instructional completion time for each learner.

In contrast to hypothesis testing, an educational researcher might seek to contribute to the knowledge base of the field by gathering data and inducing (synthesizing) a theory grounded in data (Glaser & Strauss, 1967). Such an approach to research is consistent with the empirico-inductive research tradition. Proceeding from data to a model (theory) for identifying effective K-12 teachers is the educational research scenario pursued in Section 6.4.

Consider the following examples of constructivist instruction.

2050 Energy Calculator
United Kingdom Department of Energy and Climate Change
http://2050-calculator-tool.decc.gov.uk/

The Producer (of films)
Annenberg Foundation
www.learner.org/interactives/cinema/producer/

My Corporis Fabrica (modeling anatomy)
Olivier Palombi, Guillaume Bousquet, David Jospin, Sahar Hassan, Lionel Revéret, and François Faure
www.sofa-framework.org/applications/gallery/anatomy-modeling/
www.mycorporisfabrica.org/

Machine Learning

Given training data, machines improve performance on a wide variety of tasks. For large vocabulary continuous speech recognition, algorithms have been trained to identify spoken words in real time. In seeking to make autonomous cars, algorithms have been trained to distinguish between people, animals, and other things in images. Multiple machine learning algorithms and images depicting states in the game Go were used to train the *AlphaGo* program to play Go well enough to defeat European Go champion, Fan Hui (Silver, Huang, Maddison, Guez, Sifre, et al., 2016). Using a machine learning algorithm called a binary classifier, software has also been trained to classify email as legitimate or spam.

For the research scenario in Section 6.3, a researcher might ultimately hypothesize that learners are more satisfied with customized predictions of instructional completion time than with general predictions. In order to get that far, the notion of a "customized" prediction of completion time must be operationalized and instructional apps must be able to provide such predictions of completion time. A customized prediction of instructional completion time could be a prediction of completion time based on the time it took the learner to complete similar instructional activities. In Section 6.3, we consider fictional data for predicting instructional completion time, which might reveal how to make accurate predictions of instructional completion time for each learner. In turn, learners presented with accurate predictions of instructional completion time may perceive such predictions as an improvement to instruction.

Section 6.4 addresses the second educational research scenario. In the second scenario we seek to distinguish between effective and ineffective teachers. Given measures of teacher effectiveness for teachers in a particular school district, a machine learning algorithm could seek any pattern in the data that distinguishes between two groups of teachers, effective and ineffective teachers. In machine learning, such an approach is called *unsupervised learning*. In contrast, *supervised learning* algorithms are trained using data that identify which input data sets belong to which class, such as benign or malignant tumors. In this simulated educational research scenario, the training data will identify effective and ineffective teachers. The fictitious data set on teacher effectiveness will also include, for each teacher, the mean Math test score of the teacher's students (scaled to fit a range from 1 to 7) and a rating for lesson preparation, classroom teaching, and rapport with stakeholders (i.e., students, fellow teachers, and administrators). We assume that school administrators have provided those ratings from 1 to 7, along with a designation identifying each teacher as effective or ineffective. For this scenario, we will code a machine learning algorithm to perform logistic regression in order to create a software model for distinguishing between effective and ineffective teachers. Like people, the software model will be imperfect. The better the training data set, the better the model. Conceivably, once the data analysis has been completed, teacher effectiveness data pertaining to teachers in other school districts could be input to the model to predict which teachers are effective and ineffective.

The general idea in predictive modeling is to derive a mapping between particular input variables (variously called *attributes, features, predictors*, or *independent variables*) and the output variable, which is often called either the *criterion variable* or the *independent variable*. If we speak of this (mysterious) mapping as a function represented by f, and the input and output variables depicted as X and Y respectively, then we could use the following notation to depict the goal of predictive modeling.

$$Y = f(X)$$

For both of the educational scenarios we consider below, the function will be linear, which is a good starting place for those new to machine learning, but could not be assumed when seeking an actual mapping from input variables to the criterion variable. Real-world analyses might hypothesize and test whether a linear mapping is a good fit for the data. For example, a correlation coefficient might reveal that a linear relationship exists between two variables, which would justify linear modeling. It is also possible to test linear and non-linear mappings using multiple machine learning algorithms in order to determine the best model.

Use of linear analyses in machine learning makes evident the importance of prior work by statisticians. As noted, linear models provide a fine starting place for our two simulated inquiries into predictive modeling. Subsequent work would consider non-linear analyses performed by algorithms such as Classification and Regression Trees, k-Nearest Neighbor, Learning Vector Quantization, and Support Vector Machines (Brownlee, 2017; Raschka, 2016). Both Brownlee (2017) and Raschka (2016) discuss ensemble methods, which perform analyses using multiple machine learning algorithms.

Raschka (2016) discusses reinforcement learning as a third category of machine learning beyond supervised and unsupervised learning.

6.3 Seeking to Improve Instruction

Estimates of time needed to complete tasks facilitate planning. Accurate estimates of completion time are particularly helpful. Instructional developers might estimate time to complete instruction based on the time it took someone else to complete the instruction or the average (mean, mode, or median) time it took some group of people to compete the instruction. Alternatively, instructional completion time might be based on estimates of time to complete the parts of the instruction. A reading might take about 30 minutes and a follow-up task might take another 30 minutes. Maybe such estimates are close enough to satisfy learners. On the other hand, some learners might find engagement in instruction more satisfying when an accurate estimate of completion time is available. Unsolved questions, which can be tested empirically, often make for compelling research. Our world becomes more predictable and manageable when (particular) unsolved questions are answered. Selection of the question is critical.

TARGET LEARNERS: People capable of abstract thinking (deduction and induction; formulate hypotheses; consider possibilities; analyze; synthesize) and interested in knowledge discovery.
INSTRUCTIONAL OBJECTIVE: The learner will be able to gain educational research skills by seeking to improve learner satisfaction with instruction.

Design

We seek to improve instruction by offering learners better estimates of the time it will take to complete instruction. Imagine programming the coin puzzle app in the previous chapter to store the number of minutes it takes the learner to solve the problem. Also imagine programming the app to ask the learner whether it is okay to time them and to use the time taken in a research study that seeks to improve instruction. Assume that we have also programmed a second coin puzzle in the app and have data on how long it took learners to complete each of the two coin puzzles. To proceed along this line of research, we need an app to predict how long it might take the learner to complete the second coin puzzle, given the amount of time it took them to complete the first puzzle. The method we will use to derive this predication is called *simple linear regression*, which uses one input variable to predict one output variable and assumes that the input and output variables have a linear relationship.

Development

We assume that there is a linear relationship between the times taken to complete the two coin puzzles. That seems especially plausible when the two coin puzzles are similar. The data set has fictitious values for two variables: (1) Time taken to complete the first coin puzzle; and (2) Time taken to complete the second coin puzzle. Times taken are in minutes. Figure 6.1 depicts the data in a scatter plot. Notice that a linear relationship appears to exist. We seek to predict the time learners will take to complete the second coin puzzle based on the time the learner took on the first coin puzzle. To accomplish this, we need to determine what statisticians call the "line of best fit," which is the line that minimizes errors in the predictions. Given the data depicted in Figure 6.1, a straight line cannot be drawn through all of the points, but a line can be drawn such that the total distance between all points and the line is minimized. The distance between a point and the line is the measure of the error in the prediction. There are multiple methods for determining the line of best fit. Whatever method is used, the slope and y-intercept are determined. You may recall that a line can be specified algebraically as $y = mx + b$, where m is the slope and b is the y-intercept. For consistency with other texts, we will use $y = B0 + B1x$, where B0 is the y-intercept and B1 is the slope.

We will write a program in Python to calculate the slope (B1) and y-intercept (B0) in accordance with the equations below.

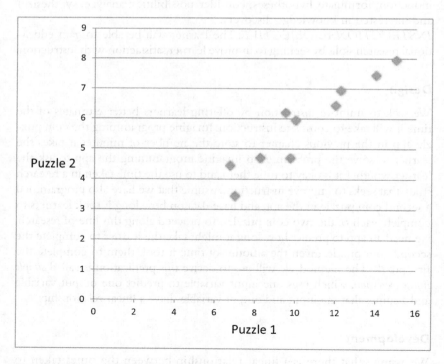

Figure 6.1 Training Data Scatter Plot.

$$B1 = \frac{\sum_{i=1}^{n}\left(x_i - \text{mean}(x)\right) \times \left(x_i - \text{mean}(y)\right)}{\sum_{i=1}^{n}\left(x_i - \text{mean}(x)\right)^2}$$

$$B0 = \text{mean}(y) - B1 \times \text{mean}(x)$$

Once we have B1 and B0, we will have the model needed to predict the time it will take a learner to complete the second coin puzzle, given the time the learner took to complete the first coin puzzle. To calculate B1 and B0, each row of the data, which represents the time it took one learner to complete coin puzzles 1 and 2, trains the model to make increasingly accurate predictions. The training data are stored in a two-dimensional array. Since there are data for only 10 fictitious learners (20 values total), the data are entered directly into the two-dimensional array `trainingData` in the Python code. (In Section 6.4, data are read from a file, which is typical in real-world apps.)

Open a new document in your text editor and enter the following Python code. Save the file as *makeCompletionTimeModel.py*.

```
trainingData = [[15,8], [12,6.5], [6.75,4.5],
[8.25,4.75], [10,6], [9.5,6.25], [14,7.5],
[12.25,7], [7,3.5], [9.75,4.75]]

sumX = sum(row[0] for row in trainingData)
sumY = sum(row[1] for row in trainingData)

#print('Training data, sumX, sumY')
#print(trainingData, sumX, sumY)

N = len(trainingData)
meanX = sumX/N
meanY = sumY/N

sumVarianceXY = 0.0
sumVarianceXsquared = 0.0

for index in range(N):
    varianceX = trainingData[index][0] - meanX
    varianceY = trainingData[index][1] - meanY
    sumVarianceXY += varianceX * varianceY
    sumVarianceXsquared += varianceX * varianceX

B1 = sumVarianceXY/sumVarianceXsquared
B0 = meanY - B1 * meanX

#print('\n')
#print(N, sumX, sumY, meanX, meanY, sumVarianceXY,
sumVarianceXsquared)
print(B0, B1)
```

Run the program by opening a command window and entering the following.

```
python makeCompletionTimeModel.py
```

The results are B0 = 0.7861923212398727 and B1 =0.486967241986615. Due to rounding error, your results may vary slightly.

Most of the program consists of assignment statements, which would be programmed very similarly in other procedural programming languages. In JavaScript, for instance, the only difference for most of the assignment statements would be a semicolon at the end of each assignment statement.

The Python statement below loops through the ten rows of the two-dimensional array, `trainingData`. As the loop progresses, the variable `row` contains the current value of `trainingData`, which is a one-dimensional array. The first element in the array, which is at index 0, is the X value. The sum function calculates the sum of each value.

```
sumX = sum(row[0] for row in trainingData)
```

The Python statement `N = len(trainingData)` assigns the number of elements in the array `trainingData` to N. In JavaScript, that Python statement would be `N = trainingData.length`.

With respect to the Python code above, notice the loop that begins with the following line.

```
for index in range(N):
```

This statement begins a loop with four assignment statements in the loop body, which are used to calculate intermediate results needed to calculate B1. Notice in the Python code above that the statements in the loop body are indented. In JavaScript, that loop structure would appear as follows and the statements in the loop body would be placed within braces { }.

```
for index = 0 to N - 1 {
}
```

In machine learning programs it is helpful to measure the extent of the error. Since the training data set contains actual values, subtracting each actual Y from the predicted Y yields the extent of the error. To emphasize larger errors and minimize smaller errors, the difference between the actual value and predicted value is squared, which is called Squared Error (SE). To calculate error over the entire data set, the sum of individual SE is calculated and divided by the number of items in the data set (N) in order to calculate Mean Squared Error (MSE). Lastly, the square root of MSE is calculated to yield Root MSE or RMSE. Add the following statements at the end of the script.

```
sumSquaredError = 0.0
for index in range(N):
  predictedY = B0 + B1 * trainingData[index][0]
  sumSquaredError += (trainingData[index][1] - predictedY)
* (trainingData[index][1] - predictedY)
RMSE = sqrt(sumSquaredError/float(N))
print ('RMSE: ', RMSE)
```

The square root function is not standard in Python so it is imported from the Python math library using the following statement, which appears as the first statement in the script.

```
from math import sqrt
```

As educational researchers, we have learned something of the benefits and limitations of a predictive modeling technique, which we might apply in pursuit of an answer to the hypothesis that learners prefer customized predictions of completion time.

This same type of predictive modeling method (algorithm) could be used to predict posttest scores given pretest scores or cost of a house given size of the house in square feet, provided the two variables are related in a linear manner. With respect to limitations, simple linear regression uses one input variable, which may not be sufficient to make particular predictions of interest. After completing the seven tasks below, continue in your role as an educational researcher in the next scenario, which provides insights into the influence of multiple input variables on predictive modeling for the purpose of predicting effective teachers.

Task 6.1 Add the following line as the first line in *makeCompletionTimeModel.py*.

```
from math import sqrt
```

Then add the Python code above for calculating RMSE as the final statements in *makeCompletionTimeModel.py*. What is the value of RMSE?

Task 6.2 Using the values calculated for B0 and B1, calculate the predicted value for x = 10.

Task 6.3 Write a separate program in Python called *predictCompletionTime.py* to display the predicted values for x = 1 through 20.

Task 6.4 After making a backup copy of *makeCompletionTimeModel.py*, change the values in `trainingData`. For example, add three to five more training instances. Run the model to calculate B0, B1, and RMSE. How did the RMSE change in comparison with the RMSE you obtained in Task 6.1?

Task 6.5 After making a backup copy of *makeCompletionTimeModel.py*, or at least saving the training data, delete five instances from trainingData. Compare the RMSE values obtained in Tasks 6.1, 6.2, and 6.3. How can the data set be changed to reduce RMSE?

Task 6.6 Write the program in *makeCompletionTimeModel.py* in JavaScript.

Task 6.7 To enable the user to enter training data, add a textarea tag to the JavaScript program you wrote for Task 6.6. You may use the following tag.

```
<textarea id="userTrainingData" rows="12" cols="20">
<textarea>
```

In JavaScript, instead of assigning values directly to trainingData, use the following declaration.

```
trainingData = []
```

Then use the following code to retrieve the data entered by the user in the textarea.

```
userDataStr = document.getElementById("userTraining
Data").value;
```

Lastly, parse userDataStr to populate the trainingData array. If you assign each line of data in userDataStr to crntInputData, you can append each line of data using the following statement.

```
trainingData.append(crntInputData)
```

6.4 Developing a Model to Identify Effective Teachers

As noted previously, a literature search would inform an educational researcher seeking measures of effective teaching. For this educational research simulation, we will use mean standardized math test score of the students of the teacher and the following three administrator ratings for teacher performance: (1) Lesson preparation skill, which would be based on a sample set of lesson plans; (2) Classroom observations of teaching; and (3) A composite score pertaining to rapport with students, fellow teachers, parents, and administrators. To enhance validity and reliability in real-world scenarios, scoring rubrics would be used to help make those ratings accurate and consistent. As noted, this simulation will use fictional data for the standardized test scores and ratings of the administrators. However, you will implement an actual machine learning algorithm, a *classifier* in this case. Since we need only distinguish between effective and ineffective teachers, we will use, as per Brownlee (2017, p. 52), the "go-to" machine learning method for binary classification, *logistic regression*. We may also refer to *logistic regression* as a statistical method. We will program the classifier in Python, using a few assignment statements and loops.

TARGET LEARNERS: People capable of abstract thinking (deduction and induction; formulate hypotheses; consider possibilities; analyze; synthesize) and interested in knowledge discovery.
INSTRUCTIONAL OBJECTIVE: The learner will gain educational research skills by seeking to develop a new model for identifying effective teachers.

Design

This app will input a file of fictitious data about effective and ineffective teachers, which will be used to train the model. The first five rows of the input file appear in Table 6.1. Each row represents a fictitious teacher. Column 1 is the scaled score (from 1–7) for the mean of the teacher's students on the standardized Math test administered in the school district. Columns 2–4 are administrator ratings (from 1–7) for lesson preparation, classroom teaching, and rapport with stakeholders. The final column is the administrator's effectiveness rating for the teacher, which is 1 for an effective teacher, 0 for an ineffective teacher. Though invisible on a page, the tab character ("\t") appears after each of the first four columns on every row in order to separate the data. Such a file is said to be "tab delimited," which is convenient for splitting the data in Python and other programming languages.

This app will output coefficients (weights) of each predictor variable and a constant value. Those values—the coefficients and the constant—define the model for identifying effective teachers. Additional input data pertaining to teachers (perhaps in another school or school district) could be input to the model in order to predict the effective and ineffective teachers.

Development

This app will perform logistic regression using stochastic gradient descent. Logistic regression is useful for binary categorization, such as when labeling a characteristic as true or false. In this case the training data specify whether a teacher is effective or ineffective. Consequently, the model will predict whether a teacher is effective or ineffective based on input data.

Open a new document in your text editor and enter the following code in order to read the input file and initialize the `trainingData` array and the `teacherEffective` array. [The first line of code below, which imports three routines from the Python math library, is not required to read the input file and initialize the arrays. However, the line is included now to eliminate the need to add it to the start of the program later.]

```
from math import exp, sqrt, pow
```

Table 6.1 First Five Rows of Input File

5.30	6	5	7	1
4.30	1	3	1	0
5.29	5	5	6	1
5.33	7	7	6	1
5.30	6	5	7	1

```
fileHandle = open('teacherEffectivenessTD.txt')

trainingData = []
teacherEffective = []

for crntLine in fileHandle:
  crntValues = crntLine.split('\t')
  numColumns = len(crntValues)

  crntPredictors = [1]
  for index in range(numColumns - 1):
      crntPredictors.append(float(crntValues[index]))
  trainingData.append(crntPredictors)
  teacherEffective.append(int(crntValues
[numColumns - 1]))
print('Training data')
print(trainingData)
print('Number of teachers in sample: ', len(trainingData))

print('\nTeacherEffective')
print(teacherEffective)
```

Save the file as *makeTEM_001.py*. (TEM is the acronym for Teacher Effectiveness Model.) Run the program in a command window by entering the following.

```
python makeTEM_001.py
```

Debug as necessary. Proceed when the two-dimensional `trainingData` array contains 40 rows of data beginning with the value 1 followed by the values in the first four columns of the input file ([1, 5.3, 6.0, 5.0, 7.0], [1, 4.3, 1.0, 3.0, 1.0], etc.) and the one-dimensional array `teacherEffective` contains the last column of the input file. The value 1 is inserted before the values of the predictor variables from the input file to facilitate calculation of the constant term. Multiplying the constant term by 1 (the multiplicative identity) will leave the constant term unchanged until it is changed during the gradient descent phase.

Copy the *makeTEM_001.py* file to *makeTEM_002.py*. In *makeTEM_002.py*, add the following code at the end of the file.

```
coefficients = [0.0] * numColumns
print('number of coefficients', len(coefficients),
coefficients)

learningRate = 0.2

numTeachers = len(trainingData)
for crntEpoch in range(10):
  sumSE = 0
  totalErrors = 0;
  for crntTeacherNum in range(numTeachers):
    exponent = 0
    for crntPredictorIndex in range(numColumns):
      exponent += coefficients[crntPredictor
Index]*trainingData[crntTeacherNum][crntPredictorIndex]

    predictionValue = 1 / (1 + exp(- exponent))
    prediction = 0 if predictionValue < 0.5 else 1
#      print('crntEpoch crntTeacherNum   predictionValue
prediction ', crntEpoch + 1, crntTeacherNum, prediction
Value, prediction)

    squaredError = pow((teacherEffective[crntTeacher
Num] - predictionValue), 2)

    sumSE += squaredError

    error = 0 if prediction == teacherEffective
[crntTeacherNum] else 1
    totalErrors += error

    for crntPredictorIndex in range(numColumns):
      coefficients[crntPredictorIndex] = coefficients
[crntPredictorIndex] + learningRate * (teacherEffective
[crntTeacherNum] - predictionValue) * predictionValue
* (1 - predictionValue) * trainingData[crntTeacherNum]
[crntPredictorIndex]
#          print(crntPredictorIndex, coefficients
[crntPredictorIndex])
    RMSE = sqrt(sumSE/numTeachers)
    accuracy = (1 - totalErrors/float(numTeachers))
* 100.0
#    print('\n')
    print("Statistics:   crntEpoch   totalErrors
accuracy RMSE: ", crntEpoch + 1, totalErrors, accuracy,
RMSE)
#    print('\n\n\n')
```

```
print(coefficients)
```

Save the file *makeTEM_002.py*. Debug as necessary. The coefficients, B0 to B4 follow (though your computer may yield slightly different values).

```
B0 = -0.1720304102725984
B1 = -0.5783649317063256
B2 = 0.48825964160975904
B3 = 0.036453654357493405
B4 = 0.8121268634501364
```

In logistic regression, the inputs for each instance (in this case, each teacher's effectiveness measures) are used to make a prediction based on the probability that the inputs belong to the default class (class = 0), which in this case is the group of ineffective teachers. In the code above, the probability that the inputs belong to the default class is stored in the variable, `predictionValue`. If `predictionValue` < 0.5, an ineffective teacher (default class) is predicted; otherwise `predictionValue` will be greater than or equal to 0.5 and an effective teacher (class = 1) will be predicted. Logistic regression is performed in the code above using the following equations.

$$\text{exponent} = B0 + B1 \times X1 + B2 \times X2 + B3 \times X3 + B4 \times X4$$

$$\text{preditionValue} = \frac{1}{1 + e^{-\text{exponent}}}$$

The following code implements those equations for each of the 40 teachers in the fictitious data set.

```
for crntTeacherNum in range(numTeachers):
    exponent = 0
    for crntPredictorIndex in range(numColumns):
        exponent += coefficients[crntPredi
ctorIndex] * trainingData[crntTeacherNum]
[crntPredictorIndex]

    predictionValue = 1 / (1 + exp(- exponent))
```

With the constant term (B0) and the four input variables (X1, X2, X3, X4), `crntPredictorIndex` goes from 0 to 4. The first time through the inner loop, `crntPredictorIndex` is 0 and the constant term (B0) is multiplied by 1 so as not to alter the constant term. That is why the first column of each row in the `trainingData` matrix is set to 1 and the remaining columns in each row of `trainingData` are the values of input variables (X1, X2, X3, X4), which are read from the data file.

Once `predictionValue` has been calculated, the following if statement sets prediction to 0 or 1.

```
prediction = 0 if predictionValue < 0.5 else 1
```

Also, for each of the 40 teachers, the coefficients (B0, B1, B2, B3, and B4) are adjusted in order to minimize error. This is done using gradient descent. In metaphorical terms, minimizing error using gradient descent is like traveling down the surface of a bowl. At the bottom of the bowl, one reaches the place of minimum error. The following equation is used to update each coefficient, *b*.

$$b = b + \text{learningRate} * (y - \text{prediction}) \times \text{prediction} \times (1 - \text{prediction}) \times x$$

The loop below updates all five coefficients (B0–B4) in this app. Since the following loop is nested within the loop for each teacher (`for crntTeacherNum in range (numTeachers) :`), the five coefficients are updated after processing each teacher's data. In other words, by minimizing error for each input instance, the model learns to make better predictions about a teacher's effectiveness. Further, the loops performing logistic regression using stochastic gradient descent are repeated ten times due to the outer loop, `for crntEpoch in range (10) :`. Each iteration through the entire set of input data is called an *epoch*. The outer loop could be changed to a while loop, which would stop when accuracy reaches 100 percent, but the input data are a sampling of data and it is not clear whether stopping at that point would minimize error for other data samples. It is also not clear that stopping after ten iterations through the entire set of input data is optimal. The optimal learning rate is also not clear. It was set to 0.2 based on the heuristic that a value in the range 0.1 to 0.3 often works well. The learning rate is the pace of learning, which metaphorically is the rate of descent along the surface of the bowl. The higher the learning rate, the quicker the descent and the faster the minimum is reached, but at the expense of less learning. The smaller the number of iterations through the entire data set, the fewer the updates to the coefficients and the less refined the model; the less refined the model, the greater the risk of inaccurate prediction.

```
    for crntPredictorIndex in range(numColumns):
        coefficients[crntPredictorIndex] =
coefficients[crntPredictorIndex] + learningRate * (tea
cherEffective[crntTeacherNum]   -   predictionValue)
*   predictionValue   *   (1   -   predictionValue)   *
trainingData[crntTeacherNum][crntPredictorIndex]
```

To check the validity of this model, accuracy and RMSE are calculated. In this case, accuracy is the number of times the model correctly identified the teacher as effective or ineffective, which is determined by comparing the algorithm's prediction with the school administrator's rating.

Copy the *makeTEM_002.py* file to *makeTEM_003.py*. In *makeTEM_003.py*, add the following code at the end of the file. The code below stores the coefficients in the file called `teacherEffectivenessModel.txt`.

```
outputFile = open('teacherEffectivenessModel.txt',
'w')
for crntCoefficient in range(numColumns):
  outputFile.write(str(coefficients[crntCoefficient]) +
'\n')
  print(coefficients[crntCoefficient])
```

The complete program (instructional app) appears below.

```
from math import exp, sqrt, pow
fileHandle = open('teacherEffectivenessTD.txt')

trainingData = []
teacherEffective = []
for crntLine in fileHandle:
  crntValues = crntLine.split('\t')
  numColumns = len(crntValues)

  crntPredictors = [1]
  for index in range(numColumns - 1):
    crntPredictors.append(float(crntValues
[index]))
    trainingData.append(crntPredictors)
    teacherEffective.append(int(crntValues[numColumns
- 1]))
print('Training data')
print(trainingData)
print('Number of teachers in sample: ', len(trainingData))

print('\nTeacherEffective')
print(teacherEffective)
coefficients = [0.0] * numColumns
print('number of coefficients', len(coefficients),
coefficients)

learningRate = 0.2

numTeachers = len(trainingData)
```

```
for crntEpoch in range(10):
  sumSE = 0
  totalErrors = 0;
  for crntTeacherNum in range(numTeachers):
      exponent = 0
      for crntPredictorIndex in range(numColumns):
          exponent += coefficients[crntPredictorIndex]
* trainingData[crntTeacherNum][crntPredictorIndex]
     #    print('\nExponent')
     #    print(exponent)
          predictionValue = 1 / (1 + exp(- exponent))
          prediction = 0 if predictionValue < 0.5 else 1
     #    print('crntEpoch crntTeacherNum predictionValue
prediction ', crntEpoch + 1, crntTeacherNum,
predictionValue, prediction)
          squaredError = pow((teacherEffective
[crntTeacherNum] - predictionValue), 2)
          sumSE += squaredError

          error = 0 if prediction == teacherEffective
          [crntTeacherNum] else 1
          totalErrors += error

          for crntPredictorIndex in range(numColumns):
              coefficients[crntPredictorIndex] = coefficients
[crntPredictorIndex] + learningRate * (teacherEffective
[crntTeacherNum] - predictionValue) * predictionValue
* (1 - predictionValue) * trainingData[crntTeacherNum]
[crntPredictorIndex]
     #          print(crntPredictorIndex, coefficients
[crntPredictorIndex])
  RMSE = sqrt(sumSE/numTeachers)
  accuracy = (1 - totalErrors/float(numTeachers)) * 100.0

  #   print('\n')
      print("Statistics:   crntEpoch   totalErrors
  accuracy RMSE: ", crntEpoch + 1, totalErrors,
  accuracy, RMSE)
  #   print('\n\n\n')

outputFwile    =    open('teacherEffectivenessModel.
txt', 'w')

for crntCoefficient in range(numColumns):
    outputFile.write("%s\n" % coefficients[crntCoefficient])
```

```
#      outputFile.write(str(coefficients[crntCoefficient])
+ '\n')
        print(coefficients[crntCoefficient])
print('\n')
print("See output file, teacherEffectivenessModel.
txt")
print('\n')
```

Task 6.8 If the input data were real, would the model be valid and reliable? That is, would the model accurately identify effective and ineffective teachers given only the predictor data from the school district in subsequent years (not the school administrator's overall teacher effectiveness rating)?

Task 6.9 Assuming another school district rated teacher performance on lesson planning, classroom observation, and rapport with stakeholders using the same rubrics as the school district from which the training data were obtained (again assuming a real scenario) and provided the mean standardized math test score for each teacher, would the model be valid and reliable? Assuming no overall rating of teacher effectiveness was provided with the data set, would the model accurately identify effective and ineffective teachers?

Task 6.10 What criteria would you actually use to distinguish between effective and ineffective teachers? Could a school administrator obtain valid and reliable measures of those criteria? Would you use a machine learning algorithm to analyze the data? What if there was no linear relationship between the data? What are the implications of valid and reliable models of teacher effectiveness on teachers and on society at large?

Task 6.11 What happens when you limit the number of epochs to five by replacing the 10 with 5 in the following line of code? Also, predict what will happen to RMSE when you change the number of epochs to 20, 50, 100, and 500? Test your predictions.

```
for crntEpoch in range(10):
```

Task 6.12 Change the learning rate to 0.3 and run the model again. How many epochs were needed to attain 100 percent accuracy? What was the effect on RMSE?

Task 6.13 Change the learning rate to 0.1. How many epochs were needed to attain 100 percent accuracy? What was the effect on RMSE? Predict what will happen if you change the learning rate to 0.05. Will you need more than ten epochs to attain 100 percent accuracy? How will accuracy and RMSE change if the learning rate is set to 0.5, 0.8, 1.0, 2.0, or to something higher? Test your predictions.

Task 6.14 Given the coefficients in the model, would a teacher with predictor values 5.12, 5, 4, and 6 be effective or ineffective? Write a program in Python to read the model's coefficients from `teacherEffectivenessModel.txt` to identify effective and ineffective teachers using additional fictitious data in the file called `dataToTestTEM.txt`, which is available in the eResources.

Task 6.15 Given your work through this chapter, what have you learned about educational research? What have you learned about machine learning and how it can be used in educational research? What have you learned about practical applications of mathematics, particularly statistics? What will you seek to learn next about machine learning, statistics, and educational research? (See Chapter 7 for information about scikit-learn, which is a Python machine learning library enabling use of linear and non-linear machine learning algorithms.)

References

Baker, R. S. J. D. & Yacef, K. (2009). The state of educational data mining in 2009: A review and future visions. *Journal of Educational Data Mining, 1*(1), 3–16.

Bednar, A. K., Cunningham, D., Duffy, T. M., & Perry, J. D. (1991). Theory into practice: How do we link? In G. J. Anglin (Ed.), *Instructional technology: Past, present, and future* (pp. 88–101). Englewood, CO: Libraries Unlimited.

Brownlee, J. (2017). *Master machine learning algorithms: Discover how they work and implement them from scratch*. Melbourne, Victoria, Australia: Machine Learning Mastery.

Cook, T. D. & Campbell, D. T. (1979). *Quasi-experimentation: Design & analysis issues for field settings*. Boston, MA: Houghton Mifflin.

Glaser, B. G. & Strauss, A. L. (1967). *The discovery of grounded theory: Strategies for qualitative research*. Chicago, IL: Aldine.

Hung, J. L. & Crooks, S. M. (2009). Examining online learning patterns with data mining techniques in peer-moderated and teacher-moderated courses. *Journal of Educational Computing Research, 40*(2), 183–210.

Raschka, S. (2016). *Python machine learning*. Birmingham, UK: Packt Publishing.

Silver, D., Huang, A., Maddison, C. J., Guez, A., Sifre, L., van den Driessche, G., Schrittwieser, J., Antonoglou, I., Panneershelvam, V., Lanctot, M., Dieleman, S., Grewe, D., Nham, J., Kalchbrenner, N., Sutskever, I., Lillicrap, T., Leach, M., Kavukcuoglu, K., Graepel, T., & Hassabis, D. (2016). Mastering the game of Go with deep neural networks and tree search. *Nature, 529*, 484–489.

Tsai, Y-R, Ouyang, C-S, & Chang, Y. (2015). Identifying engineering students' English sentence reading comprehension errors: Applying a data mining technique. *Journal of Educational Computing Research, 54*(1), 62–84.

Verdú, E., Regueras, L. M., Gal, E., de Castro, J. P., Verdú, M. J., & Kohen-Vacs, D. (2017). Integration of an intelligent tutoring system in a course of computer network design. *Educational Technology Research & Development, 65*(3), 653–677.

Chapter 7

Current and Future Considerations

Instructional app developers, like all computer programmers, can leverage Application Programming Interfaces (APIs) to extend the functionality of their apps. APIs are collections of well-tested functional routines. We will become aware of many types of APIs in this chapter and focus on one in particular, the *Web Speech API* (https://dvcs.w3.org/hg/speech-api/raw-file/tip/speechapi.html). Available since 2012 (with some corrections and additions in 2014, https://dvcs.w3.org/hg/speech-api/raw-file/tip/speechapi-errata.html), the Web Speech API enables app developers to include speech synthesis and speech recognition functionality in web apps. As instructional app developers, we will use the Web Speech API to examine how voice recognition and synthesis capabilities provide the foundation for a voice tutor. When we have completed that work, we consider some next steps toward key fundamental goals: Making instructional apps ubiquitous across diverse digital devices; incorporating machine learning algorithms in instructional apps; and vastly improving instructional development tools.

7.1 Software Extensibility

Software developers have the option to extend the functionality of their programs through use of prepackaged, well tested, functional code. Just as libraries provide books, software repositories facilitate free access to software. *GitHub* (github.com) is one such repository. Additionally, some universities, corporations, and other entities, including individual software developers, make their software available to others for free. Unlike books, which must be returned when borrowed from libraries, software is copied from libraries under licensing agreements, which in the case of particular free software requires only acknowledgement of the original developer. Further, some software free of monetary cost is also open source, which enables developers and others to view and modify the source code. Also unlike books in libraries, which are read when borrowed, application programming interfaces (APIs) provide protocols to leverage, extend, and capitalize on the software routines. Such extensibility fosters innovation.

In Section 7.2, we leverage an implementation of the Web Speech API specification, which was edited by Glen Shires and Hans Wennborg and published in 2012 by the Speech API Community group (www.w3.org/community/speech-api/) of the World Wide Web Consortium (W3C). The Web Speech API Specification provides technical specifications of the functions and variables that perform speech synthesis and speech recognition. It also provides comments about conformance, use cases, security and privacy consideration, and a few example code segments. In addition to the Web Speech API, which we will use for speech synthesis and speech recognition in the next section, it is helpful to be aware of many other uses of APIs. The following list identifies a variety of use cases.

- Interactive mapping
- Data analytics
- Social media content sharing and third party logins
- Monetize apps (advertising)
- Buying
- Selling
- Accessing fonts
- Video streaming
- Weather forecasting
- Viewing real time bus and subway data (supplied by some municipalities)
- Search for books
- Query big data
- Using machine learning models
- Make predictions
- Natural language understanding
- Game services
- Programming language extensions (e.g., jQuery, node.js, Angular).

For links to specific APIs, see the article *50 Most Useful APIs for Developers*, which was published by the Computer Science Zone online magazine and is available at www.computersciencezone.org/50-most-useful-apis-for-developers/. Google provides a list of their APIs, which you may access at https://developers.google.com/apis-explorer/#p/. The open source project, scikit-learn (which is also referred to as sklearn) maintains a library of machine learning methods for use in Python programming environments. The scikit-learn project website (http://scikit-learn.org/) provides installation instructions for the API, which includes code and sample data. Additional resources at the scikit-learn project website include a quick start guide, tutorials, API documentation, a flow chart for selecting particular machine learning methods, examples, and a list of replies to frequently asked questions (http://scikit-learn.org/stable/documentation.html). Brownlee (2016) offers a step-by-step guide to proceeding through an initial machine learning project, which includes a brief program (fewer than 20 lines of Python code) for testing the effects of six machine learning algorithms in the sklearn API.

7.2 Voice Interface for a Software Tutor

In this section we create apps that leverage the Web Speech API. To gain an appreciation for the utility of the Web Speech API, as well as to resolve any configuration issues you may encounter with your web browser and your computer's speakers and microphone, try the Web Speech API Demonstration at www.google.com/intl/en/chrome/demos/speech.html. I recommend using the latest version of the Google Chrome web browser for Web Speech API apps, including the ones in this section. Google's implementation of the Web Speech API Specification performs Large Vocabulary Continuous Speech Recognition (LVCSR) effectively in approximately 40 languages and multiple dialects. The speech synthesis function generates speech in over 50 voices. Although the default voice used by the following code is beneath present day standards, which have been set, for instance, by Apple's Siri, International Business Machine's (IBM's) Watson, Amazon's Alexa, Microsoft's Cortana, and the social robot, Jibo, we will quickly transition to a better voice after considering the code in the following example.

Sample App with Voice Synthesis

The following three lines of JavaScript code running in the Google Chrome web browser utter the following words: "What do you want to learn today?" The first line below, consistent with the Web Speech API specification, creates a Speech Synthesis Object. In the second line of code below, the words to be uttered are assigned to the variable text, which is in the Speech Synthesis Object. The third line of code below calls the speak method in order to speak the words.

```
var utterance = new SpeechSynthesisUtterance();
utterance.text = "What do you want to learn today?";
speechSynthesis.speak(utterance);
```

The first two lines of code can be combined into one line of code and the speak method can be called separately, as follows.

```
var utterance = new SpeechSynthesisUtterance("What
do you want to learn today?");
speechSynthesis.speak(utterance);
```

It is even possible to combine all three of the original lines of code into one, as shown below.

```
speechSynthesis.speak(new SpeechSynthesisUtterance("What do
you want to learn today?"));
```

Enter the following HTML and JavaScript into your text editor and save the file as *sampleSpeechSynthesis001.html*. Double-click the icon for the file in order to load the page into a Google Chrome web browser. (You may also test the web page in different web browsers.) You may choose to replace the words in the string assigned to utterance.text with other words in order to say something else.

```
<html>
<head>
  <title>Speech Synthesis Sample</title>
</head>

<body>


<p style="margin-top: 200px; text-align: center">Are
you listening? Do you hear me?<p3>

<script>
  var utterance = new SpeechSynthesisUtterance();
  utterance.text = "Hello, I hope that you are
well. I am wondering: What do you want to learn
today?";
  speechSynthesis.speak(utterance);
</script>

</body>
</html>
```

The default voice produced by that web page makes the utterance somewhat challenging to perceive. Selecting a superior voice is our next task. Before leaving this example, though, notice in the paragraph (<p>) tag above that the style attribute contains a `margin-top` setting to display text 200 pixels below the top line of the web browser's content space and a `text-align` setting to center the text.

In addition to the text variable, which contains the words (or letters) to be spoken, the Speech Synthesis Object has multiple settings that control, for instance, the rate at which words are spoken, the pitch of the voice, and the sound of the voice. The version of Google Chrome available at the time of writing includes 66 voices. After loading the voices into the array named voice, the following line of code assigns a voice to the Speech Synthesis Object.

```
utterance.voice = voices[50];
```

Note that the voices must be loaded before assigning a voice other than the default voice (which is `voices[0]`). Many objects, including the Speech Synthesis Object, include *event triggers*, which activate functions when key events have occurred. When an event is triggered, program execution continues with the statements in the body of the function assigned to the trigger.

The trigger for determining when the voices have been loaded is called onvoiceschanged. The voices load quickly; human beings perceive no delay as the voices load, but the CPU cannot wait a few milliseconds while the 66 voices load. The CPU executes other statements while the voices load and triggers the onvoiceschanged event when voice loading is complete. When triggered, program execution continues with the statements in the function assigned to the trigger. The following syntax can be used to define the function for a trigger.

```
speechSynthesis.onvoiceschanged = function() {
    // statements executed when trigger fires
}
```

A common alternative is to assign a function to a variable and then to set the trigger to the variable. In JavaScript, a function is an object and, consequently, can be assigned to a variable for use by triggers, as well as in other contexts. Following are two key statements in the onvoiceschanged trigger function below.

```
utterance.voice = voices[7];
speechSynthesis.speak(utterance);
```

The first of those two statements assigns voices[7] (called Daniel) to the Speech Synthesis Object and then the second statement invokes the speak method. Voices[10] (Fiona) speaks rather quickly; you may want to set the rate of speech to 0.85 (utterance.rate = 0.85) or some other value between 0.8 and 0.9 for that voice. Adjust as you wish and also try other voices. To help determine which voices you might try, the following loop appears in the trigger function in order to display (in the console window) the voice number and name of all voices.

```
for (var i = 0; i < voices.length; i++) {
    voice = voices[i];
    console.log(i, voice.name, voice.default ? voice.
default : "");
}
```

In the console.log statement, the code voice.default ? voice. default : "" uses the alternative if statement syntax, which in this case displays *true* when voice.default is true and null string (nothing) otherwise. Hence, when you view the list of voices, the word *true* appears for voices[0] because voices[0] (Alex) is the default voice.

Copy *sampleSpeechSynthesis001.html* to *sampleSpeechSynthesis002.html*. In your text editor, edit *sampleSpeechSynthesis002.html* until it appears as per the code below. Save the file. Run the program for numerous voices and for a couple of voices, try a speech rate around 1.7 or even 2.0.

```html
<html>
<head>
  <title>Speech Synthesis Sample</title>
</head>

<body>

<p style="margin-top: 200px; text-align: center">Are
you listening? Do you hear me?<p3>
<script>
  var utterance = new SpeechSynthesisUtterance();
  var voices;

  speechSynthesis.onvoiceschanged = function() {
    voices = speechSynthesis.getVoices();
    utterance.voice = voices[10]; // 7: Daniel; 10:
Fiona;
    utterance.lang = "en-US";
    utterance.rate = 0.8; // Fiona: set to 0.8 or 0.9
    utterance.text = "Hello, I hope that you are
well. I am wondering: What do you want to learn
today?";
    speechSynthesis.speak(utterance);

    for (var i = 0; i < voices.length; i++) {
        voice = voices[i];
        console.log(i, voice.name, voice.default?
voice.default :"");
    }
  }
</script>
</body>
</html>
```

Replace the voice, rate of speech, and words spoken as you wish. Also try a different language or languages. For example, replace "en-US" with "es-ES" to change the language to Spanish; use `voices[15]` (Juan); and replace the text spoken with "Qué quieres aprender hoy?" Additional language codes are available at https://gist.github.com/vitoziv/9108407.

Sample App with Voice Recognition

Programming this app in JavaScript is straightforward. As per the code below, create a `webkitSpeechRecognition` object; optionally set the variable for language to be recognized (US dialect of English is the default); optionally set the variable to determine whether the speech recognizer returns interim results (no interim results is the default); start the speech recognizer; insert one assignment statement in the `onresult` trigger function to store the string of words the user speaks; and include one `console.log` statement in each trigger function in order to view the results of the speech recognizer.

```
var recognition = new SpeechRecognition();
var resultString;

recognition.lang = 'en-US';
recognition.interimResults = true;
recognition.start();

recognition.onresult = function(event) {
    resultString = event.results[0][0].transcript;
    console.log('You seem to be saying: ', resultString);
}
recognition.onend = function(event) {
    console.log('You said: ', resultString);
}
```

The words spoken by the user are available through the two-dimensional array `event.results`, which in the code above are stored in `resultString`.

Open a new file in your text editor and enter the code below. Save the file as *sampleSpeechRecognition.html*. As discussed below, double-clicking the file icon will not be sufficient to run this program because permission to use the microphone cannot be granted to a local file unless it is processed by a web server.

```
<html>
<head>
  <title>Speech Recognition Sample</title>
</head>

<body>

<p style="margin-top: 200px; text-align: center">Speak
to me ...<p3>

<script>
  var recognition = new webkitSpeechRecognition();
  var resultString;
  recognition.lang = 'en-US';
  recognition.interimResults = true;
  recognition.start();

  recognition.onresult = function(event) {
      resultString = event.results[0][0].transcript;
```

```
      console.log('You seem to be saying: ', resultString);
   }

   recognition.onend = function(event) {
      console.log('You said: ', resultString);
   }
</script>
</body>
</html>
```

If using a web browser other than Google Chrome, you might want to replace

```
var recognition = new webkitSpeechRecognition();
```

with

```
var recognition = new (webkitSpeechRecognition ||
SpeechRecognition || mozSpeechRecognition ||
msSpeechRecognition)();
```

Before running this program, consider the privacy implications of a program running on the web that can listen to you and other sounds in your environment. Such programs should, and do, require explicit permission from you to use the microphone connected to your computer. The Google Chrome browser does not permit a local web page (including *sampleSpeechRecognition.html*, which is stored one on your computer's hard drive) to even temporarily access the microphone. Hence, if you double-click the *sampleSpeechRecognition.html* icon in an attempt to run the program, your voice input will not reach the program because a local program loaded directly into the web browser is not allowed to access the microphone. However, a web page retrieved by web server software and rendered in the browser is able to obtain permission to use your computer's microphone if you grant such permission. Hence, you could transfer *sampleSpeechRecognition.html* to a web hosting service and deliver *sampleSpeechRecognition.html* to your web browser through the web host's URL. If you have no such web hosting service and do not wish to create an account with a free hosting service or you just want a local solution, you can run a web server on your computer. To run a web server on a computer running Microsoft Windows, download Internet Information Service Express and install it on your computer. With Python installed, enter `python -m http.server` in a command window to run the local web server. To run a web server on a Mac, follow the instructions for the particular version of Mac OS X installed on your computer, which are available at https://discussions.apple.com/docs/DOC-3083.

Then enter the local URL to *sampleSpeechRecognition.html*, which in Microsoft Windows would be the following.

http://localhost:8080/sampleSpeechRecognition.html
On a Mac the URL will be structured as follows. Replace username with your actual user name.
http://localhost/~username/sampleSpeechRecognition.html

Sample Dialog

This app alternates between speech synthesis and speech recognition in order to produce dialog (though, admittedly at this stage, the computer is fixated on particular statements). As per the code below, after loading the voices in the `init` function, the dialog begins with a call to the `tutorSpeaks` function in which the computer (in the role of tutor) poses an initial question. When the final word of the question has been spoken, the `onend` event is triggered and processing continues with a call to the `tutorListensToLearner` function in order to "listen" for the learner's reply. This question/response (voice synthesis/voice recognition) pattern continues through two more questions before the tutor ends the dialog. In the current state of the app, the tutor's questions and final comments are predetermined. The user's replies are completely ignored, but you will begin to change that in Task 7.1. Ultimately, you may wish to learn more about dialog systems (Jurafsky & Martin, 2009; Weizenbaum, 1976), including Eliza (Weizenbaum, 1983), in order to program legitimate dialog. You may also learn more about natural language processing by considering the book *Computers and Language* (Dickinson, Brew, & Meurers, 2013).

Open a new file in your text editor and enter the code below. Save the file as *sampleDialog001.html*. Run the script though a web server and debug as necessary.

```
<html>

<head>
 <title>Speech Dialog Sample</title>
</head>
<body onload="init()">

 <p style="margin-top: 200px; text-align: center">Are
 you ready to learn?<p>

 <divid="beginButton" style="text-align: center; display:
 none"><button type="button" onclick="tutorSpeaks()">
 Click me to begin</button></div>
<script>
 var voices;
 var resultString;
 var tutorStatementNumber = 0;
```

```
var tutorsStatements = ["Hello, I hope that you
are well. I am wondering: What do you want to learn
today?",
                        "Very well. How will you
seek to attain your learning goal?",
                        "Interesting,  is  there
anything else you want to learn?",
                        "Okay. Take care."];

function init() {
  speechSynthesis.onvoiceschanged = function() {
    voices = window.speechSynthesis.getVoices();
    tutorSpeaks();
  }
} // "init"

function tutorSpeaks() {
//    console.log("In tutorSpeaks");
  utterance = new SpeechSynthesisUtterance();
  utterance.voice = voices[7]; // 7: Daniel; 10: Fiona;
Juan: 15; 49: UK English Female; 50: UK English Male
  utterance.lang = "en-US";
  utterance.rate = 1.0; // Fiona (10): 0.8;

  utterance.text = tutorsStatements[tutorStatement
Number];
  speechSynthesis.speak(utterance);

  utterance.onerror = function (event) {
//    console.log("Speech synthesis error");
  }

  utterance.onend = function (event) {
//    console.log("Speech ended");
    if (tutorStatementNumber < 3) {
      tutorListensToLearner();
    }
  }
} // "tutorSpeaks"

function tutorListensToLearner() {
console.log("In tutorListensToLearner");

  var recognition = new webkitSpeechRecognition();
  recognition.lang = 'en-US';
  recognition.interimResults = true;
  recognition.start();
```

```
        recognition.onresult = function(event) {
            resultString = event.results[0][0].transcript;
            console.log("You seem to be saying: ", result
            String);
        }

        recognition.onend = function(event) {
            console.log("You said: ", resultString);

            tutorStatementNumber++;
            tutorSpeaks();
        }
    } // "tutorListensToLearner"
</script>
</body>
</html>
```

Notice in the script above, the `<div id= "beginButton" style="text-align: center; display: none">` ... `</div>` tag. When the web page is displayed, no button appears on the web page because the display attribute is set to none. In Task 7.1 you will make the button visible. Some users may prefer to start the dialog, rather than be surprised by a "talking web page."

Task 7.1 The app asks the learner: "What do you want to learn today?" Parse the learner's reply to the question and respond with the learner's reply in the computer's second statement. Also, modify the app to begin the dialog when the user clicks the button. Display the button when `onvoiceschanged` is true.

Task 7.2 Add images to the voice dialog program in order to visually depict when the tutor (computer) is speaking and when the learner is expected to speak. For example, an animated speaker GIF file would serve well for the tutor speaking and an animated microphone GIF would serve well for indicating when the learner should be speaking.

Task 7.3 Add error checking to ensure that the user's web browser and microphone are capable of processing speech. Provide the user with effective prompts to correct any impediments to using voice apps in a web browser.

Task 7.4 Add a `<div id="tutorsStatements">` tag to the voice dialog program and use the `tutorsStatements` section of the web page to display the words spoken by the app. Add a `<div id="learnersStatements">` tag to the voice dialog program and use the `learnersStatements` section of the web page to display the words spoken by the learner.

Task 7.5 Design a voice tutor. You may involve target learners during the design, development, and testing stages.

Congratulations for creating the instructional apps in this book!

7.3 Next Steps

Design and develop instructional apps; distribute them everywhere. Given the past decade of downloading apps to mobile devices, we may imagine designing and developing instructional apps for smartphones and tablets into the future. New and effective instructional apps for those devices would help learners. Even so, consider designing and developing instructional apps that transcend typical mobile devices. For example, various models of HP printers (e.g., OfficeJet Pro 6978) include a high resolution touch screen embedded in the printer through which users may view instructional videos.

Voice technologies also offer opportunities for innovation. In February 2011, IBM Watson, programmed to play the question-answer game Jeopardy, defeated two human opponents (prior Jeopardy champions) in a two-day competition. The voice assistant, Siri, debuted in the iPhone 4S on October 4, 2011. Since those notable milestones, many other voice-enabled systems have emerged (e.g., Alexa, Cortana, Jibo), yet not one is a tutor. Will computer tutors emerge through desktops, laptops, wristwatches, eye glasses, or social robots? Perhaps the answer will be all of those devices. Additionally or alternatively, software tutors may arise in devices not yet available. The answer depends in part on us, we designers and developers of instructional apps.

In addition to developing instructional apps, we can improve instructional development tools. The development of some instruction can be automated and researchers and developers may do well to discern the extent to which effective instruction can be developed automatically by computers. In this case, too, voice technologies may enable different forms of input to instructional development tools.

Leaders in educational technology rise from multiple venues through multiple means, including research and development in corporations, the military, government, and higher education, as well as through entrepreneurship in business, and through innovative work by individuals and small groups working in their homes. Opportunities for leadership in educational technology abound through pursuit of any one of the new directions (making instructional apps ubiquitous by designing and developing them to run on diverse form factors; making robust instructional apps with machine learning algorithms; and advancing instructional development tools). We may also conceive of mash-ups, innovations encompassing all three of those directions. Imagine an instructional robot, a social robot behaving with due regard for human life, capable of providing effective instruction, making use of machine learning techniques to refine instruction, and creating instruction to specifications provided by parents and teachers. We educational technologists can and will revolutionize instruction, not learning. As learners, we need time to process information and practice. Our instructional innovations will benefit learners greatly and, over time, reshape educational institutions.

Your contribution to the future of instructional app development depends upon realizing your visions, transforming your designs for instruction into functional apps. Design, build, test, refine; repeat as necessary, and then diffuse your innovations widely. Enjoy the process and celebrate successes along the way. As you create and share innovative instructional apps and instructional development tools, you will lead the field toward your vision of effective technologies for learning. Diffusing those technologies universally and equitably bodes well for learners everywhere.

References

Brownlee, J. (2016). Your first machine learning project in python: Step by step. Available at http://machinelearningmastery.com/machine-learning-in-python-step-by-step/

Dickinson, M., Brew, C., & Meurers, D. (2013). *Language and computers*. Chichester, UK: Wiley-Blackwell.

Jurafsky, D. & Martin, J. H. (2009). *Speech and language processing: An introduction to natural language processing, computational linguistics, and speech recognition* (2nd ed.). Upper Saddle River, NJ: Pearson-Prentice Hall.

Jurafsky, D. & Martin, J. H. *Speech and language processing: An introduction to natural language processing, computational linguistics, and speech recognition* (3rd edition in preparation). https://web.stanford.edu/~jurafsky/slp3/

Weizenbaum, J. (1976). *Computer power and human reason: From judgment to calculation*. San Francisco, CA: W. H. Freeman.

Weizenbaum, J. (1983). ELIZA: A computer program for the study of natural language communication between man and machine. *Communications of the ACM, 26*, 23–28.

Index